Coming Around the Mountain

Depicting the usual scene in 1860, on what is now U. S. 50.
The men, horses, mules and wagons, filled with cargo, which brought into being
the early inns of California

The EARLY INNS
of California
1844-1869

Ralph Herbert Cross

SAN FRANCISCO, CALIFORNIA

1954

Address all communications concerning this book to:
Cross & Brandt
111 Sutter Street • Suite 1333
San Francisco 4, California

Library of Congress Catalog Card Number: 54-12548

Printed in U.S.A.

Contents

List of Illustrations

The Author's Preface

WHY THE SUBJECT of California's early inns was chosen for an historical study has frequently been asked. In August, 1936, I read Elise Lathrop's "Early American Inns and Taverns." I was puzzled by this sentence in the introduction: "As to states omitted, California's State Historian is responsible for the statement that, to the best of his belief, not a single old inn survives in that state."

My boyhood home was on the old Auburn road, in Sacramento County (now United States Highway No. 40), between what had been the Fourteen and Fifteen Mile public houses. Both of these inns had been transformed into farm houses. In traveling about the state I had seen public stopping places which dated back to the Fifties in good repair and use with name changed, perhaps. For example, the Freeman Hotel in Auburn, and the Raffles, formerly Cary House, in Placerville.

I discussed the subject with the late Dr. Herbert E. Priestly, Director of the Bancroft Library, University of California. At his suggestion, we called on the late Dr. Herbert E. Bolton, Dean of the University's History Department. He was equally sympathetic toward research for historical information, stating that in his opinion the subject had never been explored or published. The interest shown by these outstanding historians encouraged me to begin collecting data and information on California's early inns, and for many years I have pursued this thoroughly enjoyable hobby, meeting many of the state's elder pioneers and their descendants.

In 1844 the first known inn was established in California, and in 1869 the Central Pacific Railroad was completed, the latter event sounding the death knell for a great many of the roadside inns in California. My study was confined to the intervening period of twenty-five years. As the work progressed, it became manifestly impossible to deal with all the individual stopping places which flourished in California between those years in one reasonably sized publication.

A compromise was adopted, the necessity for which will be seen by reference to the map published with this book. I sincerely trust that those who have assisted in gathering data on inns not covered in this volume will recognize the difficulties and problems involved.

i

The subject has turned out to be one which could be carried on for a lifetime, but the law of diminishing returns must be recognized. The great quantity of data gathered will be placed in the archives of an historical society, where it will be accessible to researchers in the years to come. It is my hope that those who assisted me may be the source of further information, so that another volume may be published as opportunity and time permit.

It has been most gratifying to meet with such universal cooperation on the part of these fine men and women. My great regret is that so many of them are no longer here to see the result of their assistance in the presentation of the history of the old stopping places which they recalled to memory so intimately.

Introduction

MANY BOOKS had been written about California's pioneers before the Centennial of 1946-1950 touched off a literary chain-reaction that has seldom been equaled. Since that triadic celebration of conquest, gold, and statehood, the world has been told in millions upon millions of words all about the Argonauts of 1849, why they came to California, and how they got here. They were the state's true American pioneers, and while some of their experiences have been told, one all-important part of their lives has hitherto been omitted, or only lightly touched on. This is the story of where these men and women, and those who followed them to as late as 1869, stopped after their arrival, and how they lived before and after James Marshall's discovery burst in a fierce golden blaze that completely overshadowed such humble subjects as bacon, beans, and blankets. Without bacon and beans and blankets, however, there could have been no gold rush, and the saga of the pioneers who supplied these essentials to pioneering has until now been unsung.

Today there are so many stopping places that the traveler takes them as a matter of course, and thereafter scarcely ever thinks of the hostelry where he put up. But this was not the case in California in the early days. In those times the wayfarer was so hard put to it to find an inn wherein he could get himself out of the elements and be fed that it was an occasion to be remembered; sometimes gratefully, at others with more or less bitterness, depending upon how he fared. This book is an attempt to reconstruct the stories of these early California inns, and insofar as it has been possible, to tell something of the men who established and operated them.

What is planned is to tell the story of the places that came into being and flourished down to the time of the Gold Rush, and to sketch the general picture of their successors, as after 1849 their number was so great that several additional volumes would be required to tell their stories.

In undertaking the writing of the present book, a number of serious challenges were met at the outset. These early inns almost always gave their patrons something to think about afterward, and had the latter only set down their impressions while these were still fresh in their minds, as pleasant or unhappy recollections, the task would have been much easier. Unfortunately, the literati were a minority among California's early American travelers, and it is only occasionally that one of these was sufficiently gifted, or had enough time on his hands, to leave a record of his experiences. Such accounts are few and almost invariably lacking in detail, and more often than not they are no more than casual comments, which it has been a work of no small magnitude to sift out from the mass of general reminiscences of those days. Furthermore, when earlier writers have had anything to say about these inns, this has almost always been in the form of repetitions of stories and anecdotes that have been passed down from hand to hand, with little or no attempt to verify their historical accuracy. The result of this is that, with the passing of time and repetition, a number of wholly fictitious literary traditions have come to be accepted as cast-iron facts; as exemplified by the time-honored belief that the Washington, at Monterey, was California's first hotel. Such statements would be all right if they were plainly labeled as tradition, local color, or something of that sort, but when they are offered as historical gospel the reader is justified in feeling swindled. Especially when he tries to pass them along to someone who knows better, and who complacently corrects him. When this happens, it really hurts, and no doubt it is one of the things the insurance companies take into account when figuring the life expectancy of authors.

It is only too well realized that, despite the most painstaking efforts to verify the truth of every statement made here, some errors are bound to have crept into the text. The most attentive and interested member of any audience is the man who has found, or thinks he has found, an error or misstatement in an address, and the same applies to the reader of a book. With the foregoing in mind, the reader is asked to advise us of any such errors or misstatement which he knows to be such, so that the proper corrections, additions, or deletions may be made in future editions.

The difficulties encountered have made the writing of this story all the more fascinating and it has taken some seventeen years to complete the work. Of course, none of the men and women who knew the oldest of these stopping places are still living, but fortunately many of their children and grandchildren vividly recall their pioneer ancestors' tales of their experiences. These sons and daughters of the old timers (many of them old timers in their own right) have been sought out all over the state and interviewed, and their stories have been compared with and sometimes amplified by references to manuscript memoirs of those early days. The newspapers from 1846 onward have been consulted for additional information, and the foregoing constitutes the primary material that has been used to reconstruct the story of California's early inns. The secondary sources are far too many to enumerate, and all that need be said on this score is that in each case the information has been painstakingly checked for accuracy. As will be seen, the result has been the presentation of a not inconsiderable amount of material that has hitherto either been unpublished, or unassembled, and this contribution to the history of California is in itself a source of satisfaction.

It would be even more gratifying to be able to mention by name each of the men and women who have so generously given of their time and knowledge in the preparation of this work, but their number is too great to be able to do justice to the indebtedness in a brief introduction of this nature. So perhaps the next best thing to do will be to say to each of these friends that without their kindly help and encouragement this story could not have been written. It is also a sincere pleasure to acknowledge the invaluable assistance and unfailing courtesy of the staffs of the Bancroft Library, the California Historical Society, the Society of California Pioneers, the State Library at Sacramento and Sutter's Fort, and the Sutro Library at San Francisco, as well as the help of such United States government agencies as the Post Office Department, and the National Archives.

Chapter 1. Introducing the Inns

So much has been written about the great Gold Rush to California that the events of the years immediately preceding that epochal decade have been all but overshadowed. The story of gold bulks so large on the country's early horizon, indeed, that if one did not know better he might be tempted to think of the year Eighteen Forty-Nine as having been the beginning of the State's history. While this may sound fanciful it is nonetheless true, as relatively little is popularly known of the intimate story of the half decade preceding the great discovery, when history was being made in California that will outlast the gold saga of '49.

The foregoing is especially true of the story of California's earliest inns, as heretofore practically nothing has been known about them; and what little has been written is often colored by wishful thinking, if not by downright imagination. This, however, has been wholly gratuitous, as their story is amply colorful in its own right, without the necessity of any artificial embellishments.

The first part of our story is that of those stopping places which pioneered the later inns, whose countless number led Dame Shirley to write as early as 1851 that California "... might be called the Hotel State, so completely is she inundated with taverns, boarding houses, etc."[1] Apart from the fact that the first of these were California's earliest American places of public accommodation, their opening marked the beginning of two far-reaching factors in the social and economic development of the country; first, the arrival overland of the advance guard of the American settlers, and second, the increasing number of all classes of society landing at Yerba Buena (or San Francisco) and Monterey. From these ports many of the newcomers made their way to such settlements as San Jose, Santa Clara, Sonoma and Sutter's Fort, at New Helvetia. At these early centers of population the first ripple of what was destined to become the flood of overland immigration met the rising tide of seaborne arrivals, and it was at such places that the first American hostelries made their appearance. These were the true pioneers of California's stopping places, and while the accommodations offered were rough and ready, they were no more so than were most of their single and adventurous patrons. But with all this, these early inns were more than simply eating and sleeping places, for within their walls the men who were making history in those days lived and loved, and not infrequently fought and died. The last part of our story has to do with the overall picture of the innumerable inns which sprang up, flourished, and most of which disappeared between 1849 and 1869, when the completion of the Central Pacific Railroad terminated *all* stagecoach travel, except that over roads which were lateral to the railway.

Down to the time of the American occupation of the country the Californians had no need of public stopping places. As early as 1814 ships of American and other nationalities began calling at California's ports, and from time to time members of their crews deserted to settle ashore. These, together with a few hunters and trappers who wandered into the country, were the earliest of our foreign pioneers, but they were so few in number and fell so easily into the ways of their adopted land that they made little or no impression on the life of the Spanish-Mexican settlements. This centered about the home, family and friends, and was communal in the fullest sense of the word. Almost everyone was in one way or another related to everyone else, or bound to them by the closest ties of friendship, and under these happy conditions there was never an occasion when a traveler found himself without the welcome of a home, where he might stop for as long a time as suited his convenience. Therefore, for three centuries following the discovery of Alta California the only establishments that can by any stretch of the imagination be called public stopping places were perhaps a few humble *posadas* (literally, resting places) that grew up here and there in the few small settlements of those days. But however humble these places may have been, they should not be ignored, for they were the prototypes of the plush lined and bemirrored palatial American hotels of later years.

The typical early California *posada* was either an open brush and earth roofed shed, or *ramada*, a wattle and mud walled room, where all the activities of the place were carried on without discrimination or privacy. At one end, or in the center, was a low mud or rough stone *brassero,* or fireplace, on which the simple fare of the country was prepared in earthen pots over a wood or charcoal fire. A rude table and perhaps a bench or two, and of course a crucifix, or the crude picture of some favorite saint, comprised all the furniture. In such a place it was possible to be served *tortillas, frijoles* and, at times, even a bowl of *carne con chili,* or thin flat corn cakes, beans, and meat stewed with red peppers. There, too, a drink of *aguardiente* (fire-water) could generally be procured, for saloons such as sprang up with the advent of the Americans were unknown. Finally, a corner of the hard-packed dirt floor not previously pre-empted by a pig or two, chickens, or a donkey might be found in which to spread one's blanket.

Still another reason for this lack of public accommodations was the fact that there were few travelers. Apart from the *ranchos* and great *haciendas,* the population of Alta California clustered about the missions, at places such as San Diego, San Gabriel, Santa Barbara, San Luís Obispo, Monterey, San José, San Francisco de Asis (or Dolores), San Rafael, and Sonoma. These settlements were all located along a strip of coastal plain that was nowhere above fifty miles in width by some seven hundred in length, and were loosely linked together by the *Camino Real.* This was the so-called King's Highway, and despite its sonorous title it was really little better than an indifferent trail, that only in parts permitted vehicular traffic. Not that this mattered, however, as the lumbering carriages of those days might be counted on the fingers of one hand, and were used almost exclusively for feast day and ceremonial purposes, within the limits of the settlements.

The recognized method of transportation in Spanish and Mexican days (and even down to well after the American occupation) was on horseback, and traffic over the *Camino Real* was almost wholly confined to occasional government officials, aristocratic *hacendados,* priests, and the military. Others, who might be forced to go afoot, did not count. Nor is this surprising when one stops to think that during the two hundred eighty-odd years of Spanish possession the white population of California was never greater than about three thousand souls, and for the first two or three decades of this period, barely a third of this number.

In the case of all but the military, entertainment was found at the haciendas, the missions, or with friends or relatives. Unquestioning hospitality was so much a matter of course that there was never a thought of charging for the accommodation of man or beast. Officers and soldiers either camped in the open or were quartered in the *presidios*, and others of humbler social status were at liberty to sleep beneath the stars, or to dispute with the pigs, chickens and donkeys in some *posada*.

From the point of view of the Californians, these were indeed the golden days. In 1834, however, the beginning of the final act in the secularization of the missions introduced a harsh note into the hitherto kindly welcome that was wont to greet travelers at the portals of these establishments. Taken over by the civil authorities, most of the missions fell into private hands and ceased to be places of entertainment. While the secularization of the missions was only indirectly responsible for the American inns that began to appear some ten years later, there is no question but that the closing of these establishments was another reason why California's pioneer hostelries made their appearance when they did.

So much for the Spanish background of the story of the inns. The year 1821 saw Mexico's independence and the ushering in of a new era, but as the transition was purely a political one, involving little or no social change, conditions and customs under the newly fledged eagle of the Mexican Republic were the same as they had been under the Spanish crown. From 1826 onward, however, a new factor began to affect the old order. This was the arrival in California of more and more hunters and trappers, many of whom settled and began to make their customs felt by the Californians. But there was still no marked change in conditions until about 1841, when the earlier trickle of individual American immigrants began to increase to small parties that found their way into the country across the plains and the Sierra Nevada. This was the overall picture in the early Forties, but five years later sweeping, social, political, and economic transformations occurred almost overnight.

The first of these upheavals was the revolt of a small group of Americans and other malcontents who, taking advantage of an intestine conflict between the local political parties, declared themselves in arms against the Mexican government. Acting under what are said to have been secret orders from Washington, Captain John C. Frémont, at first covertly and later openly, sponsored the insurrection, and on June 14, 1846, the Republic of California was proclaimed and the Bear Flag raised over the peaceful town of Sonoma. There the authorities, far from offering resistance, regaled their self-appointed liberators with such lavish hospitality that the latter shortly found themselves much bemused with respect to just who was supposed to be doing what and to whom. By itself this serio-comic revolt would probably have been crushed by the Mexicans, but as it was predicated on our policy of territorial expansion that on the 13th of the preceding month had led the Congress of the United States to declare the existence of a state of war with Mexico, its ideals were predestined to succeed.

On July 7th Commodore John D. Sloat, commanding our Pacific Squadron, raised the American flag over the port of Monterey and formally annexed the Mexican Department of California as a territory of the United States of America. On the 11th the Bear Flag was replaced by the Stars and Stripes, and with this the history of the short-lived Republic of California ended. The conquest lasted barely six months, and on January 13, 1847, Colonel Frémont and General Andrés Pico signed the Treaty of Cahuenga that terminated official hostilities in so far as California was concerned, although the Treaty of Guadalupe Hidalgo, ending the war with Mexico, was not signed until February 2, 1848, something over a year later. With the raising of the American flag the easy-going days of California life came to an end, and within a twelvemonth the new rules of the land had completely upset the old order, that, in the leisurely course of Spanish possession, had come to be looked upon as the only reasonable way of living.

Monterey was the seat of the new military government, and it was there that California's earliest American inn might reasonably be thought to have been opened. Unfortunately the records are silent as to this, and the only known reference to the subject at that time are the remarks of the Reverend Walter Colton, who was appointed *alcalde* of the town by Commodore Sloat. On July 28, 1846, the day he took office and twenty-one days after the flag was raised, the *alcalde* says: ". . . there is not a public house or table in all California."[2] This sounds pretty conclusive, but either Alcalde Colton was misinformed or he was not acclimated to the sort of public accommodations offered by

California's stopping places as they were at that time. However this may have been, we will have to backtrack for a moment to set the matter right.

As has been said, it is reasonably certain that the earliest of California's place of public entertainment was some Spanish or Mexican shack that was by courtesy called a *posada*, but as the Winds of Time have long since scattered the unstoried dust of this little hostelry, we must, however regretfully, turn to a somewhat later date for a glimpse of what was, in so far as is known, the first American stopping place in the country. This was a sort of bachelors' boarding-house that Nathaniel Pryor was keeping in Los Angeles as early as the summer of 1832, and we are indebted to Susanna Bryant Dakin for the following description of the place, as interpreted from the letters of Hugo Reid, who was one of California's earliest Scot pioneers:

"It followed that purely by chance Hugo had come upon the one person in town with accommodations for *extranjeros*. This was Nathaniel Pryor, a Kentucky silversmith and clockmaker who had come to California in '28 as a trapper in the ill-fated Pattie party. Being a genial soul, a bachelor with extra rooms in his home, he was by way of becoming a boarding house keeper in a town where there was no hotel. At the moment it appeared that he had only one guest, Don Abel Stearns, the traveling representative of Captain Cooper's Monterey trading company. Hugo accepted the man's cordial invitation to lodge with him. The house, as he soon observed, was of the style most favored by the pueblo. The material used in its construction was *adobe* mud mixed with straw and made into large bricks, then baked in the sun. *Adobe* bricks were cemented together with a mud mortar, to form very thick walls resistant alike to heat and to cold. In Monterey and occasionally in Los Angeles they were white-washed, but Pryor's house remained dirt colored. The floors were no more than dirt, hard packed and worn to the shine and color of slate. Only in the living room had Pryor laid down a plank floor, of which he seemed very proud. His grated windows also were rather remarkable, having glass in them. Each bedroom opened through one door into the living room and through another on a spacious veranda. Pryor owned a minimum of hard-used furniture, except beds, which were plentiful — constructed of rawhide stretched over a frame, neatly made up and surprisingly comfortable. Since he had no wife, the walls were bare of holy pictures, and the windows, of lace curtains. In Pryor's home, as in everyone else's, all the cooking was done in a separate cookhouse containing a stone oven, and the food was served out of doors under a *ramada* roofed with *tules*. Indians did all the work, indoors and out, in return for food and clothing. This usually consisted of *frijoles* (red beans) three times a day, and a small piece of coarse cloth with a belt, for the men; *frijoles* and a shapeless gown, without shoes or stockings, for the women."[3]

The foregoing gives a good idea of the transition that took place between the original Spanish-Mexican *posadas* and the American inns that began to appear something over a decade later.

It now becomes necessary to again correct Alcalde Colton's statement to the effect that in 1846 there was not one public stopping place in all California. At the precise time he wrote, a Mexican *fonda* (an eating or stopping place) was going strong in Santa Clara,[4] and there is no reason to suppose that other places of the kind were not being kept elsewhere in the Territory.

Four months after the above statement, the good *alcalde* tells of the robbery of an eating and perhaps lodging house in Monterey, when, from the amount of gold and silver involved, it would appear that the establishment was a flourishing one.[5] This is all that is known about the place, and we can only regret the lack of details concerning what was perhaps one of the earliest American hostelries in the country. The Reverend Colton's information about the inns of the new Territory evidently continued to be faulty, as he nowhere mentions an establishment in Yerba Buena that by 1844 was known up and down the Pacific Coast as a popular public stopping place.[6]

As has been said, the story of California's early inns falls automatically into two periods: the first includes those establishments which appeared before 1849, and the second the stopping places which grew up with incredible swiftness between that year and 1869. In the first instance it has been possible to gather a considerable amount of detail on these places, and in the second a general sketch must suffice, as the subject is so extensive that it is quite impossible to do justice to it in one book. The historical background applying to both these periods has been seen, but before proceeding there is another and more intimate background which to some of our readers will prove equally interesting. This is a typical picture of the inns themselves, who were their operators, and the everyday life as this was lived in those days.

Chapter 2. Ash-Hopper Days

CALIFORNIA's early inns were established by American pioneers, few of whom had any experience in inn keeping. They arrived in the country, saw the need for places of public entertainment, and these stopping places were the result. As has been said, the earliest of the inns were opened in the small settlements, but with James Marshall's discovery of gold at Sutter's sawmill, or Coloma, on January 24, 1848, they spread like wild-fire along the roads leading to the "diggings," and in a matter of months their number had become almost unbelievable.

These establishments were at first simply drinking and gambling places, with perhaps a shed or lean-to where customers could sleep in their own blankets and on the ground.

The forerunners of the later inns were no more than tents or brush shacks, earth floored, and with the simplest of amenities represented by a tin wash-basin on a stump, a bit of looking glass tacked to a pole, and a broken comb hanging from a string. Sometimes these inns, and their immediate successors, further catered to their guests' ideas about personal cleanliness by providing an item that passed for a towel. This was an endless strip of coarse huck toweling or sometimes a piece of sacking that was hung on a roller. Whatever its original color had been, the passing of numerous hands and faces had altered this to a mottled gray-black shade, and each customer turned the towel to the point which he decided was the least soiled before adding his own contribution of grime.

The first of these early inns were located in the midst of the richest diggings, and as these were worked out, they followed the miners from one favored spot to another, sometimes being little better than overnight stands. Under these conditions, the proprietors were almost invariably single men, who, with perhaps a "swamper," did all the work, and such simple cooking as was required. Later, however, when mining camps became more or less permanent, and when traffic over the roads grew in volume, the earliest "joints" were replaced by more pretentious establishments, which were worthier of the name "inn."

These "second-growth" inns were not only located in the mining camps, but on level spots at strategic points along the roads, where freighting outfits (and later stagecoaches) were wont to stop for the night. The first of these inns were still rough and ready establishments, but their social tone was a cut above that of their predecessors. They were generally unpainted one-story wooden shanties, but most of them boasted a barroom, warmed by an open fireplace, a dining room of sorts, and either an annex or a loft equipped with makeshift, three or four tier wooden shelves, where the customers might sleep, if they could—again in their own blankets, and at a price, "in bed or on shelf." With this step upward from "joints" to the beginning of "inns," the character of the owners also improved. Married men now began to replace the earlier bachelor publicans; their wives and children, many

Lodging Room, 1849

of whom had come overland, took over the chores, and Indians were often hired to do the heavier work about the establishments.

The third phase in the development of California's wayside stopping places was in full swing by about 1851, when, as has been said, their number had become almost countless. Many of the original makeshift places were now replaced by more substantial and pretentious buildings, whose architecture often reflected the owner's memories of the houses in that part of the "States" from where he came. A man from Maine was apt to build a different type of house than was the man from Mississippi, and sometimes the name of the inn was a clue to its keeper's place of origin. Two story houses now began to appear, together with outbuildings, and when the cream of the placer "diggings" had been skimmed, numbers of hard-up miners began working in various capacities at the inns. Later, when the railway began to bring in Chinese laborers, some of these augmented the hired help as cooks and waiters.

With the rapidly increasing traffic over the roads, these "third-growth" inns naturally expanded to meet the demands of their customers, and while it must, perforce, be a composite picture covering the period down to 1869, this seems a good place to glance at a typical wayside stopping place of those days.

The inn itself was always close to the road, and sometimes, as at Strawberry, on the road from Placerville to Washoe, in Nevada, it was built on both sides of the roadway, a covered passageway providing means whereby stagecoach passengers could alight under shelter. As in earlier days, the barroom (which was also the inn's office) was the establishment's most frequented department, as well as being the best heated room in the house. Here the best available liquor was dispensed over bars which were sometimes ornate affairs of carved mahogany, and here the masculine social life of the place centered.

Next to the barroom was the dining room, generally entered through double doors which were kept closed until mealtimes, and before which prospective diners massed themselves. At the appointed time a waiter pounded on a tin pan or an iron triangle, the doors were thrown open and a frantic rush ensued for seats on the backless benches lining the long tables. There were no tablecloths, and the individual's equipment consisted of a tin plate, a cup, knife and fork. No time was wasted in politeness, and the man with the longest reach got the best service and finished first. In a matter of minutes the food was demolished, the room cleared, and a second or third service under way.

Bedrooms were either on the second floor, known as the "corral," or in an annex, and these invariably accommodated at least two or more male guests, one or more such apartments being reserved for ladies and, sometimes, for married couples. The furniture was of the most simple nature—beds, with bedding, a washstand, tin basin, pitcher and slop-bucket, and a chair or two. Sometimes, but not always, a small looking-glass was added and the final mark of luxury was a flowered chamber-pot lurking beneath the bed.

The kitchen presented nothing outside of the ordinary, unless this was in the size of the cast-iron range or open fireplace where the great amount of food consumed was prepared. There was, of course, no running water until later in the period under discussion, when old-fashioned, hand-lever operated pumps in wells under the kitchen began to make their appearance.

The barn and stock corrals were generally across the road from the inn, and at the more important places hay, oats, and barley were kept in sufficient quantities to feed as many as one hundred head of stock a night. The cost of feed was always high, and it was not unusual for teamsters to carry their own grain, and sometimes even their own hay. Filling a back-action wagon, or a trailer, with feed for a round trip often proved more economical than filling it with one-way freight. Feed boxes were hung on the sides of the wagons, and after the draft animals were unharnessed and had rolled in the corral, they were tied before these boxes to feed. At many places there were ranges where the inn's stock and that of guests stopping for some days was turned out to graze. Watering troughs were of hollowed logs or heavy planks, and water was led into them by gravity from a nearby stream or spring.

In the back rear of the inn were a number of buildings which were of importance in the life of the place, such as the root-house, milk-house, and smokehouse. The root-house was invariably built wholly or partially underground, the exposed portion being of stone with a thick sod roof. This was always cool, and here were stored potatoes and other vegetables which would deteriorate at a warmer temperature. The milk-house was, whenever possible, built over a running stream or spring or, if the inn had a cellar, it might be located there.

This was another important department of the inn. Artificial refrigeration was unknown, although ice and hard packed snow were hauled down from several points in the Sierra, and used in the concoction of the most expensive iced drinks. Milk, cream, fresh meat, and other perishables were kept in the milkhouse, flour and other dry staples being kept in the general storeroom.

The California smokehouses of those days were almost identical with those still to be seen in thrifty, sparsely settled rural districts—small, tightly sealed earth-floored wooden buildings with no opening but the door. In the center of the floor was a shallow pit, and on stout pole rafters the meat was hung. One of the boy's jobs was to keep a fire of damp oak chips smoldering in the pit, and filling the smokehouse with a dense smudge, the meat hanging there until properly cured.

In the backyard of the inns were two adjuncts which, while they were both of importance to the life of these places, were located at a discreet distance from the living quarters. One of these was the pigsty, whose inhabitants provided hams, bacon, sausages, head-cheese, etc., in return for the scraps from the table and kitchen, conveyed to them in never over-clean swill pails.

The other subsidiary edifice was the old-fashioned country privy, generally a "two" or "three-seater," calibrated for grown-ups, teen-agers, and small fry. These little buildings were generally advertised by a half-moon, star, or other astral-shaped opening cut in the upper part of the door, and were not infrequently covered by passion flower, honeysuckle, or similar fragrant climbers. At the more elite inns, they were papered on the inside with old numbers of such periodicals as Harper Weeklies, Leslies, the Scientific American, and Godies' Ladies Magazine. These were tastefully and practically arranged, and many a youngster acquired his first interest in literature through their perusal.

Apart from economic strategic considerations, the wayside inns were always located with an eye to water and fuel. The former was obtained from close-by streams wherever possible, and from wells when a surface supply was not readily obtainable. Wood was always plentiful, and was cut in two lengths; for the kitchen range, and for a large stove or fireplace in the barroom, and "Parlor." Two other chores that fell to the part of the boys in the innkeeper's family were fetching buckets of water to the kitchen (and seeing to it that these were kept filled), and bringing in wood from the woodshed near the kitchen.

The foregoing is the general picture of a typical California wayside inn during the period under discussion, namely between about 1851 and 1869, and no doubt to some of our readers it will recall events in their own childhood days.

Now let us glance at an elaboration of the same picture, and see how the innkeepers took care of the hungry customers who three times a day stormed their dining rooms, and three times a day devoured everything in sight.

Provisions and supplies were at first confined to bottled and canned goods, and a few staples such as bacon, beans and flour, these being brought by pack-trains from such distributing points as Marysville, Sacramento and Stockton. This simple fare could generally be improved upon by a limited supply of such exotic delicacies as tinned oysters and sardines, bottled sour cucumber pickles, and more or less ancient cheese. But as these items literally sold for their weight in gold dust, they were only for the very fortunate or very drunk miners. And, of course, the professional gamblers, who, as they were never drunk, were always fortunate. In most cases reserve stores were built up in the fall against the winter months, when the snow and rains made the roads impassable. But even so, in the early days near famines were not unknown.

As the characters of the inns and of their keepers improved, and the demand for better and more varied menus increased, and wagons replaced the pack-trains, sugar and flour were brought out in barrels, and kegs of pickles, syrup, pickled oysters, cured hams and bacon, and other imported items were added to the fare. Other delicacies were provided by nature, such as wild berries and fruits, which were both preserved and dried; wild honey, too, was eagerly sought for, and sometimes the hollow of an oak tree would yield as much as two tubs of honey. The older part of the comb was dark brown with age, and clear, golden honey as it is marketed today, was unknown.

Fresh meat was sometimes a problem, but not often. The hills and valleys were full of deer, antelope, bears, rabbits, quail and other game, and indeed, almost anything that ran was "game." There were no game laws, and pot-hunting was one of the recognized professions, the favorite hunting weapon being the double-barreled muzzle loading shotgun, loaded with shot or slugs. Apart from wild game, steers and oxen were slaughtered in the settlements, and the inns generally managed to get their share. As soon as circumstances permitted, beef cattle, milch cows, pigs and chickens appeared in the inns' barnyard, and once this was accomplished, a place became self-sustaining in the matter of meat, poultry, eggs, milk, butter and cheese.

For winter consumption beef and venison was either cut in thin, narrow strips and hung in the sun to dry, when it was known as "jerky," or it was smoked, together with hams and sides of bacon. Pickling in brine was another method of preserving meat, when it was sometimes referred to as "salt-horse." A barrel or keg was used in this process, and was filled with alternate layers of salt and meat. The container was covered and stored in a cool place, and in due time the meat was ready for consumption. Beeves were butchered throughout the year as required, and as the methods employed were the same as those used from time immemorial to the present day, no elaboration or explanation is required.

The butchering of hogs, however, was another matter. In November, when the weather cooled, hogs were killed for the season's supply. A boxlike contrivance about six feet long, two feet wide, and eighteen inches deep was made of heavy planks, with a water-tight bottom of sheet-iron. This was located over a stone or brick lined fire-pit, filled with water, and a fire lighted in the pit. When the water reached the scalding point, a hog was killed in the pen and the carcass dumped into the cauldron, and left for a minute or two, or for about as long as it takes a man to soften his beard before shaving. At one end of the scalding-trough was a table of rough planks, strong enough to bear the weight of a two or three hundred pound animal. The carcass was dragged onto this, and all hands turned to with dull knives to thoroughly scrape off the bristles. When this had been done, the hog was quite white, a few buckets of cold water were then dashed over the carcass, when it was ready for dressing. The liver and intestines were removed and set aside for special purposes, the fresh liver for the table, and the intestines, after being cleaned inside and out, as casings for sausages, which consisted of selected parts of the animal, ground and seasoned with salt, pepper and sage. After the removal of the hams, bacon sides, hocks, head, and other meat, the fatty portions of the animal were placed in a large cauldron set over a fire in the backyard, and the lard tried out, the unreduced portions being cracklings, which were especially favored by the children. The lard was used for a number of purposes, such as cooking, lubricating and illuminating oil, and in place of butter, which at first was so scarce that bear grease was a common substitute.

Lye and soap were two by-products of civilization which were made on the premises. The wood ashes from the stove and fireplace were thrown into the ash-hopper, that was a boxlike contrivance made of heavy planks, about four feet long, two feet wide at the top, five feet high and perhaps eight inches wide at the bottom. The bottom consisted of a single scantling, one end of which projected beyond the end of the box, with a groove running longitudinally down the center. When the hopper was almost full, water was added, and in percolating through the ashes leached out lye, that drained off by gravity through the groove in the bottom of the hopper, and was caught in crocks, or under tubs. The lye would quickly eat through metal.

Hard soap was made by partially filling an iron or copper vessel with lard, fats, and suet, and adding the proper amount of lye. This mixture was then boiled and stirred until the lye reduced the fats to a thick, glutinous mass, when it was set aside to cool. The resultant soap was then cut into bars and placed in the sun to dry, when it was ready for use. If for one reason or another it was necessary to boil the soap on the kitchen range, it sometimes became scorched, and emitted a very disagreeable odor. It was customary to dispel this (as well as other offensive smells, and to drive out flies) by setting a pan of vinegar to simmer on the stove.

Another home industry was the manufacturing of tallow candles, which, together with lard or whale-oil lamps and lanterns, were the only source of lighting. Toward the end of the period, about 1869, a few oil-burning lamps may have made their appearance, but if so they were novelties, which, because of the scarcity, high cost, and dangerous properties of the newly discovered "coal-oil," were not in general use. Tin moulds, inserted top down in the bottom of a shallow wooden box, were used to form the candles. A cotton wick was brought up through a small hole in the lower end of each mould and fastened to

Mule-power for pumping water

"Phillips" at west end of sign, "Bread, Milk, Butter, Eggs"

Washington Hotel, Monterey

a stick placed across the box, in such position that the wick led straight up through the center of the mould. When this apparatus was ready, melted tallow was poured into the upper end of the mould until the moulds were filled, when they were set aside to cool.

Of course it was not all work for the innkeepers, their families and their guests, although the amusements of those times would today be considered entirely too savage, or too tame, to be amusing.

During the gold rush years, and apart from drinking and gambling, one of the most popular entertainments were bear and bull fights, which were introduced by the Americans. These were conducted within a stout corral, and the principal actors were as savage a bear as could be captured, and the wildest bull in the neighborhood. The bear was chained by one hindleg in the center of the corral, and the bull, after having been sufficiently annoyed, was introduced to his opponent. The fights were savage and generally to the death, and the survivor, if not too seriously injured, was saved for the next bout. Otherwise his next appearance was on the inn's table.

Horse racing came next in popularity, and it is almost needless to say that both racing and bull and bear fights enlivened what might otherwise have been a dull Sunday. Cock fighting was taken over by the American pioneers from the California Mexicans, and while it was a recognized form of entertainment, it was not as popular as the foregoing "sports," probably because the issue was too quickly settled, one of the birds being frequently dispatched at the first onset.

A little later, when social conditions began to be more stabilized, itinerant preachers appeared, and with this, Sunday and prayer meetings began to be held at many of the inns, these being attended by the neighbors for miles around. Other meetings such as barn dances, picnics, song gatherings, and spelling bees became common, and eventually the earlier and wilder forms of entertainment fell into disrepute until by the end of the period social diversions such as were current in more settled parts of the country, came to be accepted as the normal forms of relaxation.

In a broad sense the foregoing applies to all the early inns of California, and it now becomes necessary to determine which of these was the first. Our choice lies between what was unquestionably the state's pioneer establishment and one that for years has been called "California's first hotel." Out of deference to this more or less hoary tradition, it seems no more than common courtesy to begin the individual stories of the inns with an account of this place, even though in the end it emerges sadly battered, and with its cloak of antiquity torn to shreds.

Chapter 3. "California's First Hotel"

THE ASSURANCE with which certain writers have contradicted each other as to which was California's first hotel is reminiscent of the differences of opinion among some of the early miners as to what was gold and what was something else that glittered. In digging into the story of the early inns one sometimes finds at grass roots what appears to be a golden bonanza of material, but when this is assayed much of it turns out to be literary pyrites instead of historical gold dust and nuggets.

This may be a bit harsh, but the reader is justified in expecting something better than fool's gold when he picks up a book purporting to deal in twenty-four carat facts. Back in the hair-trigger, ill tempered days of '49 they were likely to shoot a man for trying to palm off brass filings for gold dust, but today we are more civilized and can only call attention to his misrepresentation of facts. It has required a deal of pick and shovel work and panning to dig out and separate a few grains of truth from a mass of valueless material, and even with the most painstaking care it is probable that a few pieces of pyrites have slipped into the story. If these be detected the reader is asked to weigh what has just been said before wishing he could reach for his shooting iron.

It was over a third of a century ago when the old Washington House at Monterey began to be called "California's first hotel,"[1] and since that time one author after another has taken this statement into stock without troubling to find out if it happened to be true. Worse still, some writers have further confused matters by adding some of their own "facts," that at best appear to have been no more than unconfirmed hearsay, and a few of these will serve to explain what was meant by the amount of work required to sift out the true statements from those inspired by wishful thinking. The author who seems to have started this rumor about the Washington adds for good measure that the place was built in 1832, on the northwest corner of Calle de Montenegro, or Washington and Pearl streets. For a few years thereafter it is said to have been the private residence of Don Eugenio Montenegro, who married one of the Soberanes girls, and after this it was used as a hotel.[2] To make matters still more interesting, another writer says that the place was built about 1834.[3]

Getting down to facts, Eugenio Montenegro's name does not appear in the records of Monterey until the latter date,[4] so the first of the foregoing statements appears to be too optimistic by at least a couple of years. In 1836 Montenegro was officially listed as a bachelor who was living in a house described as "*Casa No. 44*,"[5] and it was not until March 14, 1839, that he became a Monterey real estate owner. On the 12th of that month he petitioned the *Ayuntamiento* for a lot having a frontage of fifty *varas* and a depth of eighty (about 139 feet by 222), and after the ground was measured, title was granted him on the same date.[6] Unfortunately, the location of the lot is not given, but from what will be seen it can only have been the ground that Alberto Tresconi bought a few years later. To conclude this initial part of the debunking process, it was not until between June and September of 1839 that Montenegro married Juana María Soberanes;[7] and in anticipation of that happy event he probably built the house whose story has been so everlastingly mauled about that its own builder would have difficulty in recognizing it.

Still another author, after making the same statements about the Washington Hotel, changes his mind and says that it was built in 1840 by a tinsmith named Alberto Tresconi, who is said to have traveled from Mexico to Monterey on horseback in the same year. The house he built is said to have accommodated one hundred lodgers, the *adobe* for its construction being obtained from the rear of the San Carlos church, and Louis Raggio having furnished the lumber.[8] To liven up the story, the first writer referred to says that Tresconi did not arrive in Monterey until 1841, but fails to explain how he got there.[9] Still another author brings him afoot from Mexico City to Mazatlán, and thence to Monterey in 1842 by the San Francisco-bound American steamer "*Julia Liedsdorf*," that is said to have been named for the wife of the American vice-consul.[10]

Dealing with the two men who are supposed to have been pioneering the hotel industry in California in 1840, Tresconi's name first appears in the Monterey records in June and July of 1844, when Thomas

A. Larkin, American consul and merchant, gave him credit to the extent of two or three dozen pieces of glass and a box of tin.[11] Luigi Raggio did not arrive in California until July 27, 1847, when he disembarked at San Francisco, and while he did establish a saw mill on the Potrero ranch, near Monterey, this was not until the winter of '47 or the spring of '48.[12] All of this must have made it difficult for either of these men to have had a hand in the business of building a hotel at Monterey in 1840.

These peripatetic dates are confusing enough, in all conscience, but when it comes to the "steamer *Julia Liedsdorf*" the confusion literally becomes confounded—unless the statement about the steamship is a distorted version of somewhat similar facts. What really happened was that on June 22, 1841, Captain William A. Leidesdorff arrived at Monterey from New York in command of the schooner *Julia Ann*, but there is no record of Tresconi having been one of the ship's company, either on this voyage or on subsequent ones made between Monterey and Mazatlán between May and August of 1844.[13] Leidesdorff was American vice-consul at Yerba Buena, it is true, but his appointment was not made until October of 1845—and he was never married![14] It is also true that Leidesdorff owned the first steam-powered vessel on the coast of California, but this was no more than a sixty-foot stern-wheel Russian launch that he brought down from Bodega in October of 1847, and her career on the bay of San Francisco and the Sacramento River was so brief and ignominious that as a steamboat she was never officially named.[15] According to the maritime records, there never was a steam or sailing vessel bearing the name of "*Julia Leidsdorf*." Finally, it is a well-known fact that the first ocean-going steamer to make a landfall on the coast of California was the Panama Mail Company's paddle-wheel steamship *California*, that anchored in the bay of Monterey on February 24, 1849.

The next thing that impresses one on looking over the foregoing assortment of statements is the size of the house that is said to have turned into the Washington Hotel. If Montenegro's private residence was big enough to have accommodated one hundred lodgers, his menage must have been more on the order of a tribe than a family. This is an improbable state of affairs, in view of the fact that in 1840 he was only a deputy in charge of a few watchmen at the Monterey custom-house.[16] Wherever Montenegro may have lived earlier, on February 18, 1849, he rented from Nathan Spear part of a furnished house located at the southwest corner of what are today Pearl, Alvarado and Polk streets and Munras Avenue, and next door to Captain Juan B. Cooper's home. He continued paying twenty-five dollars a month (or the equivalent in hides) for the place at least as late as July 27th of the same year, when Spear was negotiating with Don Manual Jiméno to sub-rent the house.[17] As has been said, Montenegro acquired his Monterey lot in 1839 and was married in 1840, and it is probable that at some time between 1839 and 1842 he built the house on the street that was named after him, and where he was living a few years later.[18]

One is tempted to speculate on the accuracy of the statement that the *adobe* used to build the Washington Hotel was taken from the rear of the San Carlos church in 1840. If what is meant is that the earth used in the manufacture of the *adobes* was dug up at that point, the story may be a true one. But this is not what is stated, and the inference is that the *adobes* were high-graded from the chapel's sequestered hind quarters. It makes a good story, admittedly, but an improbable one when the facts are examined. The church was more or less abandoned down to 1837 or 1838, but at that time Padre José María del Real left the ruined old Carmel Mission and took charge of the San Carlos chapel, where he remained until November of 1845. In the latter part of February, 1846, Padre Doroteo Ambris took over and served until 1851,[19] and it is inconceivable that either priest would have permitted the church's old walls to be despoiled. The only time when the building material might have been "obtained" without too much scandal was between November, 1845, and February, 1846, but unfortunately this is five or six years too late to agree with the statement under discussion. Apart from all this, the San Carlos church was built of stone, not *adobes*.

The claim that the Washington was California's first hotel, and that it dated anywhere from 1832 to 1840, is now further shaken by an official haymaker. As was stated earlier, on July 28th, 1846, Alcalde Colton, of Monterey, wrote that there was not a public table or hotel in all California,[20] and had the Washington been doing business at the time, right in his home town, the *alcalde* would certainly have known about it. In the meantime, between July of 1844 and June of 1846 Consul Larkin paid out several hundred dollars to various residents of Monterey for boarding distressed American seamen,[21] and despite the fact that one of these payments was made to a "boarding-house keeper" named William Mathews, this seems to definitely confirm Colton's statement about the lack of hotels. At least as far as Monterey was concerned.

The process of sorting over the loose statements made thus far now brings us to July of 1846, when we finally come across something that has the appearance of being a fact, even though it is a negative one. On March 6, 1847, Colton remarked that a public hotel had never been able to maintain itself in California,[22] and from this it might be inferred that there was once such a place. Whatever may have been meant, as will be seen later on, between July 31st and August 2nd of 1846 a hotel was opened at Yerba Buena, and however primitive this place may have been, the fact that it thus early offered the accommodations of a public hostelry proves the oft repeated statements to the effect that the Washington was the dean of California's hotels to be nothing more than a wild-cat claim. The yarn about the Washington's seniority having been exploded we would be justified in dropping the story at this point, but it will be entertaining to follow it through to the conclusion, and see what other bits of tinsel have been palmed off as gold.

Apparently with the idea of proving that the hotel was a going concern at the time (and perhaps to show that the redoubtable Judge Bean of Texas fame was not the first man west of the Pecos to deal out justice straight from the hip), the same author who is unable to make up his mind as to whether the Washington was built in 1832 or in 1840 twice tells the following story. According to him, on May 12, 1847, a party of gamblers opened a *monte* game in the Washington Hotel, and when Alcalde Colton heard what was going on he ordered out a file of soldiers and moved in on the sportsmen. Having rounded them up from beneath beds and such like hiding places, he administered summary justice to the tune of a drumhead fine of twenty dollars apiece, plus one hundred dollars assessed against the Washington's proprietor. After taking up the collection he wound up the evening's exercise by delivering a stimulating lecture on the good their contributions would do in helping build a school house and a civil administration building.[23]

While in a general way this is what happened, there are certain discrepancies between this version and the true story. To begin with, Colton's action was not inspired by the righteous indignation of the moment, but was in accord with a decree forbidding gambling that he had published on September 29, 1946.[24] According to his diary, far from indulging in a flow of rhetoric, the *alcalde* confined his remarks to a terse statement to the effect that the only speech he had to make was in the shape of a fine of twenty dollars per head. It was Dr. Robert Semple, one of the gamblers arrested, who delivered the lecture, and pointed his remarks by being the first to contribute. While the following is doubtless pure coincidence, Semple and Colton had been partners in the publication of the *Californian* down to five days before the raid, when their ways parted.[25]

To this point the apocryphal version of the affair is surprising enough, but the real pay-off comes with Alcalde Colton's unequivocal statement that the episode took place in a two-story "Hotel honored with the name of the Astor House!"[26] So, after all this beating of drums, it appears that far from being California's first hotel, the Washington was not even Monterey's first public house. And if there should be any doubt about the matter of priority, it is only necessary to refer to the April 17, 1847, issue of the *Californian*, in which still another earlier place, the Monterey Hotel, is advertised as having been opened a month before the "Washington Hotel" episode.

Thus far the alleged story of the Washington has been strung together on a frayed thread of allegations and possibilities, that is further weakened by the interjection of a number of downright impossibilities, and it is high time that the strain be eased by the consideration of a few probabilities as to when the place was really built.

On November 23, 1847, Tresconi bought one hundred thirty-six pounds of lead at Larkin's general store,[27] and from this it would appear that down to that time he was still engaged in tinsmithing, and had not yet gone in for hotel building. By 1848 Tresconi's home was a low two-story house that stood on the northwest corner of Pearl and Washington, and Montenegro's residence was located about fifty *varas* north of this, on the latter street, the space between the two houses being vacant. For a good guess at what followed we are indebted to the same writer who produced the classic about the "steamer *Julia Lieds-*

dorf," who says that in 1849 Tresconi bought the "old Washington Hotel" and remodeled it.[28] It is a bit of a strain on the imagination to accept a place that had not been built at the time as being "old," but apart from this we are probably at last getting close to the truth. On March 5th of that year Larkin sold Tresconi a considerable quantity of varnish, white paint and flat bar iron,[29] and unless the latter was erecting a house it is hard to explain what he was doing with this building material. What probably happened is that a little before this Tresconi bought Montenegro's place, and started work on what eventually became the three-story building that took up the vacant space between the two older houses. And it is certain that about this time Tresconi's home was turned into a wing on the southern end of the new building, while Montenegro's house may at the same time have been incorporated as the northern end of the place, or an extension thereto.[30] This is deductive reasoning, admittedly, but its soundness is borne out by the following first-hand account of what Tresconi was really up to in the building line in 1849.

William Redmond Ryan arrived in Monterey from the Stanislaus River country one afternoon during the first heavy rain storm of the winter of 1848-49 (probably late in September or early in October of '48), and what he learned the next morning on going to look after his horse can best be told in his own words:

"Working at a bench, at the farther end of the stable, was a carpenter, whom I immediately recognized as having served in the volunteers. The floor of the stable was covered with chips and shavings, and my unfortunate steed was endeavouring to satisfy the cravings of his stomach upon them.

'How do they feed the horses here?' I asked the carpenter; 'They don't seem to give them anything to eat.'

'Oh, yes they do,' replied Chips; 'they have their three feeds a day regular — three wisps of hay, and a promise of oats, which accounts for all the horses being so fat in these here parts. There isn't a bit of corn or grass to be had anywhere else in town, so that the tinman can lay it on as thick as he pleases.'

'And, pray, who is the tinman?'

'The chap that owns these stables, and that large block there, and the store in front. I thought everybody knew him. He came here a few years ago — a poor, ragged younker, and took to making tin cups and saucepans to earn a living. Well, you see he lived very close for three or four years, grudging himself the smallest comfort, until he scraped together money enough to buy a large stock of liquor and other things, with which he set up a grog and general store. Since then he's been dabbling in every sort of speculation, not forgetting his original calling (for he manufactures tin pans for the use of the miners), and they say he's now one of the richest men in Monterey. There isn't one of those saucepans that he turns out of his shop that doesn't fetch at least four dollars; although the same article could be bought, in any part of the States, for five shillings. He's a hard nut to crack, an' I guess shaves as close to the wind, in a bargain, as the sharpest amongst us Yankees. I'll stick to him, however, until the winter is over, and until I can earn enough to take me back to the mines.'

'What are you doing for him?'

'*He's fitting up his house for an hotel and baths, and I'm doing all the joining work for him*'."[31]

It is unfortunate that we do not know the exact date on which Tresconi bought the property of Montenegro, but it is certain that this was between 1839 and 1850. As has been seen, Montenegro was granted the lot on March 14th of the former year, and on November 19, 1850, the title to this was confirmed to Albert Tresconi, who in a petition to the Common Council of Monterey stated that he had "lost the original papers made out by the *Ayuntamiento* that conveyed title to the property," on which the Washington Hotel stood at the time of his petition.[32]

Giving the *coup de grace* to a firmly rooted and hardy old tradition is about as tough a contract as extinguishing the ninth and last life of the proverbially alley cat, but if the foregoing does not do the job as far as the Washington Hotel's antiquity is concerned then nothing ever will. The place was built between 1848 and 1849, and while some additions were doubtless made later on, it is safe to say that by the fall of the latter year the building had taken its final shape; that of a three-story house, something over two hundred feet in length by fifty in width, with Tresconi's old narrow-fronted and gabled-roofed dwelling forming a low two-story wing running westward for about one hundred feet from the hotel's southern end. The walls of both buildings were of *adobe*, plastered over and whitewashed; their roofs were of shingles, and it is reasonable to believe that the woodwork was painted white. The ground floor of the new building was taken up by the bar and billiard room, dining room and offices; a central outside stairway led from Washington Street to a recessed veranda on the second floor, that gave access to a large salon that was used for balls and other public gatherings.[33] No description is known to have survived of the interior appointments and furnishings, but these must have been in keeping with the reputation the place eventually acquired as Monterey's leading hotel.

From various contemporary statements it seems that the house was opened for business about the middle of September of '49, and while Tresconi doubtless presided at the inauguration ceremonies, he at once rented it to a former private in Colonel Stevenson's Regiment of New York Volunteers, for a consideration of twelve hundred dollars a month.[34] The Constitutional Convention of California was in session at the time, and the new hotel was filled with delegates, who paid as high as two hundred dollars a month for rooms.[35] This was the beginning of the flood tide of its fortunes, and for almost a quarter of a century the place was Monterey's most popular hostelry.

It is not certain how long the hotel continued to be operated by its first renter, but on December 13, 1854, Tresconi leased it for three years to John M. O'Neill and James A. Gray, when the rental was reduced to one hundred seventy-five dollars a month,[36] and on the expiration of the lease the owner presumably took over the establishment. At any rate, Tresconi advertised the place on April 18, 1857, as being under his own management, and offered his old friends and the traveling public the added inducement of having both a bath house and the San José stage station on the premises.[37]

So far as can be learned, Tresconi ran the Washington for the next ten or twelve years, and it must have been during this time that he solved the problem of subduing the truculency some of his customers exhibited after a prolonged session at the bar. A little circus had straggled into Monterey on its last financial legs, and despite the awe-inspiring feats of its professional Sampson, after a few performances it folded its tent for the last time. The astute ex-tinsmith thereupon hired the strong man as his barkeeper, and when the latter appeared on the scene and flexed his muscles the saloon's patrons turned into models of genteel behavior.[38] The hotel continued to flourish for some twenty years, but when by 1873 it became apparent that the county seat was to be removed from Monterey to Salinas, Tresconi prudently sold out to Messrs. Lockwood and Bryan. He was still fond of the place, however, and he and his family continued to patronize it for the next few years.[39]

By this time the Washington's days were numbered, and when the first Del Monte Hotel was opened in 1880 it gave up the struggle. From Monterey's elite hostelry it degenerated into a gamblers' resort, and it must have been about this time, or perhaps a little earlier, that a series of well patronized bull and bear fights were staged in the *corral*, that served as a backyard to the premises.[40] But not even these stimulating sports could rejuvenate the old place, and by the turn of the century it had become a tumbled down rookery that harbored a few stray bits of human jetsam, left behind by the ebbing tide of fortune. The Washington lingered on for a few years longer, and in the summer of 1914 the end came, when the crumbling and bat-infested ruin was torn down to make way for the present *Peninsula Herald* building. The wreck went down with flying colors, however, as the literary requiem fired over the last ripple of its history still acclaimed it "California's First Hotel."[41]

In so far as it has been possible to assemble the facts, this is the true story of the most prominent of the several claimants to the distinction of having been the State's pioneer hostelry. There are other places for which local patriots have from time to time claimed the title, but there is no necessity for according them any special mention at this time. Having knocked the clay-footed idol of the "First Hotel" off its roost in California's Valhalla of Fame, it seems fitting to round off this part of the story with an account of the other hotels that appeared in Monterey before '49.

As was said earlier, in view of the fact that Monterey was the first seat of the American territorial government, and before that time the town was for a century California's Spanish and Mexican capital and the most important settlement in the country, the first hostelry might reasonably be expected to have made its appearance there. But it was not until a year after California's first honest-to-goodness hotel had been opened at Yerba Buena that there is a definite reference to such an establishment at Monterey. This appears as the following editorial item in the *Californian* of April 17, 1847:

"*Monterey Hotel* — We have the pleasure to announce that our worthy friends Messrs. Taber and Isabel have opened the above house on '*Main Street*' in this city, and to assure visitors to the Capital that these gentlemen, and their good wives will do all in their power to make their house a 'home'."

Both John D. Taber and Dr. James C. Isabel arrived by the overland immigrant road in 1846, and it seems that their attempt to make Monterey's first hotel a home for the restless characters of those days met

with scant response. The partnership lasted less than six months, when
Dr. and Mrs. Isabel moved to San José, and later settled on the Calaveras River, a few miles from Stockton.[42]

In the meantime, the Astor House had been opened on Main Street,
near the old custom-house, and judging from Alcalde Colton's account
of his raid on the *monte* game that he interrupted there the night of
May 11th, gambling must have had a stronger attraction than home
life. Taber evidently came to the same conclusion, as by November
14th he and R. C. M. Hoyt (another pioneer of '46) had taken over
the Astor House and announced that it had been refitted and was ready
for customers, no mention of home life being made.[43] but this partnership was even shorter lived than the first, as four months later it was
dissolved, and Taber was left the sole proprietor of the place.[44] This
was just at the beginning of the gold excitement, and it is quite possible
that Hoyt gave up hotel keeping in favor of the placer diggings.
However this may have been, on June 29th both Taber and his wife
succumbed to the gold fever, closed the hotel, and in company with
William R. Longley, Monterey's assistant *alcalde*, departed for the
mines.[45] Monterey was thus left without a hotel of any kind, and
Colton's vivid pen picture of the straits in which the civil, military and
naval authorities found themselves in consequence gives a spirited idea
of how the discovery of gold upset California's domestic economy:

"Gen. Mason, Lieut. Lanman, and myself, form a mess; we have a house and all
the table furniture and culinary apparatus requisite; but our servants have run,
one after another, till we are almost in despair; even Sambo, who we thought
would stick by from laziness, if for no other cause, ran last night; and this morning for the fortieth time, we had to go to the kitchen, and cook our own breakfast.
A general of the United States Army, a commodore of a man-of-war, and the
Alcalde of Monterey, in a smoking kitchen, grinding coffee, toasting herring, and
peeling onions! These gold mines are going to upset all the domestic arrangements
of society, turning the head to the tail, and the tail to the head."[46]

The only known description of the Astor House is what can be
gathered from two sketches of the place, made in 1847 and 1849 by
William Rich Hutton, and from Colton's remarks about his raid. From
these sources of information it appears to have been a small and unpre-
possessing two-story building, whose box-like appearance was only
slightly relieved by a shallow central recess between two short wings
that projected from its front and abutted on the street. The fact that

it possessed at least one fireplace proves the house to have been of American construction, and not to date back to some such time as the Spanish discovery of California, and as there were feather beds with valances, with "nameless furniture" ensconced beneath these, the place must have aspired to a certain degree of gentility.[47]

Actually, this is all that is known about the Astor House, but in a well-meant attempt to liven up its commonplace story, still another writer seized upon the game that Alcalde Colton so abruptly terminated, and without any pretense of hedging her guess flatly states that this was "the first monte (gambling bank) ever run in California."[48] Unfortunately, this author ignored three facts that disprove the statement. First, the game of *monte* (or *banca*, as it is properly called) is a quaint old Spanish custom that was enthusiastically followed in California long before either John Jacob Astor or the Astor House were heard of. Second, gambling was so prevalent in Monterey that eight months before the event Alcalde Colton found it necessary to publish the decree already mentioned. Third, in his version of the affair the *alcalde* on May 12, 1847, made it perfectly clear that this was *not* California's first *monte* game:

"Mr. R----, from Missouri—known here under the soubriquet of 'the prairie-wolf'—I found between two bed-ticks, with his coat and boots on, and half smothered with the feathers. *He was the ringleader, and raises a monte table wherever he goes as regularly as a whale comes to the surface to blow.*"[49]

These two places, the Monterey Hotel and the Astor House, were the only hostelries known to have been opened in Monterey before the great Gold Rush of '49, and the story now shifts to the early days of San Francisco, or Yerba Buena, as the place was then called from the profusion of wild peppermint that used to grow thereabouts.[50]

Chapter 4. Vioget's Tavern

W<small>HEN THE</small> seafaring pioneers of the Argonauts of '49 shed their tarry breeks in favor of the broad leathern pantaloons of the Californians and began settling ashore, the counterpart of the forecastles where they had gathered to toss down pannikins of grog during their watches below appeared in the guise of a tavern that was destined to be the first of countless numbers of later resorts that ranged from drinking places and flophouses to the world's most ornate hotels.

The man responsible for this transmutation was Captain Jean Jacques Vioget, who was by profession a seaman and not an inn-keeper; and in all probability he had no idea that he was pioneering a great industry when in 1840 he built a little shanty in Yerba Buena and opened a saloon. But whatever his thoughts about the future may have been, when he laid the floor joists of the place he also laid the social foundation upon which California's first hotel was to appear some four years later. Strange as it may seem, little has been written about the man who was responsible for California's first American public house, and who made the first survey of San Francisco; who was at one time one of the State's important land owners and, finally, who was one of the last links between the old social order and the new.

Jean Isaac Vioget was of French-Swiss extraction, and was born on June 14, 1799, in the now extinct Swiss village of Cambremont le Petit, in the canton of Vaud. He changed his baptismal name of Isaac to Jacques, and when he was fifteen years old ran away from home and joined a fife and drum corps in the Grand Army of Napoleon I.[1] After the Emperor's overthrow Jean was apprenticed to a French naval engineer, and a few years later he was employed by the government of the Dutch East Indies in an engineering capacity, at Batavia. Thereafter he joined the Imperial Navy of Dom Pedro of Brazil, and rose to the rank of captain.[2] Vioget's first mercantile experience in the western Pacific was trading on the coast of South America, whence he arrived at Yerba Buena in July of 1837 in command of the Ecuadorian brig

Delmira.[3] Even that early it was becoming increasingly evident that California's future was to be a golden one, and after making the first known sketch of the settlement,[4] and an ocean voyage or two, Captain Vioget settled down to a coastwise and island trading business that was carried on asea and ashore until October of 1839, when he elected to make Yerba Buena his home.[5]

The little settlement had only four years earlier attained the status of a *pueblo,* and at the time its population did not exceed fifty souls, of whom a third were foreigners by birth. But hide trading and whaling ships were beginning to arrive in increasing numbers, and the importance of the place was growing. *Solares,* or building lots, were being called for, and late in 1839 the governor of California, Juan Bautista Alvarado, instructed *alcalde* Francisco Guerrero,[6] of Yerba Buena, to have the *pueblo* surveyed and mapped. Until this time such lots as had been sold were scattered more or less at random over the equivalent of twelve irregular blocks, that were, generally speaking, divided into six *solares* of fifty by fifty *varas.* With this as a basis, and equipped with a sextant and ship's compass, Captain Vioget, conforming to the corners already fixed by existing buildings,[7] appears to have attempted to work out a scheme that was years ahead of the comparatively modern science of hygiene as applied to city planning. Instead of orienting the blocks to conform with the magnetic cardinal bearings, he effected a compromise that agreed approximately with the lines of the solstices, thereby providing for the maximum amount of sunshine at both the north and the south declinations. But his ideas were too advanced, and San Francisco's blocks were later altered to conform with a more conventional plan.[8] Vioget's survey included the area bounded by Pacific, California, Montgomery and Dupont streets, although what at the time passed for streets were no more than sandy tracks, leading in a more or less straight line from one house to another. Again to conform with existing conditions, the width of the streets was fixed at about eighteen *varas,* or forty-nine feet,[9] and this accounts for the narrow thoroughfares that for so long hampered San Francisco's traffic. The first of these tracks to be used, and the only one that at the time bore a name, was the *Calle de la Fundación,* leading to the Presidio, that later on became Dupont Street and is today Grant Avenue. On this stood the second house built, and for a decade the most pretentious in the village,

Vioget's House (#6)

Mountain Road, showing erosion

Van Wagener Hotel (in the distance)

Strawberry Valley, 1861

the *adobe* dwelling and store erected in 1837 by William A. Richardson, Yerba Buena's first settler.[10] Scattered along the other trails were perhaps half a dozen shanties built of undressed and unpainted lumber, and beyond these there was nothing but sand hills and *monte*, or brush forest.

Captain Vioget's survey and plat were completed in October of 1839, and on November 1st Governor Alvarado ordered that he be granted a hundred *vara* square lot in the *pueblo*, presumably in recompense for his services. This order was at the time complied with to the extent of placing the grantee in possession of Lot Number 23, measuring one hundred fifty *varas*, or the equivalent of two *solares*, and forming the western third of the block bounded by Kearny, Clay, Montgomery and Sacramento streets, and that was later on bisected from east to west by Commercial Street. In the same month, Vioget paid the *ayuntamiento*, or town council, twelve *pesos* for the grant, and on January 15, 1840, he was given legal possession of the property by an instrument dated the 16th of the same month. The deed also (and without further payment) conveyed title to the remainder of his grant, which was described as being another lot of the same dimensions located at a point known as El Cañutal, west of the road to the mission of San Francisco de Asis and where San Francisco's civic center now stands. The location of this piece of property was forthwith changed to one behind the water front *solar* that had just been granted to Jacob P. Leese and adjoining Vioget's first lot, thus giving the latter possession of the four fifty *vara solares* forming the western two-thirds of the block just described.[11]

There, on the southeast corner of Kearny and Clay, and abutting on the latter street (then Yerba Buena's principal thoroughfare), Vioget in the same month began work on the house where shortly thereafter he opened his saloon. This marked his adoption of California as his new homeland, and on May 18, 1840, he applied for naturalization as a Mexican citizen, which was granted the same day.[12] Captain Vioget was forty-one years of age,[13] a bachelor, and one of the most respected and best-liked foreigners in the *pueblo*, and as soon as he opened his tavern it became headquarters for ship owners, captains and supercargos, Mexican government officials and ranchers visiting Yerba Buena on business.[14] The place was as much a public club as it was a saloon, where its patrons met to discuss and consummate public and private business over good liquor. So to add to the attractions its proprietor installed one of the first billiard tables on the Pacific coast of North America. The tavern was small and its appointments simple, but the entertainment was the best available, and Vioget's sparkling wit and genial hospitality soon became proverbial from Mazatlán to Sitka. The rough walls were decorated with his drawings, which included the water color sketch of Yerba Buena, and over the bar hung a print of the *Savanna*, the first paddle-wheel steamer to cross the Atlantic.[15] While history does not record this, one is free to imagine a group of deep sea skippers sipping their toddies the while they argued the relative merits of sail and steam, and speculating on how long it would be before such a ship dropped anchor in the bay of San Francisco. Yerba Buena was without a municipal building, and Vioget's plat of the village hung in a prominent place on one of the tavern's walls. Business in building lots became brisk, and as the *alcalde* sold one of these Vioget would pencil in its location and the owner's name, a custom that for six or seven years constituted the town's sole graphic record of real estate locations.[16]

A year after the tavern was opened it was the scene of an amusing contest that gives a good idea of a menu of those days, as well as of the hardy pioneers' endurance. Within a decade, however, such a bill of fare had expanded to include almost every kind of delicacy known elsewhere about the world, and the gold-laden diners were turning up their noses at anything less aristocratic than quail on toast, or, in a pinch, "Hangtown frys." Captain Vioget was famous as a trencherman of outstanding ability and, as his height of five foot eight and only moderate rotundity gave little hint of his hold's cargo capacity, he took no little pride in the reputation.[17] One of his particular cronies was Andrew Hoeppner, a German music teacher, whose slender build was even more misleading than Vioget's lines. These two, together with several companions, were in the saloon one day when a heated discussion arose as to who could eat the most. Boasts ran high, and Hoeppner finally challenged his host to a contest, a gauge that the latter, thoroughly deceived by appearances, instantly accepted. More than the sordid eating of food was involved, as the not-so-long past Battle of Waterloo rankled uneasily in the background. The challenge was an affair of honor, and French or German supremacy was at stake. Invitations were sent to all of Yerba Buena's elite to witness the contest, and the audience was sharply divided into two enthusiastically partisan camps; the one supporting Vioget, as Emperor Napoleon's champion, and the other backing Hoeppner, who held the list for Field Marshal von Blucher and the Duke of Wellington.

The match opened with hot cakes, stacks of which were quickly stowed away by both contestants, with Hoeppner leading by a plate when the second course was announced. This proved to be beefsteaks, that were disposed of in short order, with the challenger a steak ahead at the end of the second round. Next came plate after plate of *guisado*, or meat stewed in the Spanish style, followed by *carne asado*, or broiled beef, and *tamales* (of which each ate at least a dozen), and generous helpings of *frijoles* to top off the more serious part of the meal. Dessert began in the form of an immense pudding, during the consumption of which Vioget began to show signs of distress, while his opponent appeared to be no more than getting his second wind. This semi-final course was ballasted by several kinds of pies and black coffee (the only beverage taken), when the erstwhile champion hauled down his colors and Hoeppner was acclaimed the victor. The contestants then took wine and played billiards as if nothing unusual had taken place, and while acknowledging himself defeated, Vioget attributed his failure to maintain French honor to the fact that he was fifteen or twenty years the elder of the two, and to the day of his death insisted that had they been of the same age Hoeppner would not have stood a chance.[18]

Captain Vioget now came into considerable prominence in connection with the colonization plans of his countryman, John A. Sutter. Being good friends, Sutter patronized Vioget's house whenever he was in Yerba Buena, and on December 13, 1840, J. I. Vioget and Jacob P. Leese were witnesses to the contract whereby Sutter purchased the Russian-American Fur Company's movable property at Fort Ross.[19] This was one of the important steps toward the development of Sutter's plan for the Swiss-American colony of New Helvetia, and early in the following year he employed Vioget to survey and map the country about his fort on the American River, where the Mexican authorities had promised him a grant of eleven square leagues of land. The work was completed in the summer of 1841, but despite the two men's friendship Vioget was compelled to threaten legal action before he could secure payment for his services.[20]

In the meantime the tavern had prospered until its profits, together with those from general trading, permitted Captain Vioget to retire from active inn keeping and devote himself to other enterprises. His association with Sutter's plans may have given him the idea of himself becoming a land owner, and in 1844 he employed Captain Juan Nepomuceno Padilla (an officer in California's Mexican national guard and Yerba Buena's barber) to manage the saloon and billiard room.[21] Whatever Vioget's ideas about real estate may have been, he had a good friend in the person of General Manuel Micheltorena, the new governor and commandant general of California, and on October 14th of the same year he was granted six square leagues of land in what later on became Sonoma County. He christened this "Rancho Blucher,"[22] and thereby hangs a tale.

When Captain Vioget arrived at Yerba Buena in 1837 he was just in time to participate in the first Fourth of July celebration held in California, which was attended by all the foreigners in the *pueblo* as well as by all the Californians within leagues of the bay of San Francisco. One of Vioget's closest companions was Captain Joseph Steel, of the Boston bark *Kent*, who was also present. Steel was of the same fun-loving nature as his friend, and in the course of the festivities the conversation turned to the Battle of Waterloo. Vioget's French ancestry, together with the fact that he had served in the Grand Army, led him to take up the cudgels in defense of Napoleon. At the time (and for long afterward) Vioget affected enormous mustachios of the type worn by the Emperor's Old Guard, and this, as well as his general resemblance to the famous Prussian field-marshal, prompted Captain Steel to dub him "Blucher," a nickname that stuck to him for the rest of his life and by which he was almost as well known as by his own name.[23]

Probably in line with Captain Vioget's ideas about the value of California land, his associate, Captain Padilla, in 1845 secured grants to the *ranchos* Roblar de la Miseria and Bolsa de Tomales. These properties adjoined the Rancho Blucher on the south and east, and their total area of nine square leagues gave the two possession of no less than forty-one square miles of land in Sonoma and Marin counties.[24] Unfortunately for whatever Vioget's plans were, Captain Padilla was then ordered to duty under General Mariano Guadalupe Vallejo, on the "Northern Frontier." There, from Sonoma, he was to keep a watchful eye on the growing pretensions of the foreigners, with especial attention to Sutter, who was becoming entirely too strong for the Mexican government's comfort. Shortly thereafter a revolt broke out against General Micheltorena, and as Padilla was one of his supporters, the governor's overthrow and expulsion placed him under a cloud that appears to have effectually eclipsed the land plans. A couple of years later Yerba Buena's first building boom got under way, and on December 24, 1847, Vioget traded the Rancho Blucher to Captain Stephen Smith of Bodega Bay, for milled lumber to the value of $1500.00, and it is safe to say that he profited roundly by the transaction.[25]

In the meantime Captain Vioget made a voyage or two to the Sandwich Islands, and early in February of 1846 he leased his tavern to Robert T. Ridley.[26] His only connection with the place thereafter was in the role of owner and landlord. In July of 1847 he married María Benvenides de Vásquez (a widow with two children), and built an *adobe* home on his father-in-law's lot on Kearny, across the street from the tavern.[27] Several other voyages to the Islands followed, and in 1849 Vioget and his family moved to San José, where in the following year he bought a house and lot on the *plaza* from Doña Juana Dios de Monteros, where he died on October 26, 1855.[28]

Jean Jacques Vioget was one of the last surviving links between the easy-going Spanish life of California and the hustling struggle for existence that followed the American occupation. He clung to the old customs to the end, and to the day of his death wore the short blue jacket, black pantaloons and *sombrero* of the land of his adoption.[29] Despite the fact of his having played so colorful a role in the country's period of transition, his burial place in San José's Oak Hill Cemetery is still an unmarked and weed-grown plot, and until a few years ago had been lost.[30]

While from the scanty records of those days it cannot be proved that Captain Vioget conducted either a public eating or sleeping place in connection with his bar and billiard saloon, on occasions he doubtless served meals to and put up some of his customers, and as these unquestionably paid for this service in one way or another it is safe to say that his tavern was the forerunner of the first hostelry in California of which there is a record. And it is certain that four or five months after it was leased by Ridley the place was turned into a hotel.

If there ever was any real question as to which was California's first inn, there certainly is none whatever about who was the first inn-keeper, or at any rate the first to leave an indelible record of his work. Although an Englishman by birth, this pioneer boniface of the Pacific coast rejoiced in the classical American name of John Henry Brown.

As in those days of fast moving history, nationalities were apt to accommodate themselves to the expediencies of the time and the place, he can be said to have been a circumstantial Yankee. Born on December 21, 1810, in Exeter, Devonshire, Brown was successively a sailor, an adopted member of the Cherokee Indian Nation, a hunter and fur trapper, and finally an immigrant to California, where he arrived at Sutter's Fort in October of 1845. After paying a short visit to Yerba Buena he returned to the Fort, where Sutter employed him as overseer of the cooking and butchering activities. Two months of this was more than enough, and when late in December of the same year Brown received an offer from Finch and Thompson, of Yerba Buena, to work as barkeeper in their saloon, he gave notice. His back wages amounted to sixty dollars, and after some haggling a settlement was reached whereby he accepted a passage to Yerba Buena, a plug of tobacco and a bottle of whiskey, and donated the money due him to the Fort's school fund.[31]

What was left of the tobacco and whiskey, plus his experience as cook and butcher, represented the sum total of John Henry Brown's worldy assets when in January of 1846 he returned to Yerba Buena.[32] But this sketchy equipment in no wise daunted him. John Thompson was a blacksmith whom he had known during his sojourn with the Cherokees,[33] and "Tinker" John Finch was a fellow Englishman, so instead of being a stranger in a strange place he found himself among friends. Finch and Thompson's place of business was in a large frame house on the corner of Kearny and Washington streets,[34] and there Brown went to work tending bar and keeping the firm's accounts.

Serving drinks in Yerba Buena in 1846 did not involve the hair-trigger knowledge of the infinite number of liquid concoctions that San Francisco's later bartenders required, as a bottle of whiskey and a glass were the only ingredients that figured in a shot of liquor in those days, but keeping the accounts of the establishment was quite another matter. Until Brown's advent "Tinker" Finch had presided behind the bar, and as he could neither read nor write, he had devised a system of bookkeeping that is reminiscent of the Aztecs' pictographic method of recording events and transactions. Finch had an excellent memory for names, and to stimulate this his records consisted of sketches at the top of each account that identified the customers, and below these a stroke of the pen or pencil stood for each shot served on credit. Captain William S. Hinckley wore large brass buttons on his coat, and in the saloon's account book he was represented by the picture of a button, a local sawyer by the drawing of a saw, and so on through the establishment's clientele. Brown's connection with Finch and Thompson lasted for only three weeks, when he accepted an offer to tend bar at the saloon that Robert T. Ridley had just leased from Captain Vioget.[35]

Bob Ridley was a jovial London cockney with an astounding capacity for brandy, and in addition to this he was a naturalized Mexican citizen, Captain of the Port, and one of its most popular foreigners. By 1846, when he leased the tavern, "Vioget's House" was known up and down the length of the Pacific coast of America, and under Ridley's management it continued to be Yerba Buena's most popular resort. Vioget's plat of the *pueblo* still hung in the barroom, and it now became customary for anyone wishing to buy a lot to consult Ridley as to a location, when this would be penciled in to the accompaniment of drinks all around and over the map. Under this usage the plat soon became so soiled and torn that Captain Hinckley volunteered to make a fair copy of the original. But when he undertook to do the work the state of his nerves was unfortunately such that he was quite unable to draw a straight line, and Brown, the new bartender, did the drafting for him.[36] This public-spirited gesture, together with a bartender's natural popularity, so bolstered Brown's fortunes that in less than six months he was casting about for a broader field wherein to exercise his talents.

John Henry Brown's opportunity was not slow in making its appearance, for when on June 3rd the twenty-one gun United States sloop of war *Portsmouth* anchored off Yerba Buena the daily comings and goings of her officers and men created an immediate demand for food and lodgings, and the *pueblo* had nothing of the kind to offer. But even so, while the demand was there the supply failed to materialize until galvanized into action by a six-shooter in the hand of one of the patriots of the Bear Party.

Upon their capture of Sonoma one of the first steps taken by the leaders of the "Bears" to safeguard themselves was to prepare a list of all the foreign residents of California, which was used to determine whether the insurgents might depend on them for support or whether their sympathies were with the Mexican government. When news of the outbreak at Sonoma reached General José Castro, acting governor and commandant general of California, he issued a proclamation calling upon loyal Mexican citizens to meet him at Santa Clara, to organize the defense of the country. Bob Ridley and Captain Hinckley were the only foreigners in Yerba Buena to answer the summons, and not unnaturally the former's name appeared in a prominent place on the "Bear's" list of suspects. So prominent, indeed, that Captain Frémont ordered his immediate arrest, and on July 2nd Dr. Robert Semple, one of the most active of the insurgents, apprehended him at the point of a pistol in his own saloon. Ridley made a move to argue the matter, but Semple cut him short by telling him to stand still, adding: "If you make a move, or attempt to escape, you will be a dead man." So summary was his arrest that Ridley had only time to pocket some loose change from the till, fortify himself with a couple of bottles of whiskey and tell Brown to take charge and do the best he could during his employer's enforced absence, and in a matter of minutes he was on his way to Sutter's Fort, the headquarters of the "Bears."[37]

This was Brown's chance to show his mettle as a publican, and he lost no time. It was obvious that the saloon fell far short of meeting the requirements of the moment, and its acting proprietor took steps to rectify this. Providentially, a whaler had just discharged three members of her crew, and Brown forthwith hired one of these worthies, a man named Tom Smith (of whom we will hear more later), as cook and steward. A sketchy remodeling of the resort was accomplished hurriedly, and in a couple of days Yerba Buena's first restaurant and sleeping place was ready for business, still under the name of "Vioget's House."[38]

The early chronicles of California's first hotel are meager, but we know that one of its first patrons was Captain John Gantt, who had commanded a company of mounted riflemen raised by Sutter on behalf of General Michaeltorena during the late Mexican political disturbance, now stopped with Brown for over a month.[39] While Captain Gantt's is the only name that has survived, it is certain that most of the other local celebrities of the day were guests at the new hostelry, and had Brown kept a register, we would doubtless find them all standing up to be counted. What the sleeping arrangements were in "Vioget's House" we can only surmise, but in the matter of refreshments there is no reason to doubt that Brown profited by his experience at Sutter's Fort and as a barkeeper to set forth as substantial and varied a fare as the limited resources of the village afforded. Among the items of food known to have been served were American pancakes, unsalted native butter (as well as the very salty imported article), wild honey, corn *tortillas, tamales,* beef, venison, antelope and bear steaks, wild ducks and geese, a variety of fish and a few vegetables, with Mexican *frijoles* invariably topping off the menu. To wash this down there were several excellent California wines, *aguardiente,* brandy and whiskey, and unlimited quantities of coffee and tea. So, however uneasy a night's lodging might have been, between the bar and the dining table the memory of this must soon have been effaced.

So far as is known, only one picture of "Vioget's House" exists, a Chinese ink wash sketch by the Swedish scientist Dr. G. M. Waseurtz af Sandel, probably drawn shortly after September, 1842, and certainly not later than February, 1844. This sketch shows the place to have been a one-story buliding that faced eastward and overlooked the beach, which at the time was about seventy-five yards distant. The front door was in the center of the house, and was flanked on either side by a square window. A narrow porch, raised two or three feet above the ground level, ran the length of the building's front and gave access to the entrance from Clay Street, on which the northern end of the house abutted. The place evidently had a good sized attic, as is indicated by a third square window in the northern gable end of its two-pitch roof, and two short ells extended westward from the northern and southern ends of the house, the former parallel to and on the line of Clay Street, and somewhat lower than the main part of the building. The only additional information that can be gathered from Dr. Sandel's sketch is the fact that a masonry chimney projected from the center of the roof ridge, and from this it may be inferred that the house had a fireplace. With one or two additional lean-tos, or semi-detached shanties built to accommodate the newly added eating and sleeping departments, this was about what California's first hotel looked like in July of 1846. The only thing that can be added is that the house was built of hand-sawed lumber, and in all probability was unpainted.[40]

Regarding the hotel's nationality, as has been seen, John Henry Brown was by birth an Englishman, and this was no doubt responsible for the atmosphere of the place at first changing from that of a Swiss-California public house to one more nearly resembling the usual air of a middle-class British tavern; and when on the morning of the Fourth of July celebration, held five days before the raising of the American flag over Yerba Buena, Vice-Consul Leidesdorff pointedly asked Brown if he was an American, the latter explained his national status by describing himself as a "white-washed" one.[41] And from this it may be concluded that from that time onward "Vioget's House" reflected its proprietor's political coloring.

On July 8th young Daniel Fisher arrived from Monterey with dispatches from Commodore Sloat to Captain Montgomery, announcing the annexation of California and ordering the flag to be raised over Yerba Buena. About eight o'clock on the morning of the 9th of July the shrill notes of fifes and the ruffling of drums heralded the disembarcation of the American force, that was landing at the foot of Clay Street. This consisted of some seventy men that were led by Lieutenant John S. Misroon followed by a detachment of bluejackets with Captain Montgomery, Lieutenant Joseph W. Revere and two midshipmen bringing up the rear. The column marched up Clay to the *plaza*, where it was deployed about the flagpole. There was not a single Mexican official of whom to demand the town's surrender, nor was there a Mexican flag to be lowered, as Rafael Pinto, the collector of customs and the last officer to depart, had left the official colors and his archives in a trunk with Leidesdorff for safe keeping. But despite this grave breach of protocol Captain Montgomery ran up the Stars and Stripes, and to the accompaniment of a twenty-one gun national salute from the *Portsmouth,* nailed English and Spanish copies of Commodore

Sloat's proclamation to the flagpole. The captain was unaware of the fact, but this last act established a precedent in the posting of public notices that was to last as long as there was anything left of the flag-pole to which such notices could be attached. This marked the end of Mexican rule at Yerba Buena, but the momentous occasion was wit-nessed by less than a dozen civilians who passed as American citizens: Leidesdorff, John Finch, Joseph P. Thompson, Mrs. Ridley, Mrs. Andrew Hoeppner, Mrs. Vioget, and John Henry Brown.[42]

Chapter 5. The Portsmouth House

T HE APPEARANCE of the Stars and Stripes before
Yerba Buena and the business end of a six-shooter sufficed to accomplish the metamorphosis of Captain Vioget's House from a Swiss-California-British tavern to a quasi-Yankee inn, but it took the showing of
St. George's ensign and the muzzles of shotted cannon to complete its
transformation into California's first hotel.

For almost a year before the American occupation Commodore
John D. Sloat, commanding the United States Pacific Squadron, and
Admiral Sir George F. Seymour, with a like complement of British
warships, had been playing the roles of rival cats watching a promising mouse-hole, up and down the coast from California to Mexico. Both
officers were under orders from their respective governments to be
prepared to capitalize on the appearance of the mouse in the guise of
war between the United States and Mexico, and it was anticipated that
the conflict would not only determine California's future sovereignty
but also would have a repercussion on the vexatious Oregon question.

As was only natural, no little rivalry was engendered between the
two squadrons, and this spirit spread ashore until bets were made freely
as to which flag would be run up first over Yerba Buena. There a good
percentage of the foreigners were of British origin, and these, together
with many native Californians, were outspoken in favoring annexation
by Great Britain. Partisan feeling ran higher than ever when a rumor
was spread to the effect that British Vice-Consul James Alexander
Forbes had asked that a warship be sent to protect his country's interests, and this ship, and the British flag, were expected to arrive any day.
The issue was not believed definitely settled even when on July 7th of
1846 Commodore Sloat seized Monterey, and on the 9th Captain John
B. Montgomery, commanding the *Portsmouth*, raised the American
flag over Yerba Buena, and thus anticipated whatever plans for territorial expansion their rivals may have entertained.

The situation continued so tense, indeed, that when on the morning

45

of the 11th a heavy gun was fired and the long roll beaten aboard the American warship, John Henry Brown and a number of his friends sprang up from the breakfast table and hurried down Clay Street to the water front, expecting to witness a spirited naval engagement.[1] The thirty-six gun sloop-of-war H.B.M.S. *Juno* was indeed just entering the harbor, and the warning gun and roll of drums were to recall the *Portsmouth* shore parties. The American ship was hurriedly cleared for action, with springs on her cables; her guns loaded and run out, the decks sanded, and her crew stood to their battle stations in anticipation of whatever action the British warship might attempt.[2] But to the disappointment of many of the onlookers, the supposedly hostile ship's visit proved to be a friendly one, and after polite exchanges of civilities on the part of the naval commanders the tension relaxed.

On the afternoon of the same day the *Juno's* captain landed to pay his respects to Vice-Consul Forbes, and among his boat's crew Brown recognized an old schoolmate and fellow Devon in the person of Midshipman Elliot. A reunion followed, and in the course of this the last lingering hopes for a change of flag were dashed by the midshipman's statement that his was a surveying ship bound for Oregon, and to the best of his knowledge his commanding officer had no orders beyond the peaceful execution of his mission. This may have been a disappointment to Brown, despite the very recent declaration as to his national status. But he accepted the outcome with good grace, and philosophically remarked that if there had been an engagement the British ship would certainly have been blown out of the water. The fate of Yerba Buena (and, incidentally, of California) having thus been amicably disposed of, it developed that Elliot's father owned a large and prosperous hotel in Devonport. Brown was an opportunist, and this bit of information gave him the idea of turning his makeshift hostelry into California's first real hotel.[3]

On July 31st the ship *Brooklyn* arrived from New York, with Elder Sam Brannan and his advance guard of some two hundred Mormons, who had sailed in the belief that they were emigrating to the Mexican Department of California. There, beyond reach of further persecutions at the hands of "this evil nation" (as Brother Orson Pratt described the United States in his farewell address to the Latter Day Saints, delivered in New York on November 8, 1845) and out of sight of "that damned flag" (as the frustrated Elder Brannan is reported to have explosively commented when, on the *Brooklyn's* arrival, he saw the Stars and Stripes waving over Yerba Buena), they had planned to occupy California and found a colony. With the arrival overland from Nauvoo of the main body of their coreligionists it was expected to become the promised land of the Mormon church. When they found that the aforementioned flag had anticipated them, and later on it developed that the Mormon hegira was to stop at Great Salt Lake, many of the colonists emulated John Henry Brown's philosophy and settled down to adjust themselves to existing conditions.[4]

It was from these people that Brown hired the staff for the more pretentious establishment he proceeded to organize. His housekeeper was the widow Mercy Narrimore, his cook Sarah Kittleman, and his waitress Lucy Nutting. Two other members of the Kittleman family were employed as carpenters to make the necessary tables, benches and bedsteads, and no doubt to effect further alterations and additions to Captain Vioget's original house. With the exception of four feather mattresses bought from the Mormons, the bedticks were stuffed with moss from the Sandwich Islands. Blankets were made from two widths of heavy flannel, and quilts out of calico, while real sheets for the first time made their appearance in the town. Everything was ready in a matter of days, and the new venture launched, still under the name of "Vioget's House." The doors were thrown open not a day too soon, for by August 2nd one after another American whaling ships began dropping anchor in the bay, for stays of from two to six months.[5]

Captain Bezer Simmons, master of the New England whaler *Magnolia*, was the first guest to stop at the new hotel, where he was soon joined by most of the other masters. All together, a dozen or more whaling ship skippers made the place their shore headquarters, but of these only two left permanent records of their passages in the history of California. Whether or not he was influenced by Brown's hospitality, Captain Simmons then and there elected to abandon the sea for a life ashore, and shortly thereafter became the senior member of the pioneer shipping firm of Simmons, Hutchinson & Co. The other notable seafarer who patronized Brown's hotel at this time was Captain William D. Phelps, master of the Boston bark *Moscow*. Captain Phelps was active in aiding Frémont and the "Bears," and his most outstanding exploit was performed on July 1st of 1846. On that memorable day he used his ship's boats to ferry Frémont, Lieutenant Archibald H. Gillespie, Kit Carson and a detachment of Bear Flag volunteers from Sausalito (the favorite anchorage for whaling ships, at the northwestern corner of the bay of San Francisco) to Punta de San José, or Fort Point, on the south shore of the Golden Gate. There the moldering and abandoned ruins of the ancient Spanish *Castillo de San Joaquin* were boldly charged and captured, and its ten prostrate and unresisting brass and iron cannon thoroughly spiked with ten of Captain Phelps ship's files. So thoroughly was the job done, indeed, that with Frémont's documentary blessing the captain later on felt justified in presenting the United States government with a bill for $10,000 as the fair value of his contribution to this brilliant victory. But Lieutenant Gillespie felt differently about Captain Phelp's role in the winning of California, and on his recommendation Congress eventually settled for fifty dollars.[6] But if Captain Phelps failed in this bid for fortune he more than succeeded in carving out a niche for himself in California's literary Hall of Fame when twenty-five years later his book, *Fore and Aft*, was published, as this is still one of the most colorful (if not always wholly accurate) sources of information about the local happenings of those days.

Among other distinguished guests entertained by Brown at that time was Dr. Robert Semple, whom we have already met in a business way. Semple was a versatile Kentuckian who was a dentist and printer by profession, and in the latter capacity he and Alcalde Walter Colton on August 15, 1846, launched the *Californian* at Monterey, the first newspaper published in the new Territory. As has been said, he was one of the most active of the Bear Party, and as a member of Frémont's California Battalion his appearance at that time, as described by William F. Swasey in his book, *The early days and men of California*, is worth repeating. On July 16th of the same year Admiral Sir George Seymour's flagship, H.B.M.S. *Collingwood*, anchored in the bay of Monterey, and when the Battalion rode into the town three days later several of the younger British naval officers expressed the desire to meet the famous "Bears" at first-hand. Swasey, who knew most of the Battalion personally, accompanied the Englishmen to Frémont's camp. His description of the redoubtable doctor follows:

"Dr. Semple was a more than ordinarily intelligent man, well read in history, and of varied accomplishments; in stature he was six feet eight inches, and very slim. Blackburn used to say that he had to wear his spurs in the calves of his legs to enable him to hit his horse's belly. He was full of geniality and wit; he was dressed at the time in buckskin, including moccasins, with a coonskin cap. The buckskins had not been properly handled, and, having been recently wet, had shrunk considerably, so that his pantaloons reached about half way between his knees and ankles. He had arrested the further subsidence of his pants by a buckskin string tied around his moccasins. The shrinkage had not been confined altogether to his pants; the body and sleeves had been equally afflicted, and his arms were about as much exposed as his legs. He reminded one of a boy who had suddenly outgrown his clothes. Among the young officers mentioned was a son of Sir Robert Peel, then the Premier of England. The author brought him and Semple together and left them for a while sitting on a log. When returning from camp, young Peel said to the author that Semple was the most remarkable man he had ever met. 'Why,' said he, 'he knows more about the history of my father and England than I do myself'."[7]

After the pacification of the country Dr. Semple was elected president of the Convention of California, that met in Monterey on September 1, 1849, to frame the Constitution for the territorial government, and while his contributions to that document were notable, his stature was even more impressive. Late in September or early in October of 1846 he stopped at Brown's new hotel, when his height put the innkeeper on his mettle. To meet the challenge a special bedstead was built, some inches longer than the others, and Brown congratulated himself on having provided ample accommodation for the "Long Doctor," as Semple was known among his friends. The next morning, however, Dr. Semple with the utmost seriousness asked his host if he had any chickens that stood in need of roosts, and when the mystified Brown inquired what he meant, he gravely replied that despite the extra length of his special bed his legs still stuck out so far beyond the foot that he felt sure he could provide roosting space for a dozen hens. A new bedstead, seven feet six inches in length, was hastily knocked together, and after stretching out on this the "Long Doctor" pronounced it a perfect fit.[8] The story (as told by Brown himself) seems to prove that despite Dr. Semple's having been the man who so summarily arrested Bob Ridley, neither his late prisoner nor Brown harbored enough resentment to prevent the latter from extending both himself and his bedstead to provide the doctor with the hotel's utmost hospitality.

Thereafter this special bed was reserved for extra lengthy guests, the best remembered of whom was Alcalde William Blackburn, of Santa Cruz, who, drunk or sober, used to hand down judicial decisions that are still famous in California as much for their originality as for their justice. Major Jacob R. Snyder, one-time surveyor for the Middle Department of California and later treasurer of the United States Mint at San Francisco, was another, and perhaps Captain Charles Burroughs, who was killed on November 16, 1846, while leading the charge of a detachment of Frémont's California Battalion against the Mexicans during the fighting at the Rancho de la Natividad.[9]

While these events were transpiring Bob Ridley was still languishing in more or less strict duress at Sutter's Fort, and in July he wrote Brown asking him to see Captain Montgomery (United States military Commandant of the Northern District of California, with headquarters at Yerba Buena) and try to arrange for his release. Brown did his best for his employer, but it was not until about a month later that the latter was released.[10]

In the meantime the hotel's business had been growing apace, and all hands felt that the place should be called by some name that would be more symbolical of the stirring chapter of history that was in the making. Brown also wanted the first sign-board in Yerba Buena, but apart from the difficulty of picking an appropriate name an even more serious problem was presented by the board itself. There were neither sign painters nor paint in the settlement, but at this critical juncture the United States Navy took over, and the situation was thereafter well in hand, without benefit of the Marines. Two of the *Portsmouth's* warrant officers, Boatswain Robert Whittaker and Carpenter Whinnesy, volunteered to overcome the last two difficulties—at a price. Their terms were that for a shipshape job, executed in even better than Bristol fashion, the hotel should be named in honor of their ship, the "Portsmouth House." Brown capitulated, and the sign-board was forthwith made and painted aboard the warship, its hoisting over Vioget's tavern by the bluejackets being the outstanding event of the day.[11]

The newly commissioned Portsmouth House now saw some stirring times, and the most dynamic of these was unquestionably the midnight attack on the town by what was believed to be a band of desperate Mexican patriots, who were credited with the determination of driving the invaders into the sea or laying down their lives in the attempt.

When Yerba Buena was occupied by the United States forces a small corps of local militia was enrolled to cooperate with the Navy in protecting the place from a gathering force of Californians, who were in no wise satisfied with the Yankees' summary annexation of their country. Captain Montgomery appointed Lieutenant Henry B. Watson, United States Marine Corps, military commandant of the town, and according to Brown, it was customary for the lieutenant to stop at the hotel before beginning his nightly rounds of the sentries. As the place would be closed by that time, he would rap twice on the shutter of the proprietor's room and in a low tone say, "The Spaniards are in the brush." This was the prearranged signal, and on hearing it Brown would get out of bed and fill the officer's flask with his best whiskey, to see the latter through the night. Shortly after the arrival of the American whaling ships, five of their skippers, together with several of the *Portsmouth's* officers (including Lieutenant Watson), Captain Francisco Sanchez, the erstwhile Mexican commandant of the port, Sub-prefect Francisco Guerrero y Palomares, and several other prominent Californians, gathered in the hotel for an impromptu celebration that lasted for two nights, and when this was over Brown fortified himself with an extra allowance of whiskey and retired for a well-earned rest. Either the fatigue of the past two days and nights or the whiskey (or the combination of the two) caused him to sleep so soundly that he failed to hear Watson's customary raps on the shutter, whereupon the lieutenant (who was no doubt in sore straits) fired one of his pistols and sang out at the top of his voice "THE SPANIARDS ARE IN THE BRUSH!"

The effect was electrical. Yerba Buena's militia company was in part quartered in the old Mexican customhouse, that had been converted into temporary barracks, and there the long roll was frantically beaten. The designated point of assembly in case of an emergency was the *corral* of the Portsmouth House, and the town's defenders reported there on the double, buckling on their equipment and loading their pieces as they ran. The *monte*, or scrub oak and brush forest, grew to within a short distance of the *corral*, and as the trees and bushes were seen to be in a state of agitation considerable firing ensued at what were believed to be the advancing Mexicans. Lieutenant Watson's state of mind is not a matter of record, but whatever it was it could not have been improved by signals received from his commanding officer aboard the *Portsmouth*, to the effect that if the situation was serious enough a landing party would be sent ashore to support him. Nor do we know how the lieutenant handled the situation from that point onward, but when in the morning it was found that the "Spaniards" had been no more than the wind-swept branches of the *monte* he told Brown that he would be a dead man if he ever dared to reveal the true story of how the attack started. How well Brown complied with this injunction is another matter that is not recorded, but it was over forty years later before the story was first printed.[12]

An increasingly common occurrence at Yerba Buena was for sailors to desert their ships, and it had become customary for their captains to pay a reward of five dollars apiece for the return of such runaways, nothing being stipulated as to the physical condition of the merchandise upon its delivery. Tom Smith, Brown's first cook and steward, seems to have turned a more or less honest dollar from time to time by this means, and may therefore, with reasonable assurance, be said to have been one if not the first of San Francisco's later notorious guild of crimps. Captain John Bottene, of the whaler *Cabinet* (another of Brown's earlier guests) suffered such a loss in the person of Able-bodied Seaman R. F. Peckham, who no sooner landed than he betook himself to the *monte*. Tipstaff Smith hunted up Captain Bottene in the billiard room of the Portsmouth House, and after apprising him of his loss offered to effect the truant's return on the basis of the usual five dollar delivery charge. The captain protested that the quotation was too high, but offered to settle for two dollars and a half if Smith would let Peckham alone to go wherever he pleased, adding that it would be worth this much to be rid of him, as he was no earthly use aboard a ship. It is to be presumed that Smith accepted the compromise, as Peckham later became district attorney and eventually county judge of Santa Clara County.[13]

It was not until August 8th, 1846, that the military situation in California was considered to be well enough in hand to warrant the release of the political prisoners held at Sutter's Fort, and a few days later Bob Ridley returned to Yerba Buena. By that time he had, like Brown, turned into a good American citizen, and announced himself a candidate for the office of *alcalde* in the election that Captain Montgomery had ordered held on September 15th. His only opponent was Lieutenant Washington A. Bartlett of the *Portsmouth* (the acting incumbent) and as this was to be the first election of a civil officer to be held under the American flag, interest ran high. The only available receptacle for the ballots was an empty box that had contained lemon syrup, and that Stephen Smith of Bodega Bay had given Ridley in payment for the survey of two lots that the former had bought in Yerba Buena. Brown nailed the cover down securely and cut a slot in this and when Ridley arrived in the back room of Leidesdorff's store (in the building that later became the City Hotel, where the election was held) and Brown cast the first ballot in his favor, both men evidently thought the election as good as won. But as their fellow citizens were none too sure about Ridley's recent conversion, and feared that if elected he would be inclined to favor the Mexicans in his decisions, the crew of the *Portsmouth* was sent ashore to vote, and when the ballots were counted it was found that Lieutenant Bartlett had been elected.[14]

Elder Sam Brannan now officiated at the first American marriage consummated in California after the occupation, and while this event did not take place in the Portsmouth House it was directly responsible for John Henry Brown's own short-lived incursion into matrimony. In some way or another he and Bob Ridley had come into possession of the old Mexican *adobe* jail that stood in the *plaza*, at the southwest corner of the customhouse, and it was there that Basil Hall and Lizzie Winner were united. Brown was one of the guests, and apart from thoroughly enjoying himself, met Hattie Pell, with whom he fell so deeply in love that their own marriage followed shortly thereafter. Hattie's father, E. Ward Pell, was one of the counselors Elder Brannan appointed early on the voyage to California to assist in enforcing the strict code of morals he laid down for his flock, but, before they were well around Cape Horn Brother Pell was not only advocating but more or less openly practising polygamy with one of the weaker Sisters. Polygamy was something that Brannan refused to permit, and Pell was sternly admonished. When he refused to mend his ways, he was excommunicated, or "disfellowshipped."[15]

About September of 1846 Brown bought out Ridley's interest in the Portsmouth House,[16] and while the exact date of the transaction is not known, the following advertisement appearing in the Monterey

Californian of October 17, 1846, proves that by then he was the hotel's proprietor in fact as well as in name:

"Portsmouth House—Yerba Buena—The undersigned has opened a Public House, under the above title, where he is prepared to entertain all those who may please to call on him. His table will be furnished with the best the market affords, and his bar with the best liquors. Yerba Buena, October 16, 1846. J. Brown, proprietor."

This was the first announcement that a hotel had at last made its appearance in California, and the event called for something more than passing notice. In the next issue of the same newspaper its joint publisher, Dr. Semple, did the subject justice in the following editorial:

"Our friends who intend visiting Yerba Buena will do well to give Mr. Brown a call. He is the proprietor of the 'Portsmouth House.' It has been the custom in California to keep taverns, but our American population require something of the kind, where they may have a 'home' of their own, such as Mr. Brown's. We had the pleasure of enjoying several days of a residence with Mr. Brown, and found his table furnished with the best, and done up in the neatest manner. He is enlarging his house, and will, in a short time, be able to give you a comfortable room and bed."

The *Californian* of the same date mentions the fact that Dr. Semple had returned to Monterey aboard the U.S.S. *Constitution* after an absence of several weeks, and he probably brought Brown's advertisement back with him. It is also probable that the episode of the long bedstead took place during this visit to Yerba Buena, and his closing remark, to the effect that prospective guests at the Portsmouth House would shortly be able to enjoy comfortable beds, was no doubt a sly editorial dig at his recent host.

Brown was by this time keenly alive to the rapidly increasing importance of the hotel business, and on October 23rd, 1846, he entered into a partnership agreement with Joel P. Dedmond and Albert Packard to open two such public houses in Yerba Buena under the firm name of John Henry Brown & Company. The first of these places, that Packard was to manage, was the Portsmouth House (that Brown was already operating), and the second, that he himself was to conduct under the name of the Congress House, was to be opened in Leidesdorff's *adobe* building, the first story of which had recently been completed at the northwest corner of Kearny and Clay streets. This was the first of California's hotel-chain deals, but it was only a paper one, as the partnership was dissolved on November 23rd, with Brown succeeding to the firm's assets and obligations.[17] A previous understanding must have been reached, however, as some time between October 23rd and November 1st Brown sold out his interest in the Portsmouth House to Elbert P. Jones, who thus became California's second hotel keeper of record.[18]

Doctor Jones, as he was generally called, was a Kentucky lawyer who arrived at Yerba Buena by the Overland Trail earlier in the same year, and it appears that hotel keeping was only a temporary expedient to permit him to get his feet on the ground and his hands on some of the loose dollars that were beginning to circulate in increasing numbers. The immediate exigencies of the hotel business do not seem to have been too pressing, for, when Sam Brannan began publishing the *California Star* (Yerba Buena's first and California's second newspaper) Doctor Jones became its first editor, continuing in this capacity from January 9th to April 17th of 1847, when differences with Brannan led to his resignation. In the meantime (and no doubt with the aforesaid dollars in mind), on January 16th Jones advertised himself as one of the town's permanent residents, and offered the public his services in the capacity as an attorney-at-law who was prepared to see his prospective clients into or out of trouble, depending upon their current requirements, and as an additional inducement he also offered to attend to the collection of "Foreign Debts." This last broadly worded proposition seems to have been the first gesture in the direction of transforming as much as possible of the native Californian's possessions into domestic Yankee holdings, and if so the suggestion was so successfully prosecuted that with but few exceptions the "foreigners" were literally stripped down to their hides. Furthermore, as hides were still the basic medium of exchange in California, most of the unsophisticated Californians were eventually denuded of even these coverings. Probably Doctor Jones' first offer of legal aid did not meet with a sufficiently ready response in clients and dollars, for on February 13th he embellished his advertisement in the *Star* by offering as references the names of the Honorable Henry Clay, Thomas H. Benton and William C. Preston, and finally that of the prominent New York legal firm of Doremus, Sydam & Nixon. This broadside of legal sponsors turned the trick, and thereafter the doctor's feet were firmly anchored and both hands busy.

From the time that Jones took over the Portsmouth House (or Jones' Hotel, as it was thereafter indifferently called) the annals of the place are so meager that about the only glimpses caught of it are through the fluctuating fortunes of its new proprietor. Ten days after Jones' last advertisement a notable gathering was doubtless held in the hotel to condemn Alcalde Bartlett's proclamation of January 23rd, 1847, decreeing that thereafter the town of Yerba Buena was to be known as "San Francisco." While this document has been published elsewhere, its effect on the future history of the port was so far-reaching that it is worth repeating:

"Whereas the local name of Yerba Buena, as applied to the settlement or town of San Francisco, is unknown beyond the immediate district, and has been applied from the local name of the cove on which the town is built—therefore, to prevent confusion and mistakes in public documents, and that the town may have the advantage of the name given on the published maps, it is hereby ordered that the name of San Francisco shall hereafter be used in all official communications and public documents or records appertaining to the town."

The new name did not begin to come into general use until after the publication of the order in the January 30th issue of the *Star*, and even then that paper clung stubbornly to "Yerba Buena" until March 20th, when Sam Brannan and Doctor Jones ungraciously capitulated editorially. At the time a good deal was said with a good deal of acrimony, pro and con, about the change of name, but little or no mention was made of the real reason for this. And, like the story about Captain Vioget's nickname of "Blucher," thereby hangs a tail.

As has been seen, Dr. Semple returned to Monterey in the middle of October of 1846, after an absence of several weeks spent at Yerba Buena and thereabouts. It must have been at that time that he and General Mariano Guadalupe Vallejo agreed to found a new town on the north shore of the entrance to Suisun Bay and on the general's Rancho de Soscol, at the point where it was expected that future land traffic between Yerba Buena and Sacramento would be ferried across Carquinez Strait. An agreement to this effect was signed by Vallejo and Semple on December 22, 1846, and in this it was stipulated that the name of the proposed town was to be "Francisca," in honor of the general's wife, Doña Francisca Benicia Vallejo de Carrillo. The instrument was recorded in Yerba Buena by Alcalde Bartlett on January 19, 1847, and four days later, when the startled *alcalde* awoke to the impending threat of the new settlement's making off with the renown attaching to even the distaff version of the name "Francisco," he hurriedly issued the famous decree that assured the original town the copyright. This was a setback to the promotion of the proposed metropolis, but only a temporary one. In May of the same year Thomas O. Larkin succeeded to General Vallejo's interest in the venture, when he and Semple compromised by calling the place "Benicia," after Señora Vallejo's second Christian name.[19]

This close miss to having its name purloined seems to have had a chastening and at the same time a stimulating effect on San Francisco, and far from resting on its laurels, after summarily disposing of its rival's pretentions, the town now entered on the first cadence of its stride as the premier Pacific port of North America. And despite the attractions offered by a new hotel opened by John Henry Brown in November of the preceding year, the popularity of the Portsmouth House kept pace with the forward march of events. There were enthusiastic gatherings in both establishments to honor the third Fourth of July celebration held in California, and from the physical repercussion thereof it may be concluded that the Portsmouth House session was the more dynamic of the two. This began with an excellent afternoon dinner that was attended by the town's elite, including the officers of the *Portsmouth* and those of the volunteer militia. Many toasts were drunk, speeches made and songs sung, and perhaps as the aftermath of these commemoratory exercises, a month later Doctor Jones advertised his place as having been "thoroughly repaired and enlarged to twice its former size." It is unfortunate that the only known description of the hotel at that time refers to it as a collection of one-story shacks, but from this it may be inferred that the aggregate represented a further development of the expansions already mentioned.[20]

On the 18th of September Doctor Jones married Sarah Kittleman, whom he seems to have taken over from John Henry Brown, together with the other assets and liabilities of the business. While the event was brilliantly celebrated by the cream of San Francisco's society, it may have been more of an economic than a social consolidation. For on October 3, 1847, Captain Vioget advertised the Portsmouth House and lot for sale, and there is no evidence to prove that the business was good enough for Jones to invest in this or any other real estate at that time. Nor does he seem ever to have acquired the property, and two and a half years later it was owned by the firm of Finlay, Johnson & Company, general commission merchants. The only additional note of interest that appears in the annals of the place was a meeting of the Odd Fellows, that was held there on December 4th to organize the first local lodge of the order.[21]

Space in the premises now began to be rented for offices and stores, and early in the same month, October of 1847, Dr. Victor J. Fourgeaud, one of San Francisco's pioneer physicians, opened a clinic in "Jones Hotel." On the 13th its proprietor was elected a member and secretary of the *ayuntamiento,* or town council, a post that he had held *pro tempore* since October 28th, and as thereafter Doctor Jones seems to have devoted much of his time to public affairs and his law business, it may be presumed that the management of the hotel devolved upon Mrs. Jones, even though her husband appears as its proprietor as late as June 10th of 1848. As far as is known, this is the last date on which the establishment was referred to as a hotel, and on October 20th of the same year Finlay, Johnson & Company rented a store in the building that was "formerly known as the Portsmouth House." From this it is safe to conclude that the place ceased to be a public house some time between June and October of 1848,[22] at any rate, a public house of any importance, and while it may have continued for a while longer to be run as a down-at-the-heels and out-at-the-elbows hostelry, John Henry Brown's new establishment had by then wrested from it its one-time position as San Francisco's leading (and only) hotel.

Either the law business or the town council (or perhaps both) must have paid off handsomely, as Doctor Jones soon became San Francisco's heaviest speculator in real estate, and in consequence one of the most successful collectors of gold dust in California. At one sale he disposed of no less than seventy-one town lots, when he seized upon the occasion as a made-to-order excuse for one of the gorgeous sprees for which he became famous. During these periods of exuberance Jones was wont to treat all his friends, together with the friends of his friends' friends, to a royal tipple at Peter Sherreback's place on the corner of Kearney and Washington streets, that was known simply as "Our House." By then he had become one of San Francisco's best known characters, and when he appeared wrapped in his long, velvet-lined cloak, swaggering down the street like a Spanish grandee, the bartenders and the saloon hangers-on would one and all make ready for another prolonged season of revelry. To keep pace with his soaring affluence, Doctor Jones built a two-story house on the corner of California Street and Dunbar Alley, where, according to his most intimate cronies, his quaint conceits achieved a climax that was in keeping with the golden era. In these more expansive moments he is said to have entertained both himself and his friends by giving spirited impersonations of the dual roles of Jupiter and Danea. Spreading sheets on the floor of his bedroom, and presumably in the simple garb affected by the god when paying social calls, Doctor Jones would pour gold over himself by double handfuls, and end the performance by wallowing ecstatically in the shining yellow dust.[23] Perhaps these, and other relaxations, were the result of the doctor's no longer being under the obligation of living up to the part of keeper of California's first hotel, that by then was nothing but a more or less fragrant memory.

The last known reference to the original Portsmouth House occurs in the following advertisement, appearing in the *Alta California* of April 22, 1850:

"Valuable property for Sale. The undersigned offer for sale the Clay street property, known as the 'Portsmouth House,' fronting on Clay and Kearney Streets, fifty varas square, with the improvements thereon. It will have three fronts when Wharf street is opened, and is at present under a large rent. We will sell the entire lot, or in separate lots to suit purchasers.

Finley, Johnson & Co."

The material end of Captain Vioget's original tavern, that became California's first American inn, came less than two months later, when on June 14th of the same year the third of San Francisco's great fires swept away every trace of the old building and its rambling annexes. But the name "Portsmouth" had been one of the town's most cherished American traditions ever since the day on which the Stars and Stripes were run up over the barren and dusty Mexican *plaza*, that thereafter was known as Portsmouth Square. A couple of years after the conflagration the first of a succession of new places called the "Portsmouth House" made its appearance in San Francisco, although not on the site occupied by its predecessor of pioneer fame.

Chapter 6. Brown's Hotel

THE SUCCESS of the Portsmouth House ushered in the era of hostelries that antedated the great Gold Rush of '49, and as might have been expected, John Henry Brown started the ball rolling by opening the first place in the State that was called a hotel, rather than a "house."

In June of 1846 William A. Leidesdorff completed the lower story of a large *adobe* building that stood on his fifty *vara* lot at the northwest corner of Clay and Kearny, and directly across the latter street from the Portsmouth House. At the time it was the largest private building in Yerba Buena, and there Liedesdorff moved the general store he had been running in one of John C. Fuller's little frame houses, which stood back from the east side of Kearny and a block south of the new place. This was known as the "Big Adobe," and not without reason. The building had a frontage of one hundred thirty-seven feet on Kearny and a sixty-foot wing at each end, with a raised veranda that ran the full length of the front, as well as the length of the Clay Street wing.[1]

During the five years of its existence the "Big Adobe" was the scene of many of the stirring episodes that took place in San Francisco in those days, and while some of these have from time to time been told elsewhere, the fact that it was the setting for the most portentous event in the history of California has thus far been only casually mentioned. On the 4th of July, 1846, Captain John B. Montgomery read the Declaration of Independence from the veranda of Leidesdorff's new building, and with this served notice of our intentions three days before Commodore Sloat annexed the country at Monterey and five days before the Stars and Stripes were run up over Yerba Buena. Those present on that momentous occasion were Captain Montgomery and his two sons, Midshipmen John E. and William H. Montgomery, another midshipman from the U.S.S. *Portsmouth*, William A. Leidesdorff, United States vice-consul, who was a Dane by birth and a naturalized Mexican citizen, John C. Fuller, an Englishman, and also a naturalized Mexican, and of course John Henry Brown. It was on this occasion that Leidesdorff asked the latter if he was an American, and Brown made his classic reply, to the effect that he was a "white-washed" one.[2] This question, coming when it did, is so significant that there can be little doubt that Captain Montgomery's action was the result of his and Leidesdorff's discussion of the international situation, and designedly foreshadowed the events that took place less than a week later.

On July 15th Leidesdorff added a bar and billiard room to his store[3] in an attempt to get some of the customers away from the place across the street that Brown was still running for Bob Ridley. The attempt does not appear to have been any too successful, as by the fall of the same year Brown (who in the meantime had bought Ridley's interest in the Portsmouth House) found the place too small to accommodate his increasing clientele. Early in October Leidesdorff offered him the "Big Adobe" at a yearly rental of two thousand dollars (payable quarterly, in advance), and it was at that time that Brown entered into the chain hotel deal with Dedmond and Packard.

Beyond what has already been said, the details of this partnership are not known, but Brown's first concern appears to have been that of furniture (presumably for the proposed "Congress House"), and not a single article of this nature was to be procured for love or money. But at this critical juncture the providential arrival of another ship solved the problem. The firm of Mellus & Howard had just received a consignment of furniture from Boston by the ship *Vandalia,* and as furniture was the one item of merchandise for which there was no demand, the goods had not even been unloaded. At this point, and in the course of a casual conversation, Henry Mellus, the *Vandalia's* supercargo, offered Brown the consignment practically on the latter's own terms. This was even better than providential, and the deal was closed on the spot, and no doubt sealed by a handshake and drink, that Brown must have paid for with no little gusto. In the meantime something went wrong with the chain hotel project, for, as has been seen, late in October Brown sold his interest in the Portsmouth House to Doctor Jones, and on the first day of November, 1846, entered into a verbal contract with Leidesdorff to rent the latter's building for a period of five years on the foregoing terms. This gentleman's agreement was no doubt consummated by further handshaking and drinks, and while at the time this must have made everything seem perfectly legal, Brown later on had cause to regret the informality of the transaction.[4]

With these last formalities disposed of, Brown stepped out on the highroad to success and fortune. His reputation as an innkeeper was already firmly established, and he was now in possession of the biggest and best building in the town wherein to expand. The new furniture was installed, but before the official opening Brown was determined that his place should have the finest signboard in Yerba Buena. This time there was no difficulty in finding either a painter or paints, and eighteen-year-old John Eager (one of Sam Brannan's young newspaper factotums) did a splendid job, that in fine gilt letters announced the new establishment as "Brown's Hotel." It was unquestionably the most ornate sign in the town, and (what is more) the story behind it is even more entertaining than that of the signboard of the Portsmouth House.

At the time Brown was courting Hettie Pell, and it will be recalled that her father, E. Ward Pell, had been expelled from the church during the voyage to California because of his polygamistic dalliance with one of the more open minded Sisters of Sam Brannan's water-borne company of Latter-Day Saints. On the Pell's arrival at Yerba Buena the family was not exactly ostracised by their fellow religionists, but the ex-counselor was under a cloud that forced him to seek a home apart from the other Mormons. In this dilemma, and no doubt through Brown's not-so-disinterested intervention, the Pells found shelter in Bob Ridley's house, when (and perhaps by way of further insuring his suit) Brown promised his prospective father-in-law a job as inspector of hides. However all this may have been, John Eager's mother was none other than the widow Lucy Eager, who had been "disfellowshipped" at the same time and for the same reasons that E. Ward Pell was cast forth from the Mormon fold. The sign cost John Henry Brown one hundred dollars, but as it completely eclipsed the signboard over the Portsmouth House he considered it well worth the money. Whatever the real reason for these antimatrimonial activities, they paid off on December 12th of 1846, when Alcalde Bartlett united John Henry and Hettie in wedlock. But in the long run the investment was not a successful one, as on April 24th of the following year Brown announced that, due to his wife's having left his board and bed, he wanted it distinctly understood that he was no longer responsible for any debts she might incur.[5]

The opening of Brown's Hotel was somewhat tardily noted in the following editorial item that appeared in the December 5, 1846, issue of the Monterey *Californian:*

"Mr. Brown has taken the large and commodious house formerly occupied by Captain Leidesdorff, and is keeping a good and fashionable hotel. Mr. Brown is a very industrious, enterprising and honorable man. We wish him great success."

Once the new hotel was opened Brown's most immediate worry was to secure food enough for his table, and in this case the problem was solved by diplomacy rather than by providence. The pacification of California was still in progress, and while many of the natives resented Yankee territorial expansion at the expense of Mexican sovereignty, they felt differently about Yankee dollars. The nearby *rancheros* refused to bring in beef for the United States forces at less than twenty-five dollars a head, but they kept Brown supplied at ten dollars per animal, without inquiring too closely into his political coloring. When Captain Joseph B. Hull, of the U.S.S. *Warren*, relieved Captain Montgomery at Yerba Buena he established his shore headquarters in the new hotel, and since the procurement of fresh beef for his command was one of his first cares, Brown's traffic with the Mexicans was questioned immediately. An investigation followed, and Brown's activities were found to come so perilously close to what would today be called trading with the enemy that the commandant threatened to confiscate the hotel's supply of meat as contraband, but before any action could be taken, the fortunes of war intervened, and Captain Hull had something much more serious to worry about.[6]

On December 8th of 1846 Lieutenant Bartlett took a short vacation from his duties as *alcalde* and went out on a cattle "buying" raid through the ranches about San Mateo. As the result of his activities he and his escort of five men were taken prisoner by Francisco Sanchez, a nonconformist *ranchero* and the excommandant of Yerba Buena, who was also one of Brown's beef purveyors. Captain Hull hurriedly organized a relief column that, among other units, included about a dozen of Yerba Buena's volunteer militia, in which Brown was a private. The campaign was short and culminated in the famous "battle of Santa Clara," and when Lieutenant Bartlett and his men were rescued and the civilian defenders of Yerba Buena returned covered with glory, the matter of the contraband beef was dropped.[7]

Rumors and counter rumors were still the order of the day, and Brown's Hotel was now the scene of a major alarm that rivalled Lieutenant Watson's famous attack by the Spaniards. Captain Edward A. King, master of the brig *Elizabeth*, had brought from Honolulu a large patent coffee-pot, that was so fearfully and wonderfully constructed that years later Brown confessed he had still never seen the like of it. The *deus ex machina* of this contraption was a screw that regulated the steam pressure, and Captain King's Kanaka steward was the only one who had mastered the act of manipulating this correctly. The machine was set up in the hotel and worked satisfactorily until one day the steward was called away, when he told the cook that if too much steam escaped he was to tighten the screw. This worthy evidently concluded that if a certain amount of tightening resulted in good coffee the beverage would be improved still further by turning the screw all the way home. He proceeded to put his theory to the test, and the immediate result was that the patent coffee pot exploded with a terrific roar, blowing the cook, pots and pans out of the kitchen, and galvanizing Yerba Buena's defenders into frantic action to meet what was believed to be a bombardment of the town by the Mexicans.

When Captain Hull established himself in the hotel he had the veranda enclosed with canvas to accommodate the sailors of his shore detail who could not find quarters in the overcrowded Mexican custom-house. Turning out these bluejackets at the double, the commandant ran to the barracks and ordered the long roll beaten, formed the militia in line of skirmishers, sent out scouts to ascertain the enemy's strength and position, and signaled the *Warren* to stand by to send a landing party ashore, and otherwise support him. While all this martial activity was going forward, Brown, who had witnessed the explosion, had picked up the badly scalded cook and gone to look for the naval surgeon at the custom-house, where he met Captain Hull and received a blistering quarter-deck dressing down for being absent when the roll had been called, but when he explained what had happened, and assured the captain that the town was in no immediate danger from the Spaniards, in the brush or elsewhere, his dereliction in the line of duty was dropped, as had been the matter of the contraband beef.[8]

News of the tragedy that had overtaken the Donner party in the Sierra Nevada now reached San Francisco, and Alcalde Bartlett called a public meeting to be held the evening of February 3, 1847, to discuss relief measures. Nearly every male citizen of the town, and all the United States officers who were off duty, assembled at 7 o'clock in the saloon of Brown's Hotel, when the heroic James Frazier Reed, one of the survivors of the tragedy, addressed the meeting briefly. Thereafter General Vallejo, Commander Mervine, Leidesdorff, William D. M. Howard and Sam Brannan collected some fifteen hundred dollars to pay the expenses of a party of volunteers that Passed-Midshipman Selim Woodworth led into the mountains to supplement the work of earlier groups of rescuers. Young George Donner, the sole surviving nephew of the leader of the ill-fated party, was later taken to San Francisco, where Brown kept him at his hotel until arrangements could be made for the boy's future. It was then that one of those acts was performed that, if they are remembered at all, are so apt to be overshadowed by more dramatic events of the day.[9]

George McDougal was one of Brown's resident guests, and in the descriptive terminology of the time, a "broker," which was the polite way of saying that he was a professional gambler. But he was also very genuine and good-hearted, and took it upon himself to buy two fifty *vara* lots that were recorded in George Donner's name, and that a few years later became very valuable property.[10]

George McDougal was also full of fun, and a practical joker. One holiday he and several others (including Doctor Jones and William F. Swasey) rolled an empty hogshead to the top of the Clay Street hill at Dupont where they drove it full of nails and tied firecrackers to these, in such a fashion that by lighting the bottom cracker the others would be set off in succession. Straws were then drawn to see who should crawl into the hogshead and light the first cracker, and the long straw was palmed off on Jones. No sooner was he inside the barrel and the cracker's fuse alight than McDougal gave the hogshead a kick that sent it careening down Clay, to the accompaniment of its inmate's yells of dismay and the explosion of firecrackers. The barrel brought up with a resounding crash against the back of Brown's Hotel, and when Doctor Jones was hauled out, it was found that despite his groans he was little the worse for his involuntary ride, but for a few nail pricks and singed hair and whiskers. On another occasion Sam Brannan was bet an ounce that, after being blindfolded and turned around three times, it would take him more than fifteen minutes to find a post that stood in the middle of the *plaza,* and that was used as a sort of public bulletin board, this being all that was left of the old Mexican flagpole, on which Captain Montgomery posted the notices of California's annexation. In the rear of Brown's Hotel there was a slimy pool of filth and water that filled a pit left by the excavation for the *adobes* used in the building, and into which the slops from the hotel were emptied. Brannan was stationed across the street from this pit, hoodwinked and revolved three times. After a moment's deliberation he struck a beeline for the trap, and in less than fifteen seconds was floundering up to his neck in the noisome cloaca.[11]

This pit seems to have been a combination of cesspool and privy, and is a fair example of the hygienic arrangements of those days. There were, of course, no sanitary toilets such as we are accustomed to, and their place was taken by outhouses that, in humbler circles, were Spartanlike in their sternly utilitarian lines, and in the case of the literati they were vine and flower disguised dependencies, such as Imogene Cunningham has portrayed in her charming photographic study, "The two-seater." Even if such refinements as flushing toilets had been known they would have been useless at that time, as there was no water to waste in flushing them. There were a few private wells and a good spring at El Cañutal, but apart from these sources San Francisco's potable water was ferried across the bay from Sausalito in the hulk of Leidesdorff's little Russian steamboat, and peddled from house to house by the driver of a water cart.[12]

The next outstanding event in the annals of Brown's Hotel occurred on February 12, 1847, when Colonel Richard B. Mason arrived to relieve General Kearny as military governor of California. During Brown's trapping days he had become friendly with the colonel at Fort Gibson in the Indian Territory, and from the time of the latter's arrival he invariably put up with Brown whenever he was in San Francisco. Mason was very fond of billiards, and he and Brown played regularly every morning from ten to eleven o'clock, when the colonel would always pay a dollar, whether he lost or won. One of these morning games was the occasion for a notable gathering of celebrities, when Colonel Mason, General Kearny, Commodore Stockton, Commodore Biddle, Captain Hull and Commander Mervine all met around Brown's billiard table.[13]

The so-called second story of the hotel was completed in March of the same year, but it was no more than a garret, whose projecting eaves formed the roof over the veranda. The place was lighted by three dormer windows overlooking Kearny Street, with a fourth above Clay, and roofed with Mexican tiles so loosely laid that San Francisco's breezes were as active inside the apartment as they were out of doors. But this was a distinct advantage when the place was crowded with the none too fragrant citizens of those days.[14] In the same month Colonel Jonathan D. Stevenson and many of the officers of his First Regiment of New York Volunteers stopped at the hotel.[15]

At Brown's invitation, one Sunday morning, the following June the first Protestant services held in San Francisco were conducted in the dining room of his hotel by the Reverend William Roberts, superintendent of the Oregon missions, who was in town waiting for a ship to take him to his post. The dining room was in the center of the building, and was flanked on one side by the saloon and billiard room and on the other by the gambling room, and Brown prided himself on the fact that while preaching, billiard playing, drinking and gambling were all going on at the same time and under the same roof. His guests were so considerate of one another that none of these social activities at any time disturbed those being conducted in the neighboring rooms. The nearest approach to a breach of decorum was committed by an old sailor, who, when the services were concluded, gave the preacher a resounding slap on the back and exclaimed admiringly, "That was a damned good sermon!"[16]

On the evening of June 14th, 1847, all the prominent citizens of San Francisco gathered in Brown's Hotel to attend a meeting that had far-reaching effects on history, insomuch as that it resulted in one of the contributing factors that thwarted Colonel John C. Frémont's attempt to have himself appointed governor of California. Without going into the still hotly disputed subject of Frémont's activities in connection with the conquest of the country, suffice it to say that at the time a large number of Americans and native Californians bitterly condemned many of his military and political acts performed during and after the conquest. At Frémont's instigation, a petition addressed to President Polk had been circulated throughout the southern part of California, that purported to request Frémont's return to enable him to settle the numerous debts he had incurred during the war, and many individuals signed this under the impression that nothing beyond such settlements was involved. When the petition reached the bay region, however, it was found that its wording was such that it could readily be interpreted as a popular request that Frémont be appointed governor of the new Territory, and as a matter of fact, this is exactly what was intended. The meeting in Brown's Hotel was to draw up another petition to the president, that would make it abundantly clear that the people of northern California emphatically refuted any such interpretation of the earlier memorial, and, after pointing out Frémont's unfitness for the post, protested against his returning as governor. Nathan Spear was elected chairman of the meeting, and, after several addresses, Frank Ward presented a resolution to the above effect. This was approved unanimously, and on a motion made by Dr. Felix P. Wierzbicki a committee was appointed to collect and document the most flagrant instances of Frémont's alleged misconduct. The members of the committee were Jacob P. Leese, William A. Leidesdorff, Francisco Guerrero y Palomares, Timothy Murphy, Jaspar O'Farrell, Dr. Robert Semple, Joseph P. Thompson and Frank Ward, and, based on their report, the petition was drawn up and forwarded to Washington.[17]

The stimulating effect on the Portsmouth House of San Francisco's first celebration of the Fourth of July after the occupation has already been noted,[18] but as was to have been expected Brown's Hotel far outstripped its venerable rival in producing the thrills of the day. Joseph P. Thompson opened the ceremonies by reading the Declaration of Independence from the spot on the hotel's veranda where on July 4th of 1846 Captain Montgomery had read the same document three days before the annexation of California. Dr. Semple followed this up by delivering an impassioned patriotic oration that brought even the drunks to their feet, cheering lustily for whatever it was that had been said. These preliminaries disposed of, such of the audi-

ence as were still able to navigate, adjourned to Brown's bar to pledge
the Flag, the United States of America, California, San Francisco,
themselves, and anything else that happened to occur to them. All the
ships in the bay were decorated, and resounding salutes were fired
from every cannon that was able to articulate, to the boundless edifica-
tion of everyone but perhaps a few not-so-edified Mexican patriots.
But these anachronisms had sense enough to keep their feelings to
themselves, and the day was unmarred by any political misunderstand-
ings. Among other ships firing the national salute was the *Vandalia*,
and her contribution to the festivities all but resulted in a holocaust
that doubtless would have brightened the day for the aforesaid patriot
Mexican minority. The ship was anchored close inshore, and to make
the last round worthy of the occasion the gun was loaded with a
double charge of powder that was rammed home with an extra heavy
oakum wad. The piece must have been trained on Brown's Hotel, as
when it was fired the wad struck one of the heavy wooden shutters,
splintered this into matchwood and imbedded itself in the *adobe* wall
across the room. A couple of minutes before the receipt of this testi-
monial fifty people had been standing before the window, but as no
one was hurt the marksmanship of the *Vandalia's* gunner only added
to the zest of the occasion.[19] The anti-climax to this near tragedy,
together with the general picture of San Francisco's observance of the
national holiday, are best told in the words of Chester S. Lyman, who
had landed the day before from New York and was an observer of
these stirring events:

"Taking a turn through the principal street of the Town nothing struck me so
forcibly as the immense amount of drinking & gambling & horse-riding done.
Almost every 3d person you met was drunk. Passing the hotel, a drunken fellow,
just able to sit on his horse was attempting to spur the animal to ascend the steps
of the front piazza, while Dr. Townsend with a large stick was assisting in the rear
& a lot of drunken swearing gentry stood looking on and applauding. But the
horse, the only sober creature in the group, showed more sense than them all &
utterly refused to submit to his drunken master. Among those standing around &
in the Hotel the officers of the navy were numerous & conspicuous. Not far from
the hotel I passed a grog shop and bowling-alley from which the sounds of
drunken revelry & awful profanity were issuing most hideously. The streets were
filled with drunken cut throat-looking horsemen, riding at full speed, with oaths,
shouting & the rattling of huge Spanish spurs at their heels. A little further on I
met a company of horsemen in masks & fancy white & red dresses riding full tilt

into the town from Ridley's Ranch a little to the west. I supposed them bent on some sort of frolic of course & afterwards learned that they were practicing a favorite mode of making money in the country, by stooping to pick up a piece of money from the ground while riding at full speed on horseback. Persons who choose throw a quarter of a dollar or half on the ground & instantly, with unfailing accuracy, the horseman rises in his saddle with the piece in his fingers which he retains for his pains."[20]

The occasion was entirely too good a chance to celebrate for this to be brushed off with a single day's festivities, and moreover, some of the junior officers and sailors of the U.S.S. *Congress* had been unable to make shore leave on the Fourth, so an impromptu continuation of the holiday was staged four days later. On the evening of July 8th a group of midshipmen met at Brown's Hotel, and the ceremonies opened with one of their host's famous suppers. Wine, and every other liquid refreshment the place had to offer, flowed so freely that before the meal was finished the table was overturned, the chandeliers and furniture wrecked and barrage after barrage of empty bottles were fired through the dining room windows into the street. Tempers flared along with the liquor; one word led to two, and knives and pistols were drawn. George McDougal was on the point of shooting Midshipman John G. Whitaker when Jasper O'Farrell (the surveyor) rushed in and knocked the pistol out of his hand. At this unpropitious moment Brown attempted to restore order, with the result that he was himself violently discharged through one of his windows, to join the spent bottles. No sooner had this post-Fourth of July demonstration quieted down than another and even more furious one broke out as the culmination of the bluejackets' patriotic activities. The town authorities had tactfully overlooked the mishipmen's celebration as a manifestation of the exuberance of youth, but this last affair was quite a different matter. The participants were rounded up before Alcalde George Hyde, who fined them ten dollars apiece and ordered them thrust into the calaboose, to ponder on the error of their ways. But far from being chastened by this treatment, they promptly tore down one of the *adobe* jail's walls and erupted into the night life of San Francisco like giants refreshed. The constabulary was utterly unable to cope with this latest situation, and a naval shore patrol had to be called to haul the celebrants off to their ship's brig for safe keeping.[21]

About this time Brown's Hotel was the scene of San Francisco's first robbery, or at any rate the first robbery that became a matter of general public interest. George McDougal and Benjamin S. Lippincott, another "broker," had gone into the livery stable business, and what with this and that they had prospered. The two shared one of the hotel's rooms that opened onto the veranda, and one day while they were at dinner a writing desk containing some sixteen hundred dollars in Mexican gold coins was stolen from under their bed. The loss was not discovered until the evening, when every able-bodied man in town turned out to help hunt for the money. While the search was in progress a Mexican arrived from the Mission, and on being interrogated said that he had seen a man engaged in some enterprise or other under one of the trees in the sand hills, who afterward took himself off in the direction of the bay. The searchers converged on the tree pointed out by the *paisano,* and after half an hour's digging Purser James H. Watmaugh of the *Portsmouth* unearthed the desk, with the money intact. The finger of suspicion pointed strongly to certain parties as being responsible for the theft, and in the following year this suspicion proved well founded, when on his deathbed in the hotel a man confessed to the robbery and named his accomplices. Brown charitably refrains from giving the names of the thieves, but as he says that a miner, who came to California from Valparaiso, died in his hotel in 1848, it is possible that this individual may have been one of the culprits.[22]

Toward the end of September Governor Mason arrived in San Francisco on his first official tour of California accompanied by his aide-de-camp, Lieutenant William Tecumseh Sherman. Quarters had been prepared for the governor and his staff in the old Hudson's Bay Company's building, but he preferred stopping with his old friend of Indian Territory days. A ball and elaborate dinner party were held at Brown's Hotel in the Governor's honor, and though Mason's character was sternly severe to the point of harshness, he said afterward that never in his life had he enjoyed himself as much as he did on that occasion.[23]

The rent (in advance) for the first quarter of the second year of Brown's tenancy of the "Big Adobe" was due on November 1, 1847, but when on the first of October he tried to pay Leidesdorff the five hundred dollars agreed on, he was told that the future rent of the place was three thousand dollars a year. Despite the verbal agreement between the two men having been sealed by a handshake and drinks, Brown could do nothing about what he temperately characterized as "an imposition." Leidesdorff then offered to take the hotel off his hands for the original cost of the furniture, but Brown refused this proposition. He disposed of his fittings piecemeal at a profit of one hundred per cent, and the only item he sold Leidesdorff was the kitchen stove, that had cost him one hundred dollars and for which his late landlord was forced to pay two hundred fifty dollars, and with this transaction terminated his interest in the place on October 28, 1847.[24]

Chapter 7. The City Hotel

Brown's removal of his furniture, his ornate gilt lettered sign and himself, does not seem to have caused the hotel to suspend operations, as is to be gathered from the following announcement that appeared in the Saturday, October 23rd, 1947, issue of the *California Star:*

"THE HOTEL of this place formerly known as 'Brown's Hotel,' will hereafter be called the CITY HOTEL, and will be conducted from Monday next, by Mr. and Mrs. Skinner. Boarding at the former prices, and the Table as good as the Market can afford."

Horace A. Skinner and his wife were members of Sam Brannan's Mormon colony, and appear to have managed the hotel for Leidesdorff. The most interesting thing about the place at the time is that the new name was inspired by that of the City Hotel of New York, that a couple of years earlier had been the first public house in America to be called a "hotel."[1] The first notable event that marked the Skinners' short-lived incumbency was the first public Thanksgiving dinner and ball celebrated in California, both affairs being held in the hotel's dining room, where they were presided over by Admiral Charles W. Wooster, late of the Chilean navy.[2]

In his reminiscences of this time Brown speaks of the City Hotel (to which he refers impartially both by this name and as Brown's Hotel) as if he still retained an interest in the establishment, but as will be seen this seems improbable. However, and in default of any positive evidence to the contrary, the setting of the following episode is as Brown records it, but with his chronology of events rearranged to conform with historical facts rather than as he recalled their sequence, forty years later.

Gold had been found in the tailrace of Sutter's and Marshall's sawmill at Coloma on January 24, 1848, but it was not until two or three weeks later that news of this epochal discovery reached San Francisco, together with the first sample of the precious metal. John Bidwell and Sam Brannan are respectively credited with having been the bearers

75

of the first news and the first gold,[3] but this is not the way that John Henry Brown tells the story. According to him, early in February a tall gangling individual arrived at the hotel and introduced himself to Brown as Charles Bennett, of Oregon, and more lately of Coloma. He said that he was looking for someone with a thousand dollars to invest, and the following day Brown introduced him to George McDougal, who was still living at the hotel. Bennett's proposition was to use the money to buy red and blue blankets, which he said would fetch a good price up country, and as proof of his responsibility he fished out of his pocket an old fashioned English snuff box, and opening this showed Brown and McDougal the first California gold seen in San Francisco. He assured them that they would be running no risk in financing him as he could get any amount of gold where his sample came from. McDougal, however, was not to be taken in by any such bare-faced confidence game, and told Bennett that he had best look elsewhere for his thousand dollars.

Brown then introduced the man to Isaac Humphrey, who before his

CITY HOTEL – BIG ADOBE – BROWN'S HOTEL

arrival in California had worked in the Georgia gold mines, and knew gold when he saw it. Humphrey proved a more sympathetic listener, and two days later he asked Brown the whereabouts of a carpenter known as "The-devil-take-the-hindermost." The man's real name was Spencer, and on learning that he lived with William M. Foster, another carpenter, Humphrey hired the two to build so strange a looking machine that no one could imagine what it was supposed to do. Bennett then departed for Monterey on the business that really brought him to the coast, and this had nothing whatever to do with either red or blue blankets.

When Marshall told Sutter about the discovery and showed him the first gold found at Coloma, it was agreed to keep the matter secret until the latter could get in touch with Governor Mason and try to secure a preemption claim to the quarter section of land on which the sawmill stood, and where the gold had been found. Bennett was the confidential agent sent on this delicate mission, with positive instructions to say nothing about the discovery to anyone, and how well he followed his orders has been seen. In the end, however, his loose talking and boasting did no more than hasten the beginning of the Gold Rush, as Mason declined to comply with Sutter's request, and within a few weeks the story was public property and the stampede to the gold diggings had begun.

As soon as Spencer and Foster had completed the mysterious machine its designer packed this up and departed for Sutter's mill, where he arrived on March 7, 1848. When the advance guard of gold miners appeared on the scene shortly thereafter, they found Isaac Humphrey snugly ensconced in a rich and secluded spot on the South Fork of the American River, where he was hard at work operating his contraption—that turned out to be the first gold rocker used in California—a very efficient rocker it must have been, since Humphrey later told Brown that its recovery of gold exceeded his expectations.[4]

When John Henry Brown hauled down his sign from over the "Big Adobe" he was so well heeled financially that he made a trip to Honolulu, with the idea of buying an estate there and settling down. But when it transpired that he would have to marry a native woman before he could secure legal title to any real estate, and, furthermore, he found he could make a handsome profit in trade, he invested in a lot of ready-made clothing and returned to San Francisco. He arrived late in December of 1847,[5] and after looking over his invoice, Robert A. Parker bought his hand-me-downs at the usual one hundred per cent profit to the seller. This transaction was the beginning of a close personal and business association between the two men that lasted for years. In the meantime, the City Hotel does not seem to have flourished under its new management, and shortly after Brown's return Leidesdorff made him an attractive proposition to take over the place. Brown was inclined to accept, but after talking the matter over with Parker it was decided to refuse the offer and build a bigger and better hotel of their own.[6]

By February of 1848 Brown and Parker were hard at work on the project of their hotel, but within less than three months practically every able-bodied man in the bay region had succumbed to the gold fever, and dropping whatever they happened to be doing, they had hurried off to "see the elephant," as the first sight of the gold diggings soon came to be referred to by the old-timers for the benefit of the new-comers.[7] Timber cutters and carpenters joined the first wave of local gold hunters, and Brown and Parker were forced to suspend work on the new building. Brown himself then caught the fever and was on the point of trying his luck at the diggings, when an unexpected event transpired that brought him back to active hotel keeping.[8]

On May 18th of 1848 Leidesdorff died suddenly of brain fever, and this gave Parker an idea that was the reverse of Mohammed's attitude toward the mountain. The City Hotel was closed on its owner's death, and Parker argued that if he and Brown were unable to build their hotel because the workmen had gone off after gold, there was now no reason why they should not take over Leidesdorff's place and wait for the gold to come to them. This reasoning sounded logical to Brown, and as it also sounded as if it involved much less back-breaking work than gold digging required, he agreed. On June 10th Governor Mason appointed William D. M. Howard administrator of the Leidesdorff estate, and on the 28th the latter gave Parker a year's lease on the hotel for two thousand dollars, payable quarterly in advance, and effective as of July 1st. A penalty of five thousand dollars was involved for failure to fulfill the terms of the lease, and in consideration of one thousand dollars Brown signed the instrument on July 5th, as Parker's guarantor. From an inventory taken on the day the lease was signed, it appears that the hotel was prepared to offer the first score of guests beds whose furniture included not only mattresses, pillows and blankets, but real sheets and pillow-cases, together with bedspreads. Furthermore, the first lucky dozen patrons were also supplied with chairs, tables, tumblers, looking-glasses and wash-bowls, and even with the gentility of chamber-pots. The final touch of luxury was supplied by a set of curtains that adorned one of the beds, but whether this couch was reserved for visiting royalty, or occupied by some local celebrity, there is now no means of telling.[9]

The City Hotel was reopened on the Fourth of July, and as by that time everyone had more money than they knew what to do with, the double celebration was a grand success that lasted until the 5th, and included two dinner parties and balls. It was not until the 15th that the reopening was announced by the following notice appearing in the *Californian* of that date:

"CITY HOTEL. Located on the south side of the Portsmouth Square. The proprietor informs his friends and the public generally, that he has again leased the above large and well known establishment, which has been recently fitted up and furnished in the most modern style, and from his experience in business as the conductor of a public house, he hopes to gain a liberal share of patronage. The purveyance department is attended with care and attention, and his table supplied with all the varieties the market affords. His bar contains the choicest brands of cordials, wines and liquors. In fact, no pains will be spared in any department to render his guests agreeable during their sojourn. J. H. Brown, Proprietor."

All the references heretofore made to the City Hotel at that time state that Parker was the proprietor, but from what has just been said it is plain that he was the lessee of the place, under Brown's financial guarantee, and that the latter was the real proprietor. The new deal was bound to be a success, as the dining department of the hotel was leased to Jackson, Ward and Steward for seventeen hundred dollars a year, thus leaving a slack of only three hundred dollars to be taken up by room rent, the saloon, and gambling. To begin with, the lessees of the dining room had some fifteen regular customers who paid forty dollars apiece for board, and while the cook received the princely salary of seventy-five dollars a month it seemed, off hand, that this department of the hotel ran no risk of showing a deficit.[10] But food prices began to rise, and before long Brown was forced to take over the management of the dining room. As has been seen, at first fresh beef was supplied by the neighboring *rancheros* at twenty dollars a head, but in common with other prices, that of meat went up until a small roasting pig cost from ten to fifteen dollars. Eggs were worth from six to nine dollars a dozen, potatoes seventy-five cents, onions one dollar, and fresh butter a dollar and a half a pound. Old Jacob Herman came in daily from his truck garden near the Mission with many fresh vegetables, such as lettuce, cabbages, turnips, radishes and carrots, for which Brown paid him fifteen to twenty dollars a day. Two hunters and a whale-boat were hired to make semi-weekly trips up the various creeks after wild game, and while they kept the table supplied with venison, ducks and geese, it was at a considerable cost. Other provisions, such as hams, bacon and pickled tripe, were ordered from Oregon, and staple stores bought of ships' captains at ruinous prices. So dear had everything in the food line become, indeed, that had it not been for many dinner parties at which a thousand dollars worth of wine was consumed the dining room of the City Hotel would have run into the red at the rate of a hundred dollars a day.[11]

In spite of the rising price of food Parker's idea of waiting for the gold to come to them instead of Brown's going off after it began to pay off handsomely from the day the hotel was reopened. The beginning of the grand rush of '49 was still six months in the future, but by July of 1848 it was estimated that a quarter of a million dollars worth of gold dust and nuggets had already reached San Francisco,[12] and Brown and Parker were getting their full share of this treasure. There were but few permanent residents left in the town by that time, as everyone who was not making money hand over fist in one way or another had either left for the mines or was only waiting to get together a stake. By the fall of the year, however, this exodus had been more than offset by the number of miners returning to spend the rainy season and their gold, and among these were Humphrey and Bennett. Both had done so well at the diggings that the latter gave Brown twenty-seven pounds of gold to keep for him, and this was only one of many similar incidents. By December there were between eighty and ninety miners wintering at the hotel, all of whom were weighted down with heavy pokes and beset by an itch to forget the hardships and privations they had gone through to fill these. At first they were content to pass their time playing billiards, but this sport soon palled, and Brown was induced to take out the billiard table and install ten or more card tables. These were at a premium for monte, faro, roulette and other gambling games, and at the height of the gold fever the hotel's cut from the games amounted to between seven hundred and a thousand dollars a day.[13]

The miners were out for fun, and the faster and more expensive this was the better they liked it. Gold was so plentiful that they did not think of it as of intrinsic value, but only as a commodity to be carelessly exchanged for whatever amusement took their fancy. This attitude was not shared by the purveyors of entertainment, however, and the situation was quickly capitalized on. The professional gamblers refused to play for dust, and their patrons had to exchange this at the bar for currency at the rate of six or eight dollars an ounce, depending on how much of a hurry they were in and how much cash Brown happened to have on hand. Board, lodging and bar bills at the hotel were all paid for at the rate of eight dollars, and at the time ten or twelve dollars an ounce was the most that anyone paid for gold.[14]

"Dust" the stuff was called, and like dust it was so carelessly handled that the swamper in the City Hotel's saloon panned two hundred dollars in gold from the floor sweepings, which had been thrown into an old barrel that served as a dust-bin. A not uncommon superstition among the miners was that it would be unlucky to take any gold back with them when they returned to the diggings in the spring, and many of them did their best to avoid this risk. One of Brown's customers was known as "Flaxhead," and before his departure for the mines he poured six pounds of dust (all that was left of over twenty pounds of gold he had brought to town) into a boot, and thrusting a stick through the boot-straps slung this improvised poke over his shoulder. He then proceeded to make the round of the saloons, where he treated everyone in sight until his gold had been reduced to the point where he felt that it would be safe for him to leave. Another patron, known as "Dancing Billy," would spend hours dancing on the hotel's veranda and treating everyone who stopped to look on at his performances. On one occasion an auctioneer named Montgomery started to jump his horse through the big barroom window, but Brown stopped him and promised that if he did so it would prove a very costly ride. Montgamery asked him how much it would cost, and Brown, thinking the figure would discourage the project, said five hundred dollars. Scarcely were the words out of mouth when Montgomery threw a bag of dust through the window and yelled "Weigh out your five hundred dollars, and take out enough for a basket of wine!" Before Brown could pick up the sack, horse and rider had crashed through the window into the saloon.[15]

After the Fourth of July exercises had subsided, the next occasion on which San Francisco pulled out all the stops was August 11th, when the town did full justice to Governor Mason's announcement of the ratification of the treaty of Guadalupe Hidalgo, that terminated the war with Mexico and ceded California to the United States. Ships and buildings were decorated with American flags, and innumerable salutes were fired by cannon, pistols and muskets, and even by such of the small fry who could buy, borrow or steal a little gunpowder to burn. In the evening the windows of every inhabited house were illuminated; tar barrels and bonfires blazed on every hand, and the day's rejoicing was topped off by a grand ball and dinner party at the City Hotel.[16]

By the fall of '48 the price at which gold was being accepted in trade had become a paramount issue. For several months after Marshall's discovery it does not seem to have occurred to anyone that gold was as permanent a medium of exchange in California as it was elsewhere, and depending on how both buyer and seller felt about the matter at the moment, its value fluctuated wildly. As a consequence of this unstable market much of the gold brought down from the diggings was shipped back to the "States" where its bullion value was between seventeen and eighteen dollars an ounce. Metallic coinage was very scarce, and it was obviously bad business for San Francisco to force so much potential wealth out of the country instead of doing something to encourage its being put into local circulation. An incident occurred at that time that of itself was of no special moment, but, happening when it did, helped crystallize the growing conviction that gold had come to stay, and was therefore to be treated more respectfully than as "dust." At four o'clock on the afternoon of August 16th the famous racehorse "Canela" was auctioned from the veranda of the City Hotel, the terms of the sale being that the minimum price of the horse was four hundred dollars, payable on the spot in coin or gold dust, the latter being valued at ten dollars an ounce.[17] It is needless to say that no one had four hundred dollars in cash with which to bid in the horse, and this transparent scheme to depreciate the value of gold turned the trick.

On September 9, 1848, a public meeting was held to discuss what steps should be taken to strengthen the foundation of San Francisco's economic structure by stabilizing the price of California gold, and on the 16th a still larger meeting resulted in all the principal citizens of the town pledging themselves to accept pure gold at sixteen dollars an ounce.[18] This action had the desired effect: the merchants' invest-ments in stocks were protected, and the miners received much better value for their gold. Prices went up like skyrockets, it is true, but this was lost sight of in the general excitement over the increasing amount of bullion that was pouring in from the mines. The bonanza days were beginning, and nobody cared a hang about what anything cost.

Despite the enforced curtailment of John Henry Brown's earlier investments in gold at from one-half to five-eighths of its real value, the City Hotel continued to do a "smashing business," and the receipts from the bar, gambling tables, board and lodgings, together with the rental from several stores and offices that occupied part of the prem-ises' ground floor, amounted to between four and five thousand dollars a day.[19]

It was at that time (the winter of '48) that another meeting took place in the City Hotel that led to the making of history, since this encounter laid the groundwork for the Indian war touched off a year later by the blow, struck in the gambling saloon of the Plaza Hotel. John M. Murphy and James D. Savage (whom we have already met) were both stopping at the City Hotel, and one rainy day they got to talking about what was happening at the Southern Mines, which were just beginning to be opened up. Murphy was established near Mari-posa, where he was trading with the Indians in an original way, which was bringing him in as much as twenty-five pounds of gold a day in return for the absolute minimum in effort and merchandise. He would hold a pair of cheap blankets in his outstretched right hand and an ordianry tin cup in his left, and into this the unsophisticated savages would pour gold dust and nuggets. As the cup was filled, Murphy would gradually lower his left hand and raise his right until a balance was struck, when the trade would be completed by the transfer of the blankets. The idea of balanced trade was nothing new to the Indians, but Murphy's technique was, and after thinking the matter over Savage hit upon a novel application of the principle, and proceeded to put this into effect at a trading post he thereupon opened on the South Fork of the Merced River. He had a tin cup made with a leather strap instead of a handle, and lying on his back in his tent he attached this to one foot and draped a pair of blankets over the other. He then rapidly raised and lowered his legs, alternately, and the Indians saw at once that Savage's legs represented a much more delicate arrangement than Murphy's arms, and would require less gold to balance them. Also, as they themselves were strongly averse to work, the fact that Savage rested comfortably on the flat of his back during the transaction, whereas Murphy had to stand upright, appealed to them and they forthwith transferred their trade and their allegiance to the former.[20]

By the beginning of 1849 Brown found it next to impossible to keep domestic help in the City Hotel, for no sooner had his employees earned a few dollars than they were off to the mines. So serious had the situation become, indeed, that he was considering closing the dining room, when for the third time the providential arrival of a ship saved the day for him. This vessel brought an Englishman from the Sandwich Islands, who had with him a dozen Chinamen whom he offered to farm out to the highest bidder. Brown at once struck a bargain with the *patron* for his services and those of his Chinamen for twelve hundred dollars a month, and they all worked well and faithfully for three months. But at the end of this time the diggings lured them away, as had happened to their predecessors. With the exception of two Chinese men and one woman, who arrived in February of the preceding year aboard the brig *Eagle*, direct from China, these were probably the first of the Chinese immigrants to California, who a few years later were the victims of such bitter racial hatred and persecution. If this be true, Brown and his hotel had once again scored an historical "first."[21]

On the 28th of February, 1849, the steamer *California* anchored in the bay of San Francisco with the first contingent of four hundred fifty Forty-Niners. Thereafter, as ship after ship followed, to add their complements to the ever swelling tide of gold seekers and adventurers, the crescendo of San Francisco's life surged upward until it reached a climax of tumultuous human activity. The day the *California* arrived there were only about three hundred people in the town, but with this accession their number was more than doubled, literally overnight. By September the population was estimated to be fifteen thousand, and three months later it had grown to thirty thousand souls, the great majority of whom were single men.[22] There was a constant clamor for accommodations, of any sort, so long as they offered a place where a man could shelter himself. The City Hotel was swamped; the last unencumbered space was the floor of the garret, where the lucky ones were more than glad to pay a dollar a night for just enough space to spread their blankets. But more and more men kept pouring into the town, and in an effort to furnish them sleeping places (and also, no doubt, in an effort to separate the newcomers from their dollars) discarded crates and boxes, containing a little packing straw, were ranged along the side of a shed which adjoined the hotel. The latest arrivals were equally thankful for the privilege of paying a dollar to crawl into these receptacles and pass their first night on California's golden strand. Nor did they quibble at paying Brown a dollar for a meal of boiled beef, indifferent bread, and a decoction that, after the addition of what they were told was sugar, passed for coffee.[23]

It seemed that every time a man opened his mouth it cost him a dollar before he could get it closed, and a few days of this caused many of the would-be miners to wonder how they were to keep going until they could get to the "diggins." This was a bad attitude for trade, and something had to be done to prove that California's strand really was golden. Thanks to the careless way in which gold dust was handled, there was color to be found almost anywhere in town, and this gave Robert Parker another idea. The night before the first of the water-borne Argonauts landed he scattered two or three thousand dollars worth of coarse gold dust up and down Clay Street in the vicinity of the City Hotel. At the time Clay was more of a gully than a street, and next day the banks of the thoroughfare were lined with amateur miners, busily engaged in washing out their first pans of California's "placer gold." Parker's contribution was not wholly altruistic, however, as the most natural thing for the fortunate "miners" to have done was to adjourn to the handy saloon of the City Hotel to celebrate their luck. Nor was the psychological effect of this civic-minded gesture purely local, as many of the newcomers forthwith wrote home to the "States," saying that gold was so plentiful that it could be found anywhere in San Francisco's streets.

Inspired by Parker's idea, an unnamed party, representing equally anonymous principals, one night salted Kearny Street in front of the *plaza* with a couple of ounces of dust, and the next day casually remarked to another group of newly arrived Forty-Niners that Clay Street was not the only placer ground in San Francisco. By then Clay had been pretty well washed out, and this statement was received with open skepticism. Whereupon the local city slicker produced a tin pan, worth about ten cents, and to the amazement of his audience proceeded to wash out almost two ounces of gold. There was an immediate stampede for tin pans (which, strangely enough, proved to be for sale in a nearby store at two dollars apiece), and while one lucky individual was rewarded by some twenty cents worth of gold, none of the others found so much as a color.[24]

Bayard Taylor, the world traveler and author, landed in San Francisco on August 17, 1849, and left the following description of the City Hotel's accommodations as they were in that hostelry's latter days:

"Our room was a sort of garret over the only story of the hotel; two cots, evidently of California manufacture, and covered only with a pair of blankets, two chairs, a rough table and a small looking-glass, constituted the furniture. There was not space enough between the bed and the bare rafters overhead, to sit upright, and I gave myself a severe blow in rising next morning without proper heed. Through a small roof-window of dim glass, I could see the opposite shore of the bay, then partly hidden by the evening fogs. The wind whistled around the eves and rattled the tiles with a cold, gusty sound, that would have imparted a dreary character to the place, had I been in a mood to listen."[25]

In the spring of '49 (and presumably after July 1st, when Parker's lease expired), the City Hotel was rented for sixteen thousand dollars a year. Part of the building was cut up into small stores and offices which were sub-leased at an enormous profit, and with this its days as a public house were numbered.

By that time San Francisco was literally glutted with humanity that, pending its departure for the mines, sheltered itself wherever shelter could be found; in makeshift tents, boxes and barrels, in the lee of a wall, or under a tree. Lodging places of all sorts were springing up daily, and among the first of these was a class of infamous tenement that today would be called a flophouse, where a "gite," or night's lodging, could be contracted for at the usual rate of a dollar. These gite houses of '49 were either tents or flimsy wooden buildings, fitted with two or three rows of bunks, three or four tiers high. On these bare shelves anywhere from eighty to one hundred guests huddled down in their own blankets to sleep and snore, or stay awake and scratch, as best suited the individual's mood and state of sobriety. These noisome dens were always so crowded that it was not unusual for a sleeper to be rudely awakened by a late-comer's booted feet being deposited on his face, since no one ever thought of undressing before bedding down. Tobacco chewing was universal, and the occupants of the lower bunks were apt to be the targets for carelessly expectorated streams of tobacco juice, or worn out cuds. There was no pretense of ventilation, and by morning the atmosphere of one of San Francisco's gite houses was something that had best be left to the imagination. The next upward step in the order of accommodations were places fitted with cubicles that resembled ships' cabins. These little pens were called "private apartments," as they contained only two shelves, and as much as twenty-five dollars a week was charged for each shelf, including board and fleas; but as in the case of the humbler accommodations, the guests supplied their own blankets. By the summer of 1849 several places had been built which more or less justly claimed to be hotels, and where board and lodging (including bedding) cost anywhere from seven to twenty-five dollars a day.[26]

Low priced competition by the gite houses, and the better accommodations offered by the more pretentious establishments, soon ended the City Hotel's career as the town's one-time leading hostelry, and thereafter it degenerated into a rowdy gambling resort.[27] While the building may have been damaged in San Francisco's first fire that occurred on December 24, 1849,[28] it was not destroyed until the great conflagration of May 4, 1851, swept it away, together with the city's other old landmarks.[29]

Under the name of "Brown's Hotel" the establishment was the first place in California to be called a hotel rather than a "house," and because of this it has frequently been referred to as "California's first hotel." The City Hotel was in reality the fourth, if not the fifth, in order of seniority, and like the Washington Hotel at Monterey, it must cede its unearned laurels to its betters.

As in the case of the Portsmouth House, the City Hotel's name survived, but unlike its predecessor, in the first instance, this was more of a recrudescence than a survival, as the name reappeared before its original bearer's memory had been decently interred. In 1849 Sam Brannan and John Fowler pirated the name and used it for the new three-story hotel they built around the framework of Sutter's uncompleted grist mill at Brighton, that had been dismantled and hauled in to Front Street, in Sacramento.[30] It was not until 1852 that the name reappeared in San Francisco, when a new City Hotel was located opposite the steamboat landing at the Pacific Street wharf, and by 1854 the place was advertised as catering to transients and families arriving by the river steamers. Little is known of the fortunes of this third City Hotel, but it could not have been any too successful, as by 1856 the name is no longer listed among those of San Francisco's hostelries.[31]

Chapter 8. The Parker House

THE ANNALS of San Francisco's famous old Parker House are so much a part of those of the City Hotel, and its fortunes are so intimately identified with those of Robert A. Parker and John Henry Brown, that these are really all parts of the same story.

When Brown and Parker turned down Leidesdorff's proposition that the former reopen the City Hotel, and decided to build a place of their own, they went energetically to work getting out the lumber for the building that they had decided to call the Parker House. But by early summer of 1848 the lure of the gold diggings had practically depopulated the San Francisco bay region, and work had to be stopped. With the setting in of the rainy season, however, most of the miners began returning, and as some of these had found only enough gold to whet their appetites, by paying as high as twenty dollars a day it was possible to hire enough carpenters and other workmen from among these and Colonel Stevenson's disbanded regiment of New York Volunteers to resume construction.[1]

As originally designed, the Parker House was a two-and-a-half story frame building with a sixty foot frontage on Kearny Street that stood on the site of San Francisco's present Hall of Justice, facing Portsmouth Square. By the end of September it was nearing completion, but the upper part of the house was still in the hands of the builders as late as April of 1849.[2] The cost of labor and materials was almost as high then as they are today, and as Parker's affairs were becoming involved in what a few months later degenerated into a complete financial failure, Brown was forced to use all the profits of the City Hotel to meet the construction bills. The closest he could come to estimating the cost of the place was the fact that he put all his earnings into the venture, which is not surprising, in view of the fact that at one time he had to pay as high as a dollar a foot for lumber. Toward the end it was found necessary to send a ship on a special voyage to the Sandwich Islands for glass to fit the window sashes, which by mistake had been made too large for the glass that was obtainable

89

locally. But Brown and Parker did not waste time worrying over the cost, as they were determined to build the biggest and best hotel in the new Territory, for that matter, west of the Mississippi River.[3]

The lower part of the building was completed in the fall of 1848, and consisted of three rooms on the ground floor that were immediately occupied as offices by Henry M. Naglee (Captain "Black-Jack" Naglee, of Baja California military notoriety) and Richard H. Sinton, exchange and real estate brokers; Dr. Alexander Perry (lately surgeon of Colonel Stevenson's regiment) and Parker. Some time after September a bar and billiard room was opened for business on the same floor, and thereafter another bar and billiard saloon was added on the second floor, and a third billiard room in the basement. With these places of entertainment going full blast it was not long before the hotel began to pay for itself, but this was only the beginning of its prosperity.[4]

It is possible that neither Brown nor Parker had ever heard of Napo-

PARKER HOUSE when first built

leon's statement that a victorious army marches on its belly, but one of their first cares was to provide the Parker House with a first class dining room. Brown had in mind his current difficulties in keeping the dining room of the City Hotel going, and the boarding department of the new place was turned over to James Crane, who paid his rent by boarding the hotel's barkeepers.[5] How Crane made the stake that enabled him to equip and open the new dining room really has nothing to do with the story of the Parker House, but it is nevertheless worth telling.

As early as March of 1847 Crane had opened the pioneer American eating house in Monterey, in part of José Abrego's billiard and gambling saloon, where he specialized in honest-to-goodness American beefsteaks, good-but-not-so-honest English mutton chops, and undisguisedly Californian eggs. He was an inveterate gambler, and a game of more-or-less honest *monte* was a side dish. It was fortunate that Crane's menu did not take in any more territory, for by the winter of '48 the food purveyors of Monterey (together with most of the food consumers) had stampeded to the gold diggings, and an occasional piece of questionable meat was about the only food item that could be obtained. Milk, butter, and fresh bread were not to be had at any price, and potatoes and even Mexican beans had come to be luxuries.[6] This was a serious handicap to Crane's budding restaurant business, but like Brown and Parker, instead of joining the rush after gold, he sat tight and waited for the gold to come to him, and cashed in with comparable success.

On February 24, 1849, the *California* put into the bay of Monterey in distress, having burned all her coal and most of her wooden cabin fittings in the effort to arrive that far on her maiden voyage from New York, and spent two days taking on enough firewood to enable her to proceed to San Francisco. By the time the ship reached Monterey the three hundred sixty-five passengers who embarked at Panama had been living for almost three months on salt-horse, beans, hardtack, and such-like deepsea delicacies, and despite a brief interlude of such Panamanian dishes and fruits as had not killed or disabled them, they were one and all clamoring for pie—that crowning grace of all well regulated American meals. How Crane managed to meet the emergency is a mystery, but for two days and three nights he supplied the demands of the newcomers, to the exclusion of his local customers, and when one of the latter diffidently asked him for a piece of pie he exclaimed: "Pie! Pie! For God's sake don't ask me for pie today! Give the strangers a chance!"

Crane was the hero of the hour, and when the first sea-borne contingent of Forty-Niners and their attendant professional gamblers moved on, what with pies and *monte* he had cleaned up over two thousand dollars, and was in position shortly thereafter to take on the dining room of the Parker House.[7] Doubtless because of the same difficulties that beset Brown at the City Hotel, the dining room of the new establishment seems to have been the only department that did not pay, and Crane soon sold out to Isaac M. Hall, of whose fortunes there seems to be no record.[8]

The bedrooms on the second floor were finished in the summer of '49, and as soon as these apartments were ready they were occupied as offices. Among the well known men who established themselves in the Parker House at that time were John Owen, a veteran of the Mexican war and a successful importer and merchant; the law firm of Hall McAllister, Frank Turk and Francis J. Lippitt (San Francisco's McAllister and Turk streets being later on named for the two senior members of the firm); Judge John Satterlee, the jurist; Dr. S. Russell Gerry, and J. H. Rodgers, the Port Health Officer. With this the hotel was officially opened with a grand ball and free-for-all supper, for which Brown had for months been saving all the exotic delicacies he could lay his hands on, and no expense was spared to make the occasion a memorable one.[9]

At first the principal ornamental features of the façade of the Parker House were eight dormer windows, lighting the upper floor, a series of decorative recesses between the windows of the first and second stories, and pilastered and linteled ground floor entrance that may have been inspired by Parker's recollection of the colonial houses of Boston, where he was born. A few months later a handsome arcade was added, that ran the full length of the house and made it look more like the elite stopping place that it was.[10] Rooms at the hotel were at a premium, both as living quarters and for business purposes. There was more gold in San Francisco and more miners trying to spend it than anyone had ever dreamed of, and the number of gamblers who swarmed in to take care of the situation was even more astonishing.

Places of business were snapped up at any price, and as money meant nothing to these gentry (especially if it happened to be someone else's money), shortly after the hotel was opened Parker closed with a tempting offer that turned the place into the town's gambling headquarters.

The billiard tables were hustled out without ceremony, and on the ground floor three faro tables were installed, two tables for *monte* and one for *roulette*, with a seventh general utility table, where the customers could call for any game they chose to name, and the professional gamblers paid ten thousand dollars a month for the privilege of running these games. Back of the bar was another room that rented for three thousand five hundred dollars a month, and on the second floor there were three other apartments, each of which brought in the same rental. All of these were public gambling rooms, where anyone who had gold and a sporting spirit was welcome to the chance of winning, and the certainty of one or more free drinks and cigars an hour, depending on how fast he lost his pile. Apart from these there were two other rooms on the second floor that were reserved for private poker games, and while it is not known what they rented for, the fact that it was not unusual for blind bets of as high as a thousand

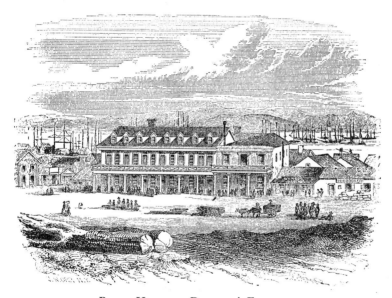

PARKER HOUSE AND DENNISON'S EXCHANGE

dollars to be made before the draw suggests that by the end of one of these sessions the kitty must have been pretty well sweetened. There is no means of telling how much money changed hands in the Parker House, but it was nothing out of the ordinary for each dealer to have on his table a bank of anywhere from ten to forty thousand dollars in gold and silver coins to guarantee that the players' guesses would eventually prove to be wrong.[11] It may sound like a pretty tall story to say that at the height of the Gold Rush there must have been at least half a million dollars on the gambling tables at one time, but the following first hand description of the Parker House as it was in April of '49 will prove that the statement is not a latter-day attempt to palm off literary pyrites for historical gold:

"This is not only the largest, but the handsomest building in San Francisco; and, having been constructed at enormous expense, and entirely on speculation, a concurrence of fortunate circumstances alone, such as had followed upon the discovery of the gold mines, could have ensured its prosperity. It was now one of the most frequented, fashionable, and firmly established hotels in the country; and in so far as it presented a model to the builders and settlers in the town, was a signal illustration of the shrewdness and enterprise of the Yankee character, and a standing credit to the projectors and proprietors. It is built entirely of wood, and contains two very spacious principal rooms; the one a dining-room, the other set apart for billiards. Beside these, there are three saloons of lesser dimensions, especially devoted to gambling, and two well supplied bars—one below, to the right of the entrance, the other in the billiard-room. The portion of the hotel that is not set apart for the usual offices and conveniences is divided off into innumerable chambers, which are occupied by the superior classes of emigrants—lawyers, doctors, money-brokers, *cum multis aliis*. The saloon contains two very handsome billiard-tables, which are constantly occupied by players, chiefly Americans, some of them of first rate excellence. The charge was a dollar a game of one hundred, and they were no sooner vacated by one party than another came in. At one of them I saw Mr. C--, of Monterey, whom I have already alluded to.[12] He was engaged in a game with a New Orleans man, who, with some difficulty, beat him. He paid his loss with great *sang froid*, and crossed over to the *monte*-tables, where he lost eight ounces; but soon won them back, and finally went away the winner by thirty ounces besides. The establishment contained nine gambling tables, which were crowded, day and night, by the citizens and the miners; many of the latter staking very large sums upon the turn of a card. The stakes, however, varied from twenty-five cents to five thousand dollars; and the excitement of some of the losers was frequently fearful to contemplate. Some who gained largely prudently withdrew; and I was informed that, a few days previously to my arrival, a newcomer from the States, who was bound for the mines, having come into the saloon, and tried his fortune at the *monte*-tables, luckily made twenty thousand dollars, with which he returned home, by the steamer, two days afterwards."[13]

With money rolling in at this rate it would seem impossible for Parker to have failed, but if he had one weakness this was his readiness to help out his less fortunate friends. In the end this open-handed generosity led to his affairs becoming so involved that by September of 1849 he owed Brown over eighty thousand dollars, and the latter agreed to take over his partner's interest in the Parker House and manage the business. But when an audit of the accounts was made, it developed that Parker's equity was so heavily mortgaged that to get out the best way he could Brown first leased the building to Wright and Haight, and on December 20th sold out to George McDougal and a man named Hart.[14]

At the time Brown felt he was taking a heavy loss in being forced to dispose of so profitable a business, but, as it turned out, the transaction was a fortunate one for him. Four days after the sale the Parker House was totally destroyed in the first of San Francisco's great fires. With the exception of how this was supposed to have started, most of the details of the conflagration have been told too often to bear repeating, but it remains for John Henry Brown to tell the story of this suspicion in his own way:

"All that I could ever learn in regard to the Parker house fire, was through the watchman, Robert Driscoll and Samuel Dennison, who built the house adjoining, which was used as a saloon and for gambling purposes. The name of the house was Dennison's Exchange. A short time prior to the fire, Dennison sold out his lease to a person by the name of Tom Bartell. A few days after he took possession of the house, a colored man, who did small jobbing around town, came to the bar and asked for a glass of whiskey. Instead of giving it to him without pay, and telling him not to call too often, as was the rule, Tom Bartell thought the best way to keep him away from his house was by abuse, and he got a club and beat the man most shamefully so that he was confined to his room for many days, and he always said he would have revenge on Tom Bartell if it cost him his life. About ten days prior to the fire, the watchman saw the colored man laying around the Dennison Exchange; also many times after. On the night of the fire he was in the Parker House, and no more notice was taken of him than any other person; but after the fire the man could not be found, and has never been seen or heard from since by any person that knew him. The general supposition was that this man was the cause of the fire, although there were no proofs."[15]

The ashes of the Parker House were still smoking when the new owners decided to rebuild, using brick instead of lumber for the outer walls, and within a week the floor timbers of the basement had been laid. By May 3, 1850, the new building had been completed at a cost of forty thousand dollars, but the day after it was finished it was again burned, when the holocaust of May 4th left nothing but a smoke blackened shell. Thomas Maguire, one of San Francisco's earliest promoters, and B. F. Williams, as Thomas Maguire & Co., then came into the picture, and expanded the original building by the addition of a playhouse. Thereafter the establishment became the Jenny Lind Theatre, and the ground floor was again in operation by May 27th, the first performance being given in the theatre in August of the same year. The cost of this building was one hundred thousand dollars, but it was no more fortunate than its predecessors. Just a year later it too was destroyed in the same conflagration that wiped out the City Hotel, and with this the last vestige of the Parker House disappeared.[16]

The very site of the old hostelry has been so altered by San Francisco's growth that it is no longer recognizable, but its name has survived, and is far more widely known today than it was a century ago, at the height of its fame. The memory of the one-time premier hotel of the west and of its builder are perpetuated in the latter's home town by the stately Parker House, of Boston. Beyond this, the rolls made famous by this hotel have carried the name into every home in the land and made it one of daily usage, not only in the United States but in every English speaking country in the world.

It is fitting that the story of so famous a hostelry as the Parker House should be closed with a word about the two men who had the foresight and courage to promote the building of such a pretentious place at a time when San Francisco's fortunes were fluctuating so wildly that it was next to impossible to tell from one day to another whether a new business enterprise would succeed or fail.

Robert A. Parker was born in Boston in 1820 and arrived on the coast of California in April of 1947 as supercargo of the United States store-ship *Mount Vernon*. Strangely enough, in view of his subsequent well known generosity, Henry Mellus (who it will be remembered was supercargo of the ship *Vandalia* at the time) introduced him to Thomas O. Larkin as "a tough customer," but this was no doubt due to some hard bargain that Parker drove with the firm of Mellus & Howard rather than to his personality. In 1848 he opened a general store in Captain William A. Richardson's old *adobe*, the "Casa Grande," on Dupont Street, and was so successful that by the end of the year he and Brown were able to start work on the Parker House. As has been seen, Parker's affairs then became so entangled that by the fall of '49 Brown took over the hotel and did his best to settle his partner's debts, that amounted to almost one hundred sixty thousand dollars. For a while Parker continued his store business in San Francisco, and in 1850 departed to try his luck in the north. In April of that year he laid out the site of Trinity City on Humboldt Bay,[17] and by 1854 he had moved to Crescent City. From there he went to San Quentin, Baja California, and died in San Diego on October 21, 1865.[18]

Something of John Henry Brown's early story has already been told,[19] and it now remains to recount what little is known of the later years of the man who can without any exaggeration be said to have been the father of California's pioneer inns. After disposing of the Parker House, he was at Lovejoy's Hotel on Broadway, San Francisco, either as a guest or the hotel's manager, as late as September of 1850, and thereafter he moved to Santa Cruz, where he farmed for thirty years or more. There he married his second wife, probably in 1850 or 1851, there being several children by his last union, whereas his first marriage was childless. Some time in the 'Eighties Brown returned to San Francisco where he went into the grocery business. It was during this period of his life that he wrote his inimitably quaint little book, *Reminiscences and Incidents of "Early Days" of San Francisco*, which after the lapse of over sixty years is still the richest source of intimate and gossipy information about the men and events of those far off and colorful days. By 1898 he was back in Santa Cruz, where he died on April 6, 1905, at the ripe old age of ninety-four and a half years.[20]

NIANTIC HOTEL

Chapter 9. San Francisco's other Hostelries

T HE ANNALS of what might be called the blue blooded artistocracy of San Francisco's earliest inns have been recounted, and it now remains to tell the stories of these hostelries that, while also of ante-Forty-Nine vintage, were of humbler social stature, or of somewhat later origin.

The Shades Tavern was one of the earliest of the saloons that the 1848 stampede to the gold diggings turned into so-called hotels in the spring of '49. The original establishment stood on the northeast corner of Pacific and Stockton streets, and the earliest mention of the place is on July 1st of 1846, when a dance was held there in celebration of the arrival the day before of the ship *Brooklyn*, with Sam Brannan's party of Mormon colonists. This was the first American dance given in the little settlement of Yerba Buena, and the first occasion on which American women appeared at such a public gathering in California, and in consequence the affair was doubly noteworthy. Unfortunately nothing more is known about this pioneer *baile* except that the music (probably that of a fiddle) was furnished by a man who in all probability was William J. Reynolds,[1] an English sailor and carpenter who left his ship in 1843 and settled in Yerba Buena. We are indebted to "Chino" Reynolds himself for even this meager scrap of information, but as this pioneer was rarely detected in telling the truth about early events, the statement must be accepted with this reservation.[2] In the beginning the Shades was no more than a common grog shop, where bowling and food of sorts could be indulged in, and that catered to the none too fastidious tastes of sailors ashore for a spree. If not the first, it was certainly the most notorious of these hybrid places, and a pretty fair idea of its social status can be gathered from the fact that its senior proprietor was none other than Tom Smith, California's pioneer American crimp. Tom was by this time associated with Henry Smith, another crimp, whose calling was so well recognized that his bills for apprehending sailors were acted on by the town council as early as November of 1847. When these two worthies joined forces and opened the tavern they must have come to the conclusion that it was better business to have their items of prospective merchandise safely warehoused on their premises and thus ready to hand, rather than to lose time and money hunting them up among the sand dunes and in the *monte*.[3]

The first reports of the discovery of gold doubtless induced the Smith boys' stock of potential deserters to make good their status by decamping to the diggings, and thus putting themselves beyond the reach of their hosts. To offset this loss the two sailor-catchers turned their attention to the rapidly increasing number of less problematical transients *en route* to and from the mines, whose patronage they solicited by advertising good beds *and* bedding in addition to the tavern's earlier attractions.[4] But notwithstanding this suggestion of gentility, the place had a hard name that grew worse before it improved.

By September 5th the Smith boys' partnership had been dissolved, and ten days later the Shades was reopened by Isaac Montgomery (a liquor dealer who came to San Francisco from Honolulu and in 1849 was elected a member of the town council), William F. Upham (of the firm of Upham & Talbot, of Monterey) and John A. Patterson (who was later elected a member of the California Convention, notwithstanding his earlier activities), under the firm name of I. Montgomery & Co.[5] The advertisement that they inserted in the *Californian* of September 16, 1848, is a masterpiece of both optimism and caution that speaks volumes for the spirits of the times:

"Shades Tavern (Re-opened). This well known establishment has been reopened with a large and superior assortment of Brandy, Wines, Cordials, Cigars, etc., which will be sold in quantities of from one bottle or case, to a pipe of 60 gallons, as may suit purchasers. Terms — *Cash, or Gold Dust* at 16 dollars an ounce."

Apart from its unquestionable reputation, the Shades earliest claim to fame is the fact that at two o'clock on the morning of January 15, 1849, it provided San Francisco's first noteworthy fire, when despite the utmost efforts of volunteer firemen the building was totally destroyed. A few days later work was begun on a considerably more pretentious place, but for some reason or other, by February, Montgomery seems to have had enough of the business. The firm of I. Montgomery & Co. was in turn dissolved, and Upham and Patterson completed and opened the new "Old Shades Tavern," where in November of the same year over one hundred sixty guests were lodged.[6]

In all probability the new tavern was built on the fifty *vara* lot at the northeast corner of Pacific and Dupont streets, which Patterson and Upham purchased of Tom Smith, John H. Couzens and John Ilig in the same year,[7] but in any event it is certain that by September of 1850 the place was located on Pacific Street between Kearney and Dupont.[8]

By the middle of 1849 Patterson appears to have been the sole proprietor of the tavern, and under his management the place for a while achieved an even worse reputation than it had enjoyed under Tom Smith.[9] A gang of ruffians known as the "Hounds," and later as the "Regulators," had been formed by San Francisco's criminally-minded riffraff who, taking advantage of the fact that there was no adequate provision for maintaining law and order, practically took over the town, and under the pretense of protecting the English speaking citizens from foreigners (especially Mexicans and Chileans) committed every sort of outrage that occurred to them. The Hounds' rallying place was in a large tent known as "Tammany Hall," that was pitched in the rear of the Portsmouth House,[10] and their leaders

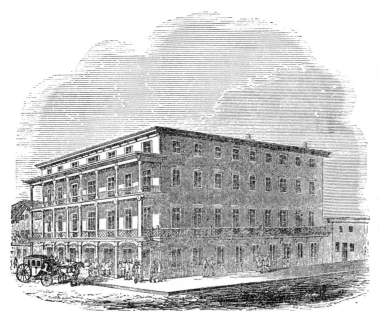

ORIENTAL HOTEL

stopped at the Shades Tavern with Jack Patterson, who was not only their host but also treasurer of the gang.[11] Like San Francisco's fires, much has been written about the Hounds, but a better idea of these characters can be gathered from the following account written by William Redmond Ryan, who at the time was living in a tent directly opposite the Shades and was an eye witness to the events that culminated on July 16th of '49, and sowed the seed from which San Francisco's vigilantes sprang eighteen months later:[12]

"Their headquarters were at a tavern called the 'Shades,' the resort of the wildest characters in San Francisco.... Crimes of almost every hue were openly perpetrated with the most audacious recklessness; for there existed no law to which the citizens could, with any degree of confidence, appeal ... The numbers of these wild and lawless men who thus infested the public thoroughfares were perfectly astounding; some of them would gallop headlong through the most frequented streets, and, alighting at any hotel, demand what they wanted, and often refuse to pay for it ... At other times, a party of them might be seen, attired in the most gaudy clothing, with rich-coloured *serapas* thrown over their shoulders, their hats ornamented with feathers and artificial flowers, perambulating the streets in the company of the most abandoned Spanish women or Indian squaws, and shouting the most ribald songs and jests, interspersed with oaths and imprecations of the most horrid kind ... Frequently, on such occasions, the party would be preceded by a motley band of music, consisting of a violin or two, perhaps a horn, but always a banjo, and several pairs of rib-bones.... In illustration of their lawless practises, and of the manner in which they harassed the poor Chilians, three of them one day entered the store of a native of that country, and demanded goods on credit to the amount of seventy-five dollars, saying they resided at the 'Shades,' and were well known.... The poor fellow, who was totally unacquainted with them, declined their patronage ... Upon this refusal, they assumed a threatening attitude, and so effectually terrified him by their menaces, that he supplied them with what they wanted; and even offered no resistance, when, on their taking their departure, they helped themselves to several articles to which they had, apparently, taken a sudden fancy.... Not very long after the outrage alluded to above, a party of the association was seen parading the streets, with drums beating and colours flying. That same night the store of a Chilian was broken into by them, and the unfortunate proprietor nearly murdered; he being so severely beaten, as to have been left for dead.... The next day, however, due information of this act of ruffianism having reached the authorities, several hundred of the citizens, among whom were several Chilians and Spaniards, armed with guns, pistols, and other weapons, proceeded through the town, towards the 'Shades,' crying out the names of several well-known members of the gang. On reaching the hotel, they arrested first two of the principal leaders, and subsequently six or eight more, all of them notorious characters ... They were all brought to trial; and though some escaped, for want of sufficient evidence, the proofs against the principals were too strong for them to escape conviction; and they were accordingly sentenced to be transported to the United States."[13]

It is not clear whether or not the new Shades Tavern was burned in the town's fourth great fire, which on September 17, 1850, ravaged the greater part of the blocks bounded by Montgomery, Dupont, Washington and Pacific,[14] but it may well have been, for in so far as is known the foregoing is the last reference to the place. In October of 1856 a saloon called "The Shades" was being run by Pat Ward on the northeast corner of Kearney and Commercial streets,[15] the site of "Tammany Hall," and with this even the name disappears from San Francisco's annals.

Of about the same vintage as the Shades Tavern was another of Yerba Buena's so-called hotels, that was kept by Alfred J. Ellis on the east side of Montgomery Street, near Jackson. This was a one-story *adobe* house that Benito Diaz, the Mexican Collector of Customs, is said to have built in 1844 and sold to Ellis three years later.[16] The only noteworthy event that is known to have taken place in this hostelry

St. Francis Hotel

occurred late in October of the same year, just after John Henry Brown gave up his lease on Leidesdorff's house and moved to Ellis' place, when this establishment was the scene of a peculiar tragedy that Brown must describe in his own words:

"A few days after taking up my quarters in Mr. Ellis' house, an incident occurred which I will relate here: One night we had a very heavy rain and wind storm, and on the side of the house there was a well twenty-three feet deep. The storm was so heavy that it was next to impossible to hear anything. Between twelve and one o'clock that night Ellis came to my room and called me, saying that there was a man in the well. People would often come to the house late at night and inquire for me, and I thought at the time Ellis called me it was only a ruse on the part of some person to get me up, so I took my time. Another man, by the name of Griffin was called at the same time, he also boarding in the house. When I reached the bar-room, I found that they had got the man out of the well, and it proved to be George, a ship-carpenter, who belonged to Saucelito. Ellis gave him a couple of drinks, when George observed that the other fellow made a terrible grunting when he fell on him. There was not much notice taken of his remark, as he was a very hard drinker and was usually 'two sheets in the wind' when he left town. Things went on as usual for about four days, when the water became too bad to be used for drinking purposes. It was even too bad for washing, so Ellis got some men to clean the well. When part of the water was out, a man's hair was seen floating on the water, and it was found that there really was a person there. When the man was taken from the water it proved to be a Russian sailor, belonging to a vessel which came after wheat. There had been a large reward offered to anyone who would bring the above mentioned sailor on board the vessel, as it was supposed he had run away. When it became generally known that a dead body had been taken from the well, there was the greatest time I ever saw. Most of the citizens had been to Ellis' saloon and had drank the water. With some of them it went very hard; Captain John Patey laid in bed for two days, also Robert A. Parker, and many others were very sick."[17]

To round out Brown's story, the first of these events took place about midnight on Sunday, October 31st, the victim having been one of the crew of the Russian bark *Naslednik*, of Sitka, and when retrieved on Friday, November 5th, he was found to be in possession of a full bottle of rum and (stranger still) of twelve unspent silver dollars. The well's second customer, after having been fished out and provided with a fresh skinfull at Ellis' expense, was asked how he felt. To this he replied that as far as *he* was concerned he was "as happy as a clam," later on (and no doubt as an afterthought) adding the remark with which Brown credits him respecting the reaction of the well's first occupant to his arrival.[18]

Next door to and east of the Shades Tavern, on Pacific Street, was

Vardaman Bennett's groggery, bowling alley and sailor's retreat, that is said to have been opened in 1845, or the early part of 1846.[19] Although referred to as a hotel the place never achieved this status, even under the elastic interpretation of those days, and this despite the fact that in the winter of '48 the house was so crowded with customers that even the bowling alleys were used as sleeping apartments.[20] Nothing of any special note seems to have occurred to enliven the story of this place, and no more is heard of it after Bennett's death in 1849.[21]

Another of these early pothouse hotels was kept by George Denecke on the southwest corner of Pacific and Sansome streets, opposite the ship anchorage, and while this was of a somewhat better character than some of the other places just described, its career started with a first-class murder. Denecke was a German baker who arrived in San Francisco in 1846, when he opened California's first public bakery diagonally across the block from Ellis' hotel, and in the following year began selling liquor along with his bread.[22] Whatever it was he served must have been pretty deadly, as it was responsible for one of the

New Rassette House

town's earliest killings, and at the same time for starting California's pioneer American desperado on his career of crime.

On the evening of Sunday, November 14, 1847, McKenzie Beverley and several kindred spirits (probably runaway sailors, or deserters from Colonel Stevenson's regiment of New York Volunteers) gathered at a grog shop owned by John Ilig, and began a drunken carousal that presently overflowed to Denecke's establishment. Denecke's liquor was evidently of the "chain-lightning" variety, as after a few jolts of this a quarrel broke out that led the party to withdraw themselves and their patronage, with threats of reprisals. Securing a rifle they returned shortly and after expressing disapproval of both Denecke and his place, Beverley punctuated their remarks by firing through the closed door of the saloon. The shot mortally wounded C. Dornte, one of the town's oldest citizens, who was sitting in a chair and minding his own business. The victim was very well thought of, but despite this and the fact that Beverley was known to have been the killer, the authorities did nothing about the matter and the culprits seem to have gone scot-free to work out a program of bigger and better paying crime.[23] By March of 1848 Beverley and his associates were operating in the Pulgas redwoods, to the northwest of San José, as an organized gang of marauders. While little is known of their activities, it is not improbable that some of them came to a bad end, as in the same year the irate citizens of San José and Santa Barbara hung, scourged, cropped and in other ways left the mark of their disapproval on a number of these highway murderers and robbers.[24]

By the middle of May of '48 Denecke had either enlarged his original place or put up a new building on the same lot, which he advertised as a commodious public house, whose bar was stocked with the choicest liquors and whose table offered the best the market afforded. As an additional attraction, he stated that his bakery was prepared to supply fresh bread, pies and such-like delicacies at all times,[25] but this promptly got him into trouble with John Henry Brown.

Two of Brown's compatriots, John Rose and William J. Reynolds, had brought a cargo of flour down from Napa in their little schooner the *Londresa*, and Brown took three tons of the cargo on consignment. This must have been about the time that Denecke decided to expand, as Brown unloaded the entire consignment on him at a figure that compares favorably with today's prices. There must have been a

pretty bad slump in business immediately thereafter, since when it
came to a settlement Denecke was unable to pay the full value of the
flour, and in an attempt to recoup his fortunes took to gambling and
lost what loose change he had left. So hard pressed was he, indeed, that
on February 7, 1849, he sold his house and business to Frederick Wissell & Co., and was preparing to leave town. Brown heard just in time
of what was in the wind, and before Denecke could get away relieved
him of his fifty *vara* lot in settlement of the unpaid balance of fourteen
dollars due on the flour transaction. As had happened when he was
forced to dispose of the Parker House, Brown felt that he was being
imposed upon, but when later on he sold the same lot for six thousand
dollars he must have come to the conclusion that with a little luck
generosity sometimes pays off. By July the name of the place had been
changed to "Wissell's Hotel," and thereafter it disappears from the
picture.[26]

The Colonnade Hotel was another of San Francisco's old timers

BRYANTS HOTEL

whose reputation was above that of the pothouse hostelries of those days. It was a one-story building that stood on Kearney Street a few doors north of the *plaza*, and its most notable architectural feature was a pillared veranda that gave it its name, and was probably copied by the Parker House. The place was opened as early as the middle of March of '48 by William Conway and Francis Westcott, but a fort-night later suffered a temporary reverse when on Monday, March 29th, Westcott decamped, leaving his partner and his creditors to wonder where he had gone.[27] Conway carried on, however, and, by adding an all-day and all-night restaurant and a reading room to the original establishment, built up the reputation of his place until it ranked as one of the town's leading hotels.[28]

By April of '49 the Colonnade House had been taken over by J. Mead Huxley (an ex-member of Company A, New York Volunteer Regiment), who initiated a startling innovation by refusing to permit either gambling or drunkenness on his premises.[29] This must have been a disagreeable shock to the town's sporting fraternity, but at the same time a welcome boon to its soberer transients, and had the place survived it would be interesting to have followed its career. Unfor-tunately, the experiment was cut short a year later by the great conflagration that on the morning of May 4, 1850, swept away practi-cally every building in the blocks bounded by Montgomery, Dupont, Jackson and Clay streets.[30]

The last of San Francisco's old hostelries worthy of note as having flourished before the Gold Rush of '49 is Merrill's American House, which has the unique reputation of having been California's first temperance hotel. The annals of the place have become almost hope-lessly confused with those of the later American Hotel, as each of these hostelries is repeatedly referred to both as a house and a hotel, and in each case the name has shifted around to almost a dozen differ-ent locations. To make it still more complicated, Merrill's place was known unofficially as the "Irving House" at least a year before a hotel by this name was opened.[31]

John H. Merrill was a carpenter who arrived in California with the New York Volunteer Regiment, and upon his separation from the military service he built a two story wooden house on one of San Fran-cisco's hills, where for something over a year he and his wife did a thriving business. There is some dispute as to just where the place was located, but it is safe to say that it stood either on Dupont or Powell Street, between Broadway and Vallejo, the latter being the more probable location.[32] On May 16th of 1847 Merrill was appointed superintendent of San Francisco's first Sunday School,[33] and when by November his American House was opened to the public this fact doubtless contributed to its becoming the most popular gathering place of the town's better class of society.

The first of these affairs was what would today be called the dinner dance celebrating the marriage of William Heath Davis (one of California's earliest and best known American pioneers and writers) to María de Jesus, a daughter of Don José Joaquin Estudillo, who was the head of one of California's oldest and best families, and owner of the famous Estudillo estate, on which the city of San Leandro is now located.[34] This affair was so colorful and so typical of the Spanish and Mexican entertainments of the higher class of society that it is better to let Davis himself describe it in his own words:

"About a week before the wedding, Don Joaquin sent about twenty milch cows from his rancho around the bay to San Francisco to be used in the preparation of the marriage feast, for milk was scarce in town. He also sent a caponera of his fine horses for use during the festival. . . . Miss Maria Estudillo and I were married at the Mission of San Francisco de Asis, sometimes called Mission Dolores, in November 1847. The bride was carried by her uncle, Don Jose Martinez, to the church on a spirited jet black horse from Pinole, taken from his own caponera of blacks. It was in keeping with the ancient custom on such occasions for a relative thus to convey the bride, if she was not mounted by herself; as carriages and buggies were not in use at so early a period. The animal was superbly caparisoned with gold and silver mounted saddle and bridle, and Don Jose was dressed in the costly festal habiliments of olden times. At the ball in the evening Don Jose was a prominent actor. He danced the Jarabe, an ancient dance of the country, which is performed by a gentleman and lady facing each other. At a certain stage of the amusement both would stop, when one would deliver several verses in rhyme, at the end of which the dancing was resumed, the lady approaching in a circle, round and round her partner and back to her place, bowing gracefully to her companion, her dainty feet in full view. This was repeated by the Don in a similar manner; and both would then dance with the rapidity of lightning in a circle of small diameter, going round and round artistically and with grace, accompanying their movements with appropriate gesticulations. Sometimes two ladies and gentlemen would dance the Jarabe and then it was even more amusing and attractive. This elicited applause from the audience. The order of dances embraced quadrilles, waltzes, contra-dances and la Jota. The festivities were kept up continuously as the company was eager to commemorate the occasion with a genuine marriage festival such as was enjoyed by their forefathers. At intervals during the night a cold luncheon of poultry, ham, cakes, coffee, champagne and other wines was served."[35]

In January and February of the following year a series of popular masquerades was held in the hotel's hall, which was the largest place of its kind in town.[36] At about this time Merrill must either have rebuilt or added to the original building, as on September 9, 1848, he advertised the place as being in progress of completion, and anticipated Huxley by announcing that the American House would "be conducted purely on the temperance principle." A decision that was doubtless due to the fact that by that time gambling, drinking and carousing were the order of the day (and night) in all the other hostelries in San Francisco.[37]

This is the last record found of the American House as a hotel, but once again the name lingered on for a few years. In 1852 John Davis was running a saloon by this name at No. 6 Commercial Street, and two years later the same establishment was under the proprietorship of Simonds & Co. In 1858 a Miss C. Dyer was managing some sort of a place on Pacific Street, below Battery, which was called the American House, and by June of 1859 the name itself is lost sight of.[38]

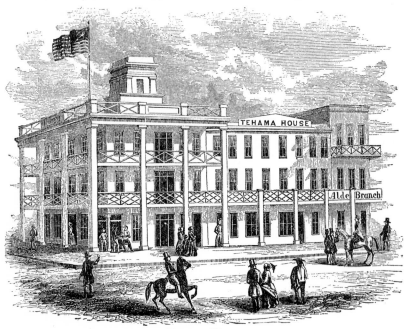

TEHAMA HOUSE

Chapter 10. San Jose's Earliest Inns

SAN JOSE DE GUADALUPE was the first of Califor-
nia's settlements where the overland immigrants met the sea borne
arrivals, and after San Francisco's pioneer hostelries it was here that
the earliest of the country's inland hotels had their beginning. The
pueblo was moved to its present site about 1797,[1] but while after Monterey it was the most important Spanish-Mexican settlement in northern California, half a century later the place consisted of not above
fifty one-story *adobe* houses, built in a meandering parallelogram
about a barren, dusty and ground squirrel infested common that is
today the city's *plaza*, and the population did not exceed eight hundred
souls.[2] Not including Indians, who naturally did not count.

As far as can be ascertained the first public house in San José to
afford any sort of accommodations to the traveling public was a litte
fonda kept by a native Californian as late as 1846,[3] and this was doubtless just the sort of *posada* that has been described as having been the
prototype of the later American inns. Whatever this place may have
had to offer must have been of the crudest, as on August 4th of the
preceding year James Clyman (a hunter, trapper and plainsman) spent
the night in San José with Charles M. Weber, and four days later wrote
that there was "no such thing as a tavern in California so I am informed."[4] The same statement was repeated more specifically by Edwin Bryant, who says that when he visited the village on September
19th of 1846 there was no hotel there, or anywhere else in California.[5]
which makes it appear that either the Americans of those days were
softer than the native Californians or that San José's *fonda* did not
cater to foreigners, as there is no question that it was doing business
at the time.

By 1847, however, the rapidly increasing number of newcomers
arriving in the town had created an insistent demand for both transient
and permanent accommodations. There was still no hotel in the place,
but by paying as high as fifty dollars a month a sleeping space could
be rented on the floor of the second story of Weber's *adobe* store, on

the east side of the *plaza* at the corner of what was later called Light-ston's Alley, as well as in other buildings in the *pueblo*.[6] Opportunity, if not fortune, was hunting for a door on which to knock, and Zacha-riah Jones was the man who supplied the portal.

Zachariah, or "Buffalo" Jones, as he was nicknamed "because his deep, powerful voice reminded oldtimers of a herd of 'bellerin' buf-falo," arrived overland in 1846 with his wife and five children.[7] Taking an old *adobe* building on the east side of the *plaza* near San Antonio Street, he began by taking boarders, and shortly thereafter turned the place into a hotel that he called the Half Moon. When asked why he had selected this name Zachariah explained that as there was but little enlightenment in San José he did not wish to appear too bright by drawing attention to his house, as anything more brilliant than the name suggested.[8] Jones was a man who took his religion so literally that he was in the habit of carrying on loud (if one-sided) conversa-tions with the Lord, as he went about his mundane affairs. But regard-less of such eccentricities he was sincerely religious, and the features that made his place popular with the more serious minded travelers were the services and psalm singing held every Sabbath in the Half Moon.[9]

San José was without a resident physician until early in December, when young Dr. Benjamin Corey arrived from Oregon and estab-lished himself at the Half Moon. When he reached the *pueblo*, Dr. Corey was literally without two *reals* to rub together, and after stopping for a few days at Peter Davidson's home (where he paid a dollar a day for board and lodging) he moved to the Jones menage, "where the necessities of life were obtained at a much reduced rate." As far as is known this is the only reference to the rates Jones charged for accommodations, and judging from this Dame Fortune's knock could not have left any noticeable golden dents on the door of the Half Moon.[10]

So probable is this that, when word that gold had been discovered on the American River reached San José, Zachariah and Dr. Corey were the first to hurry off to Mormon Island, to see for themselves. They are said to have been gone for the proverbial Spanish "eight days" *(ocho dias*, which may mean anywhere from a week upward), and on their return brought with them a small sack of gold dust they

Cary House, Placerville

Placer Hotel, 1850–55 (*Hangtree Inn*)

Yank's Station, at Meyers

bought to prove the truth of the story.[11] Jones and Dr. Corey got back late in May, and by then the *pueblo* was in the throes of a furor of gold excitement that can best be described at first-hand by Thomas O. Larkin, who was an eye-witness of the events he describes in the following extract from his letter to Colonel Robert B. Mason, military governor of California, dated San José, May 26, 1848:

"I arrived here after two days travel. Every Body is in the greatest state of excitement. We can hear of nothing but Gold, Gold, Gold. An onze a day, two a day or three – every one has the gold or yellow fever. Last night several of the most respectable American Residents of this town arrived home from a visit to the gold regions – next week they with their families and I think nine tenths of every Foreign Store Keep. Mechanic or day Labourer of this town and perhaps San Francisco leave for the Sacramento. Mellus & Howard have taken several thousands dollars of gold for goods. I can not vouch for half of the reports in circulation; Mr. Brannon the Mormon, I understand claims some two or three miles by some right of discovery or preemption. In this town 6$ per day will not put a man to work. Mr. Belden informs me that Carpinters on the Anita obtain that pay. Mr. Semple takes from Passengers some 20$ per day. Has not a single Boatman to help him. Only one man has offered to remain and he only for 2 weeks at 25$ pr week.

"I have seen a writen statement of the day labour of one man for 16 days Washing it came to 24$ pr day. This paper from the character of the man who showed it to me I believe – Some Men have done better. 5 or 6 men have to club together and pay one of their number 1½ oz. a day to *Cook*. Mr. Jones the Inn Keeper of this town has just returned. Is now packing up with his Family to open a Hotell *out doors* – at the gold regions, at 3$ pr day for Boarders – Messrs. Link, Taylor, Ross and in fact most every Body are gone. Alcalde Townsend wishes to go. Mr. Belden today from San F. says Mr. Tobar says he and family are going – Mr. West Stable Keeper of this town, informs me his two Brothers have wrote down to him, if he can do no better to burn the Stable and bring up his family – he says having much hay on hand he will leave the doors open. Forbes miners are leaving the Mine. Baskets, tin pans, shovels, Etc. bring any price imaginable. At gold washings 20 to 30$ pr day is asked for to spend a day to go for a quarter of meat. Now of course all this is not true, but much of it is. Santa Cruz and Monterey in 30 days will lose most of their American population. Unless bloodshed, or fever & ague stop the Excitement. We can not imagine the bad results of this fever to C. if it continues. The improvements of Yerba Buena for the present is done. Those men yet there are wishing to leave – Nine men in ten who meet me ask and have you left home to look for gold."[12]

Dr. Corey probably accompanied Jones and his family back to the mines, when they carried the equipment for the proposed "out doors hotell" in an ox-drawn wagon. On arriving at Carquinez Strait the party found so many other gold hunters waiting to be crossed in the ferry that the "long Doctor," Robert Semple, had established the previous year that they were delayed for eleven days. Semple had advertised that a four-horse powered paddle-wheel ferry would be in service by the first of September, but at the time he was using a lateen sailed ship's long-boat to ferry his passengers across the strait.[13] By the first week in July, Jones was established at the "Upper Diggings," on the South Fork of the American River, about a mile and a half below Sutter's mill,[14] and while no record seems to have survived of what must have been one of, if not the first, of the "hotels" opened at the mines, there is every reason to believe it was a money-maker. Early in November Jones and Dr. Corey were back in San José, Jones with enough money to enable him to build a sawmill at Los Gatos, and Corey with about four thousand dollars worth of gold that he had acquired in one way or another.[15] The only additional reference to the first hotel in San José is on Sunday, December 2, 1849, when during a religious service held in the place there was no fire to warm the few who attended.[16] Zachariah Jones' interests were evidently elsewhere, and the Half Moon had passed through its final phase.

The later sequence of San José's hostelries is not entirely certain, but from the evidence available it seems that Weber's hotel was opened about the time the Half Moon was eclipsed. This was another place that from time to time has been put forward as a candidate for the honor of having been "California's first hotel," but in this case the belief in its seniority has been an honest one, based on misleading statements made years after the events under discussion transpired, rather than an attempt to polish up San José's patina of antiquity.

Charles David M. Weber was a German and one of the earliest of California's foreign settlers to arrive overland, having been a member of the first party of immigrants that in 1841 crossed the trackless wilderness of the Sierra Nevada. On his arrival he went to work for Sutter at New Helvetia, and in the spring of 1842 settled at San José. There, on the southeast corner of what later came to be Santa Clara and Lightstone streets, he opened the trading store already mentioned, which later included a saloon and gambling place, and eventually became the town's second hotel.[17]

John A. Sutter, in his reminiscences written in 1876 and referring to the winter of 1841-42, was responsible for the first statement that (taken at its face value) suggests that Weber's Hotel was established by the latter year, and was therefore the earliest of California's American inns. He says:

"Weber ... clerked for me that winter, then went to San Jose and kept a hotel for a while."[18]

William F. Swasey appears to have confirmed this impression two years later, in the following extract from his recollections of early events in San José:

"... in the latter part of February, 1846 ... at San Jose were Chas. Webber, who kept a hotel ... and Peter Davidson, who kept another hotel there."[19]

While both of these statements seem too categorical to admit of any but the obvious interpretation, it must be remembered that the pioneer writers quoted were recalling events of more than thirty years earlier, and furthermore both were thinking of Weber in terms of later dates than those of which they wrote. As a matter of fact, two and a half years after Sutter says Weber was keeping a hotel, and six months after Swasey makes the same statement, Weber's place of business was still a store. It was there that on July 9, 1846, his friend General José Castro took him prisoner, charged with being a naturalized Mexican citizen who was a notorious American sympathizer, and carried him off to Los Angeles for safe keeping.[20]

After three months of what was probably not too arduous captivity Weber returned to San José early in October,[21] and about May 1st of 1847 announced that thereafter his business would be conducted in partnership with his countryman, Francis Lightstone, under the firm name of "Webber & Lightston."[22] No mention of a hotel was made at that time, but by August 10th of the same year he certainly was keeping a hotel in connection with his store and saloon, where there was so much drinking, gambling and carousing that on October 17th the establishment merited being described as a "terrible place."[23] From this it may be concluded that instead of having been established in 1842, Weber's Hotel was not opened until some time between May and August of 1847, and was therefore just a year too late to qualify for anything better than a questionable third place in the race for the honor of having been California's first hotel.

The most notable event that occurred in the hotel took place in

February of '48. One day a man came into the barroom, and in payment for some purchase offered the first native gold seen in San José, saying that it came from Sutter's mill, on the American River, where everyone was going to work. The story was received with open skepticism until an old Georgia miner assured the audience that what the man had was really gold, when it was somewhat doubtfully accepted at the rate of four dollars an ounce.[24] Shortly thereafter, when Zachariah Jones and Dr. Corey returned from "seeing the elephant" and told their story, the *pueblo* was forthwith emptied of all but two of its male inhabitants, and for a couple of months thereafter R. F. Peckham (the runaway sailor from the ship *Cabinet*[25]) and Francis Lightstone were the only adult foreigners left, while old Don Luis Peralta and his sons were the sole Californians who did not join the stampede.[26] When his townsmen began decamping Don Luis called his boys about him and said:

"My sons, God gave the gold to the Americans. If He had wanted the Spaniards to have it, He would have let them discover it before now. So you had better not go after it, but let the Americans go. You can go to your *rancho* and raise grain, and that will be your best gold field; because we all must eat while we live."[27]

Charles Weber was neck-and-neck with the leaders in the race to the American River, and there in partnership with Dr. Isabel, John M. Murphey and others from San José he built a brush shack and opened a trading store at the mouth of the creek named after him. This enterprise turned out to be one of the most remunerative retail businesses ever known, as apart from selling his goods to the miners at prices that ranged upward from twenty-four dollars for a box of Seidlitz powders, he drove a thriving trade with the Indian gold diggers. These unenlightened savages were gravely assured that their dust and nuggets were only worth their weight in silver dollars in trade for glass beads, breech clouts and such-like articles of luxury, and of course nothing was said about the original profit on the beads and clouts.[28] From the foregoing it will be gathered that these bartering transactions were consummated at the rate of sixteen to one, and in consequence Weber must be credited with having gotten away with bimetalism half a century before William Jennings Bryan failed to put across the same happy doctrine.

Thanks to his having been the successful originator of "Free Silver" (or perhaps it would be more appropriate to say free gold), it is said

that in about a year's time Weber collected no less than a *fanega* of
gold from "his friendly Indians" on Weber's Creek and the Stanislaus
River, or in round figures some $650,000. This may seem like a some-
what more than rotund figure, but one of Weber's partners, John M.
Murphey, did much better, as it is claimed that for safe keeping he
buried nearly two million dollars worth of loot. To keep the record
straight, it may be added that Murphey later dug up his gold and
spent it.[29]

Whatever Weber's profit from glass beads, breech clouts and Seidlitz powders may have amounted to, it was sufficient to permit him to
withdraw from trade and devote himself to the development of a
little settlement he had started a year earlier at Stockton, or Weber's
Embarcadero, as the place was generally called at the time. The hotel
in San José was no longer a necessary part of his financial structure,
and in 1849 he deeded it and the rest of his real estate in the *pueblo* to
his partner, Francis Lightstone, as a wedding gift on the day of the
latter's marriage.[30]

The next place to make its appearance in San José was announced
in the following advertisement, appearing in the December 15, 1847,
issue of the *Californian:*

"Peter Davidson, begs leave to inform his friends and the public that he has
opened a House at the 'Pueblo de San Jose.' His table will be constantly supplied
with the *best* the country affords; his rooms are large, airy and commodious; at his
Bar will be found the choicest liquors and wines. N.D.— Oysters supplied at short
notice."

Davidson (or Daveson, as the name is also spelled) was another of
the *pueblo's* early American settlers, having arrived in 1843,[31] when
in competition with "Webber & Lightston" he set up a trading store on
San Pedro Street. While his advertisement did not appear until the
middle of December of 1847, as has been seen, Dr. Corey stopped with
him on the first of the same month, so his hotel must have been opened
before that time.[32] Whatever the correct date of its debut, Peter
Davidson's house was the first of San José's hotels to be advertised in
the press, and the fact that, in addition to its other attractions, oysters
(that were presumably fresh) were available to a discriminating clientele goes far toward suggesting that it was the elite place of entertainment. If this reasoning be correct, it must have seen some colorful
times, but like the town's other hostelries it was engulfed in the roaring

golden maelstrom of '48 and '49. All that is known of its subsequent history is that Peter Davidson departed for the diggings along with the rest of the male inhabitants, and later on a Chilean firm was doing business in his old adobe.[33]

By the latter part of August of 1848 there were two or three so-called hotels in San José that were doing a thriving business in spite of the extravagantly high prices charged for accommodations,[34] and one of these was a place that Pete Brannan had recently opened. Pete was an Irish bricklayer, another of the arrivals of 1846,[35] and his typical Yankee house was popular with travelers because of its good and abundant table, and the excellent fire that warmed the large common room. This last was by no means a minor attraction that winter, as about Christmas time three inches of snow fell in the Santa Clara valley. But perhaps the principal inducement to patrons was the fact that Brannan took gold at nine dollars an ounce, more than twice what the local rate had been a few months earlier. To offset this, how-ever, he charged an ounce for supper, a bed (on the floor, and in the guest's own blankets), breakfast and horse feed (the latter consisting of a handful of corn and a few wisps of dry grass).[36]

Notwithstanding the fact that by this time the town's hotel keepers were in a fair way to doing better than the average miner, toward the end of '48 Pete Brannan became another gold fever casualty, and pulled out for the diggings, via San Francisco. There he was joined by a boat load of deserters from the U.S.S. *Warren*, and after a last rousing drunk that almost landed the sailors back aboard their ship in irons, the party made the best of its way to the American River. There between drinks Brannan settled down to mining in Log Cabin Ravine, off Weber's Creek, and for a while seems to have done better than he did at keeping a hotel. But he was one of those souls who thrive better in an atmospehre of convivial companionship than they do in Nature's great open spaces, and after acquiring a poke full of dust and a thirst that the elementary facilities of the mines were wholly inadequate to cope with, he departed for New Helvetia to take care of the matter. There, after getting very drunk, he concluded that the place did not offer a sufficiently wide scope for his activities, and proceeded to San Francisco where he got very much drunker. So drunk, indeed, that he shortly found himself beset by a soul shaking attack of delirium tremens, and in a frantic attempt to escape from the unwelcome attentions of two-headed plaid crocodiles, pink winged elephants, and such-like fauna, he jumped into the bay and was drowned. Thus closing the accounts of the last of San José's earliest hostelries.[37]

Chapter 11. Ex-Mission Stopping Places

FOR ALMOST eight decades the Franciscan missions of California were the only places where the public found accommodations that can in any way be compared to those offered by typical wayside inns, and as has been said, down to the time of the American occupation there was not one establishment of this nature in all the land. In view of this it might be supposed that, when the need for such places arose, the old mission buildings would in part, at least, have been turned into hostelries. As a matter of fact this was what happened in the cases of a few of the most strategically located church establishments, and that it was not generally true was due to two all-important considerations.

The first of these had to do with the missions' locations with respect to the principal roads, and only a dozen of the twenty-one missions were located on these early arterial highways. The second factor was that of proprietorship. By the time that the American immigrants began to settle California, all but the missions of San Francisco de Asis, or Dolores, and Santa Clara de Asis had been sold or rented to private individuals (mostly Americans who had become naturalized Mexican citizens), and were being held by their new owners.

Despite this last consideration, and the fact that San Francisco and Santa Clara were still nominally in possession of the secular clergy, a few more or less successful attempts were made by newly arrived Americans to capitalize on the past reputation of these and other old missions, as places where travelers could always find a kindly welcome. But the onetime spirit was lacking, and the open handed hospitality of the *padres* was replaced by tight-fisted Yankee commercialism. What happened at San José de Guadalupe is a typical story of these make-shift hostelries, and about the same fate overtook most of the other once flourishing church institutions.

Founded on June 11th of 1797, fifteen miles north of the *pueblo* of the same name, by the good Father Fermin Francisco de Lasuen, San

José was for two generations one of the most important agricultural missions in the two Californias. For almost forty years it continued to grow and prosper, but with the first steps taken in 1834 toward secularization the Franciscans' authority began to be wrested from them, and twelve years later, when the great westward American immigration began, the place was little more than a silent memory of what it had been in the past. With the departure of the *padres*, San José's two thousand Indian neophytes drifted away; its fifty thousand head of stock was either sold or stolen; the broad agricultural lands, where twenty-five thousand bushels of grain were once harvested, lay abandoned, and the well-planned system of irrigation ditches were dry and fast disappearing. All was desolation, and the primeval *monte* was fast reclaiming what had been a fair and smiling scene of manifold industries. With the exception of the church and the fathers' two-story *adobe* dwelling, the mission buildings were menacing ruin, and where a few years earlier the traveler had met with a kindly welcome, all that could be found was a makeshift meal and a corner on the filthy and flea infested floor of the least disreputable of the surviving rooms. This was the picture on September 18th of 1846.[1]

By a perfectly legal transfer of title dated May 5, 1846, Governor Pio Pico, the last Mexican ruler of California, sold the property of the ex-mission of San José to Andres Pico and Juan Bautista Alvarado.[2] But this did not deter Alcalde Colton and Dr. Semple (who, it will be recalled, were publishing California's first newspaper at Monterey) from printing a scant five months later the following editorial, urging the newly arrived American immigrants to move into the old mission's buildings, settle on its lands and otherwise make themselves at home:

"To the Emigrants — It is a matter of importance to persons recently arrived in this country, to know where to go, and to find shelter and provisions for the winter. We feel called upon to make suggestions for their consideration. There are a number of Missions mostly unoccupied, where the emigrants may find shelter for the winter, or rainy season, and in the neighborhood they may be able to purchase provisions ... On the South side (of the bay of San Francisco) is the mission of Santa Clara and San Jose, both in the Puebla valley, and will afford room and provisions for thirty families ... We will mention further, that there is at each of the above Missions, as much public land as they may think proper to cultivate."[3]

Without stopping to look up the remarks that this ingenious idea must have elicited from Señors Pico and Alvarado, suffice it to say that the "recent arrivals" took the exhortation as the obvious interpretation of the time honored motto, "To the victor belong the spoils," and proceeded to make free with the mission property along the lines recommended by Messrs. Colton and Semple. The fact that the immigrants themselves were no more the victors in the current unpleasantness than was the private property of the native Californians the spoils of war, was ignored in the scramble to get as much of everything for as little as possible or nothing, and they moved in without even the pretense of saying "by your leave." Nor was this all, as they speedily took care of what ruin was left to be accomplished.[4]

George Harlan was the leader of a group of immigrants that separated from the ill-fated Donner party at Weber's Canyon, just east of Great Salt Lake and, after overcoming the almost insurmountable difficulties of that portion of the newly discovered Hastings' cut-off, succeeded in crossing the Sierra Nevada ahead of the winter storms that brought about the Donner tragedy.[5] The party arrived at William Johnson's *rancho* (some forty miles northeast of Sutter's Fort), about October 25th of 1846, and on the strength of the recommendations that had appeared a week earlier in the *Californian*, Harlan sent his nephew, Jacob W. Harlan, on ahead to select their winter quarters at the allegedly ownerless and abandoned mission of San José.[6] By the spring of '47 George Harlan and his family, consisting in part of his two married daughters and his two nieces, Sarah and Malinda Harlan, were well established at the old mission,[7] and it must have been to these young ladies that William Redmond Ryan referred to appreciatively in the winter of 1848-49, when he wrote:

"I strolled out into the courtyard to see how my horse had been provided for, when I was agreeably surprised at finding assembled there a group of fresh-looking Yankee girls, chatting and jesting together. They must have come across the mountains, and seemed to have been well taken care of on the route."[8]

A trading store was set up in one of the mission buildings, where goods were sold at a profit of at least eight hundred per cent, and a heavily backed *monte* game took care of any loose change the customers happened to have left after making their purchases. It is improbable that George Harlan had anything to do with the *monte* game, but he certainly did with the rest of the establishment, and in another part of the mission one of the young ladies just mentioned presided over a table at which meals of sorts were served. Thereafter the guests were at liberty to seek repose on a pile of straw in what had once been the *padres'* stable, and in justice to these enterprising "recent arrivals" it must be recorded that the straw was not second hand, and was therefore reasonably clean.[9]

The mission of Santa Clara de Asis, or Santa Clara de Thamien, as the original establishment was called after the Indian tribe that dwelt thereabouts was more closely identified with the *pueblo* of San José than was the mission that has just been described. One reason for this is that it was the older of the two by twenty years, having been officially founded by Father Junipero Serra on the 18th of January, 1777. Another reason is that it was only about three miles northwest of the settlement, with which it was joined twenty-two years later by the first real highway built in California. This was the shady, park-like *Alameda*, whose three rows of immense elm and willow trees and cooling irrigation ditches delighted the first American immigrants plodding along the *Camino Real* with their sun-baked and dust coated ox-drawn wagons.[10]

The first hint of a place in Santa Clara where travelers might find refreshment occurs on September 19th of 1846. At that time Mrs. Mary Bennett was living in one of the least ruinous of the old mission buildings, and while there is no definite allusion to her having kept a public house her immediate background makes this a distinct possibility. In contradistinction to her lackadaisical husband from Georgia, Mary Bennett was very much of the Amazonian type, and when a year earlier Vardaman Bennett's grog shop in Yerba Buena failed to support her and their eight children she demanded a separation, and with her brood of sons moved to Santa Clara.

There her aggressive spirit and command of forceful language earned for her the sobriquet of the "Strong Woman of Santa Clara," and when her spouse died in 1849 she married Harry Love of San José, the reputed killer of Joaquin Murieta. Twenty years of stormy wedded life should have taught Harry Love better, but in 1868 he made the tactical error of trying to mistreat his wife, with the result that he was in turn killed by Chris Iverson, a bodyguard the lady had hired to ward off her husband's unwelcome attentions.[11] Some color is added to the suggestion that Mary Bennett kept a public house by the fact that a few years later she was one of the claimants for reimbursement for services rendered during the pacification of California by the United States forces, and her occupation of the mission building may have been the sort of shotgun settlement that would have been in keeping with the lady's forthright character.[12] Unfortunately, no further reliable information is available on the early history of the building that a few years later became Santa Clara's California Hotel, and we must, however reluctantly, turn to a far less dynamic establishment.

Santa Clara was too close to San José to have been one of the early strategic points for hotels, and the only place that is known definitely to have been opened there before '49 was the Santa Clara House, that George W. Bellomy was operating as early as February of 1848. Beyond the usual claim that his table was set with "the best the market affords," and that his bar was supplied with "the best wines and liquors,"[13] nothing is known of the history of this place. As far as its proprietor is concerned, about all that is recorded of him is that he seems to have been in more or less constant legal difficulties that at one time landed him in jail at San José for disobedience to the mandates of the redoubtable Alcalde Burton, a magistrate whose decrees equalled in originality, if they did not exceed, those of his famous contemporary jurist, Alcalde Blackburn of Santa Cruz.[14]

The mission of San Juan Bautista was founded on June 24, 1794, by Father Lausen, some forty miles south and east of Santa Clara, and there grew up another of California's pioneer hotels. While it cannot be stated positively that the place had its beginning before the Gold Rush, the evidence in favor of this having been the case is sufficiently strong to warrant assigning it a place in the ranks of these old mission stopping places, and the fact that it is suggested semi-officially that the place was still another claimant for the title of "California's first hotel" is a further reason for this.[15]

To sketch the background of this hostelry, with the exception of the church, the adjacent *padres'* quarters and the famous old orchard, the San Juan mission was secularized in 1834, and on May 4th of 1844 Governor Pio Pico sold the latter piece of property to Olivier Deleissieque.[16] Prior to this, however, by the end of 1839, José Tiburcio Castro, the Mexican government's *mayordomo* or administrator of the ex-mission, had built one or more *adobe* houses on land that originally belonged to the church.[17] One of these buildings faced the southeast corner of the *plaza,* and while the official version is that it was erected as early as 1825,[18] this date was later altered to about 1838, when the builder was said to have been General José Castro, a son of José Tiburcio.[19] Whichever version is correct, General Castro was living in the house by the latter year, and made it his headquarters down to the time of the American occupation, when he absented himself from California until the political situation had become stabilized.[20]

In the meantime the ghastly tragedy of the Donner party had taken place near Truckee Lake (as Donner Lake was then called) in the winter of 1846-1847, and among the survivors of that ill fated group of immigrants was Patrick Breen, his wife Margaret and their seven children. After their rescue the family spent a year looking for a place to make their home, and in February of '48 they finally settled at San Juan.[21] There the Breens opened a sort of tavern in a building by combining two small adobe buildings, the larger one being the barracks, and then adding a second story of wood, that they called the United States Hotel. Despite the fact that it left a great deal to be desired it was the only stopping place in the settlement, and is said to have made money during the ensuing Gold Rush days.[22] On February 7, 1849, General Castro sold the place to Breen,[23] and in the summer of the same year J. Ross Browne, the distinguished writer, traveler and diplomat, stopped overnight at the hostelry. It is to his pen that we are indebted for the following description of the place and its owners, and while Browne's reference to its proprietoress' alleged cannibalism at Truckee Lake no more than reflects the contemporary belief, his version of what took place is, nevertheless, open to question:

"The only tavern in the place was the 'United States,' kept by an American and his wife in an old adobe house, originally a part of the mission establishment. Having secured accommodations for my mule, I took up my quarters for the night at the 'United States.' The woman seemed to be the principal manager. Perhaps I might have noticed her a little closely, since she was the only white woman I had enjoyed the opportunity of conversing with for some time. It is very certain, however, that she struck me as an uncommon person — tall, raw-boned, sharp, and masculine — with a wild and piercing expression of eye, and a smile singularly startling and unfeminine ... The man was a subdued and meloncholy-looking person, presenting no particular trait of character in his appearance save that of general abandonment to the influence of misfortune ... In the course of conversation with the man, I found that he and his wife were among the few survivors of a party whose terrible sufferings in the mountains during the past winter had been the theme of much comment in the newspapers. He did not state—what I already knew from the published narrative of their adventures—that the woman had subsisted for some time on the dead body of a child belonging to one of the party. It was said that the man held out to the last, and refused to participate ... The room allotted to me for the night was roughly furnished, as might reasonably be expected; but, apart from this, the bedding was filthy; and, in common with every thing about the house, the slatternly appearance of the furniture did not tend to remove the unpleasant impression I had formed of my hostess. Whether owing to the vermin, or an unfounded suspicion that she might become hungry during the night, I slept but little."[24]

According to John Breen, his father Patrick was an invalid, and this fact no doubt prevented the latter from trying his luck at the gold diggings. But in the summer of '48 John went to Mormon Island and later to Hangtown, where he did well at mining, and on his return to San Juan in March of '49 he may have helped his father to settle for Castro's house and to acquire the farm that Breen and his sons later cultivated.[25] In the latter part of July, or the early part of August, of 1849, the Swiss traveler Carl Meyer arrived at San Juan, and while he does not mention the Breens his description of the only stopping place in the settlement must refer to their tavern, and this notwithstanding the fluent Spanish expletives with which the innkeeper is credited:

"Immediately on our arrival in San Juan I went directly to an old building which we had been told was the only *Mesón* in the town. As soon as I entered I heard a shrill voice shouting 'no hai! no hai nada!' (I have nothing) but even with the best sense of location and auditory perception I was unable to discover whence it came. Somewhat surprised and annoyed at this rude reception I shouted back in good German 'Hey peasant!' '*No entiendo! No hai!*' was the reply to my incomprehensible answer. 'The devil take it! What haven't you got that I want?' I finally asked in Spanish while Witfield let a *Peso duro* clang sharply on the floor. The dollar produced magic results; it sounded sweeter than honeyed Spanish words. The door of the room opened and before us stood the old inn-keeper who, it seemed, had retired to the subterranean room to protect himself from the heat of the day. He said he regretted very much that he could give us neither food or lodgings as his house was very badly off and everything had become so expensive 'since so many strangers roamed about the country.' Then he paced restlessly back and forth in the room as if he had eaten pepper or ... but after he heard again the clang of a dollar he turned about so quickly that he stumbled and fell through the trap-door into the cellar. '*Santa Maria purissima! Dios de mi alma!*' (Holy blessed Maria; God of my soul!) was his first outburst but then he let loose a torrent of invective while he attempted to set to rights the many pots and baskets filled with provisions which he had upset by his fall. This was undoubtedly his supply storeroom which he would probably not have shown to strange guests without a great deal of money. Quite amused we left the pitiful *Mesón* and with no alternative camped out of doors."[26]

From this humorous sketch of the *mesón* and its keeper it would appear that business was none too good, but as has been said, the Breens eventually made an excellent thing out of the hotel. It was probably about this time that the place began to be called the United States Hotel, and while it no doubt saw stirring times and was patronized by some of the famous characters of those days, Browne's and Meyer's accounts are the only known sources of information about this pioneer inn. All that is ascertainable beyond this is that by October of 1860 the place was no longer a public house, although Patrick Breen continued to live there until his death, which occurred on December 21st of 1868.[27]

San Francisco de Asis was founded by Father Francisco Palou on June 29, 1776, and was another of the Franciscan missions secularized in 1834 by orders of the Mexican government. With the exception of the church, an adjacent building on the north that was occupied by the curate, two garden orchards and the cemetery, the balance of the church property was in the following year distributed among the Indian neophytes, and thereafter called "Pueblo de Dolores."[28] As happened at the other missions that became Indian *pueblos*, the neophytes were at a loss to know what to do with their little plots of land and *adobe* houses, and on the pretext that they had abandoned their property Governor Pio Pico on October 28, 1845, ordered their holdings to be sold.[29] No one seems to have made a bid for any part of the *pueblo* proper,[30] and this was indiscriminately squatted on by both Mexicans and Americans down to March 3, 1858, when the remnants of the mission lands were returned to the Church by the President of the United States.[31]

By the early part of 1846 Manuel Castro, the government's *mayordomo*, was living in one of the mission buildings, where he sold brandy,[32] and his grog shop was the forerunner of the so-called inn that shortly thereafter made its appearance. After Bob Ridley sold out his interest in the Portsmouth House to John Henry Brown he settled for a while at Dolores (as the Mission is familiarly called), and there, just north of the *padres'* dwelling and at about the northwest corner of what are today Dolores and Sixteenth streets, he opened a tavern.

Mansion House, at Mission Dolores

Wood Hotel and Store

Pacific House Stage Barn

This immediately became famous for a drink that until then seems to have been unknown in California, and by 1854:

"The center of attraction (at the mission) was the Mansion House where Bob Ridley and C. V. Stuart dispensed milk punches to crowds of cavaliers, to whom the frequent Mexican attire gave a picturesque coloring."[33]

The only additional glimpses caught of this place are in 1854, when the Mansion House was being run by Captain L. T. Wilson, and in 1867, when M. O'Brien was its proprietor, and thereafter it disappears.[34] There was another drinking place called the Milk Punch House that was owned by John Williams in 1854, but this was on Mission Road, and was a different establishment.

By the latter part of '49 Bob Ridley and John Landers had opened an inn called the Cabeza del Toro, or the Bull's Head, on Dolores Street just south of the Mission cemetery, but with so little success that in the same year William Redmond Ryan could procure neither food nor lodging there.[35] The career of this place was short lived, and on May 28, 1850, the proprietors were sold out by the Sheriff of San Francisco,[36] and in so far as is known this closes the annals of California's old mission stopping places.

Chapter 12. Santa Clara's Fremont House

 I N SO FAR as it has been possible to draw together the frayed threads of its historical fabric, this is the story of what seems to have been the first of California's typical country stopping places. The tale goes back to the spring or summer of '48, when a pioneer American settler built his cabin beside one of the primitive tracks that passed for roads, and a few years later the place had grown into one of the earliest of the innumerable wayside inns, that were strung like beads along the highways and byways throughout the length and breadth of the State.

In Spanish and Mexican days the *Camino Real*, running northward from the mission of Santa Clara, skirted the sloughs and backwaters of the southwestern end of San Francisco Bay by two routes, one of these running directly across the low flat lands and the other winding over higher ground, along the eastern base of the coast range of hills. The lower road was used during the long dry season, when the flats were baked hard by the summer sun, but when the rains set in the lowlands between the Cuperlines and San Antonio *arroyos* were covered by a continuous sheet of water, and such travelers as were forced to be abroad followed the upper road.[1] For several years after the Americans began to settle in the Santa Clara valley the situation remained unchanged except for the increasing number of travelers over these old Spanish roads, and it was due to this combination of circumstances that the earliest known of California's wayside inns had its beginning at this point.

Some time before December of 1847, George W. Harlan (a nephew of the George Harlan who less than a year earlier had established himself and his family at the "abandoned" mission of San José) built a little clapboard redwood house on the east side of the lower *Camino Real*, about ten miles northwest of Santa Clara and a quarter of a mile south of the present Bayshore Boulevard.[2] George Harlan and his wife Sarah (who was one of the young ladies who presided over her uncle's stopping place at the mission of San José) were the second American settlers in that section, having been preceded a few months earlier by John W. Whisman, who established himself half a mile to the northwest on the Posolomi Grant, made in 1844 to Lope Yñigo, a Santa Clara Indian, and in the extreme southwestern corner of what is today the United States Army's Moffett Field.[3]

In those early days, before stage lines and stage stations were thought of, it was customary for settlers along the roads to put up travelers overtaken by nightfall, and as Harlan's place was conveniently located on the *Camino Real* he and his wife followed the established custom. While such accommodations were paid for, their house does not seem to have been a regular public stopping place down to as late as March of 1848,[4] but shortly thereafter the rapidly increasing number of wayfarers (and perhaps Mrs. Harlan's earlier experience at inn keeping) induced Harlan to turn his home into a wayside inn that was christened the Frémont House. The place had barely been opened when Harlan succumbed to the gold fever and followed his cousin, Jacob W. Harlan, to the Coloma diggings, where he remained at least as late as the end of October.[5]

Shortly thereafter Jacob Harlan and his family left the mines for San Francisco, and whether George accompanied them or remained near Coloma is not clear.[6] However this may have been, Jacob spent the winter at his cousin's hotel, and judging from the fact that he devoted most of his time to hunting to keep the table supplied with wild game (that ranged from cotton tails to mountain lion), the place must have entertained numerous guests. While it cannot be stated positively that mountain lion steaks were served at the Frémont House, the fact that packs of timber wolves at times raided the hotel's out-buildings and carried off pigs makes this a distinct possibility, especially in those rugged times.[7]

During George Harlan's absence at Coloma the newly established inn was either closed or it lost its original popularity, as by February of 1849 travelers instead of stopping there were putting up at John W. Whisman's place, half a mile to the northwest.[8] By the time that Harlan returned Whisman appears to have taken most of his trade away, and by the end of March of '49 George and Jacob Harlan and their families departed for the southern mines. A month later they were established at the site of Columbia, and in a few months more had accumulated some fifteen thousand dollars by mining and trading.[9] With whatever competition was left thus eliminated, Whisman was now getting all the business, and in the summer of '49 he began advertising his place as follows:

"WILDGROVE INN—ON THE SAN JOSE LOWER ROAD.—The traveling public are respectfully informed that a House of Entertainment has been opened under the above name, on the Monterey route, via San Jose, for the reception of persons frequenting this important thoroughfare. The table will be well supplied, the Bar amply furnished with choice Wines and Liquors; while the convenience and beauty of the locality—its excellent water and abundant pastur-age, render it a desirable stopping place for those visiting the interior. The Inn is situated about forty miles from San Francisco, and twelve miles from the Pueblo de San Jose. J. W. Whisman, San Jose, July 2, 1849."[10]

While John Whisman was not responsible for the first of Califor-nia's wayside inns he was the originator of the first stagecoach service to be put in operation in that part of the State, and it is thanks to his enterprise that stage lines and stage stations began to make their ap-pearance at that time. In the fall of 1849 he initiated an irregular service between San Francisco and San José with an old French omnibus, drawn by mules and mustangs, his first drivers being Tom Calloway, Dawson Calvin and Henry C. Ward. It is difficult to say whether Whisman's inn inspired the stage service or his stage line inspired the inn, but in any event, his coaches were well patronized (even at the fare of two ounces of gold dust per passenger), and in the summer of 1850 he sold out to Warren F. Hall, William Hall and Jared B. Crandall, all of whom had until the discovery of gold in California been drivers on the Mexican mail line between Vera Cruz and Mexico City.[11]

By the time that George Harlan returned from Columbia the inn business had evidently outgrown the capacity of the Wildgrove, but as he no longer needed the Frémont House as a means of livelihood he sold out in November of '49 to James Lynn (or perhaps it was James S. Linn), who with his son-in-law, Washington Moody, took over the operation of the place.[12] In the spring of 1850 Ackerly and Morrison (also from Mexico) put on an opposition stage line, and with this a new era of prosperity dawned that was only temporarily dampened by the fact that the winter rains of '50 and '51 were so heavy that the roads became impassable for vehicular traffic, and all stages were withdrawn for four months.[13] It was during this time that the Frémont House was the scene of one of those mysterious dispensations of divine providence that cause men to bow their heads and humbly repeat the majestically simple credo, "Thy will be done."

Cholera was raging in San Francisco, and after a trip to the metropolis Jacob Harlan and Dr. John Townsend were making the best of their way on horseback over the flooded roads to San José. Upon leaving San Mateo Harlan began to vomit and suffer severe cramps, and Dr. Townsend was forced to tell him that he had contracted the dreaded Asiatic disease. By the time the Frémont House was reached Harlan was so ill that he was unable to continue in the saddle, and as the doctor could not stop he left some medicine with the landlady and gave her instructions as to what little could be done for the sick man, but those were forthright days, and as he evidently considered Harlan's case all but hopeless he bluntly told him that he might have one chance in a hundred of seeing another sunrise, gave him a last encouraging handshake and rode on.

Jacob Harlan lay awake all that night, suffering and praying as he had never prayed before, and about four o'clock in the morning he felt that his prayers had been answered and that the crisis was past. Just before daybreak he arose and went to the door of his room to anxiously watch the brightening eastern sky. With the first rays of the sunrise that the doctor had told him he might never see he knew that he was cured, and after breakfasting continued his journey with a heart full of thankfulness for his all but miraculous recovery. The day was either December 31, 1850, or the 1st of January of 1851, and on riding into San José the first man Harlan met told him that both Dr. Townsend and his wife had died of cholera only an hour earlier.[14]

As soon as the roads were dry enough stage service was resumed, and it was then that Palmer, Cook & Co. either rebuilt the original Frémont House or put up a new building on the same site, when Cyrus G. Sanders managed the place until the end of 1851. The township of Frémont was created shortly after August of the same year, and the fact that the Frémont House was so well known was doubtless responsible for the naming of the new subdivision of the county. Sanders was the township's first Justice of the Peace until December, when he was appointed Associate Justice of the Court of Sessions and moved to San José.[15]

By September of 1852 Campbell and Gillis had established another line of stages and built their own stage station on the upper *Camino Real*, where this was joined by the country road that led from the southern end of the growing settlement of Mountain View to the boat landing at Alviso.[16] Traffic was beginning to be diverted from the lower road and the Frémont House, but worse was to follow. The country was fast being settled and farms, orchards and pastures were reclaiming the one-time rain flooded flats. The land was becoming too valuable to be criss-crossed by meandering old fair-weather roads, and the county highway that replaced the lower *caminos* of Spanish days were eventually located along the trace of the upper *Camino Real*.

The Frémont House was still holding its own on March 24th of 1853, when a strip of land along the southern edge of Mariano Castro's Rancho Pastoria de las Borregas (at the northern end of which the inn stood) was surveyed for Peter Davidson, of San José, as the marriage portion of his wife, who was one of Castro's daughters.[17] The first school house was built in Mountain View in 1858, and as two of the pupils were children from the Frémont House the place must have survived down to that time.[18] But its days were numbered, and two years later the only hotel reported in the township was Campbell and Gillis' old stage station, that since it was opened had been kept by W. A. Elliot, and that by 1863 was being run by his widow and her sister as the Mountain View Hotel.[19] The old place may have continued to enjoy a vicarious sort of existence during the construction days of the San Francisco and San José railroad, as the tracks were laid only about three-quarters of a mile south of its front door. On January 16, 1864, however, when the whistle of the first train announced the inauguration of regular railway service its portals must have been closed upon its last departing guest.[20]

This is the end of the story of California's first wayside inn, and the only subsequent references that have been found to the place are that in 1881 the property was owned by John Sullivan, and Dan Murphey lived until 1889 on the site of the old Frémont House.[21]

Chapter 13. Sonoma's Blue Wing Hotel

ACROSS THE STREET from Sonoma's restored mission stands a well preserved two-story *adobe* building that, were one given to believing in signs, should have been given the place of honor in the story of California's pioneer inns. This is the old Blue Wing Hotel, and a large bronze plaque that adorns the front of the house informs the trusting pilgrim that General Vallejo built the place about 1840, for the accommodation of emigrants and other travelers, who presumably were Americans. This statement is guaranteed to get immediate and respectful attention from the aforesaid pilgrim, as were it true the Blue Wing would be the hoary dean of the state's innumerable hostelries.[1]

From the aesthetic point of view it is really too bad that this scattergun claim is untrue, but it is an awkward fact that it is in no wise supported by history. But if the Blue Wing's inception had nothing whatever to do with the 1840 vintage of immigrants, of American or any other persuasion, the place is unique among the earliest buildings in the state for an equally interesting historical reason. It is the sole survivor of the true pioneer inns of California, and on this account, if for no other, it is worthy of much more than passing notice in the chronicle of those long forgotten hostelries. Furthermore, the story of the house that eventually became the Blue Wing goes back almost two decades earlier than the foregoing lapse from historical accuracy claims, as it began about July 4, 1823, when Padre José Altamira founded the mission of San Francisco Solano at "New San Francisco" in an unsuccessful attempt to force the transfer of the mission and settlement of San Francisco de Asis, or Dolores, to a new and more healthful location.[2]

Ten years later the presence of the Russians at Fort Ross and Bodega Bay became a source of acute worry to the Mexican government, and on April 11, 1833, Governor José Figuéroa ordered Mariano Guadalupe Vallejo, a young sub-lieutenant commanding the presidial com-

137

pany of San Francisco, to proceed into the zone of Russian influence and select a cite for a new *presidio*, where he was to offer free land to induce colonists to settle the country. Lieutenant Vallejo attempted to carry out his orders at several places between the missions of San Rafael Arcángel and San Francisco Solano, but the *padres* of these establishments in each case outmaneuvered what they looked upon as an encroachment on their domains, and Vallejo was forced to withdraw. For the time being a stalemate existed between the Franciscan fathers and the Mexican government, but on August 9, 1834, the Governor promulagted the law requiring the secularization of the missions, and in October ordered Vallejo to take over the temporal affairs of San Solano (as the mission was familiarly called), as administrator for the Republic of Mexico.

A month earlier a party largely made up of the riff-raff and gutter sweepings of the City of Mexico, and known as the "Metropolitan Company," had arrived at San Diego under the leadership of José María Híjar and José María Padrés. These worthies were politicians from the capital who had cooked up a neat scheme whereby they, with their so-called colonists, planned to capitalize on the forthcoming decree of secularization by possessing themselves of the best of the mission lands of California. It is almost needless to say that the California politicians had already laid their own plans for the disposition of these selfsame lands, and no sooner did the Híjar-Padrés scheme become apparent than there was a rare ruffling of political feathers to thwart the designs of the "foreigners." So effective, indeed, was this reaction that before the would-be colonists quite knew what was happening to them they found themselves forcibly settled at the ex-mission of San Solano, where Lieutenant Vallejo had the business of secularization well in hand and was in no mood to brook interference with what promised to be the cutting of an especially juicy melon. Messrs. Híjar and Padrés did not waste any time ruffling *their* feathers, but forthwith began promoting a revolution that was designed to overthrow General Figuéroa and seize the government of California, as in those days this was the recognized method of adjusting differences of Mexican political opinions. They were well supplied with arms and ammunition, and the proposed coup might well have succeeded had it not been for the treachery of one of the leaders' accomplices.

Antonio Ortega was one of the more disreputable of Híjar and Padrés' importations, and if the word of men who knew him is to be credited, it would have been difficult to have found a greater rascal in all of the two Californias. But despite this, he was one of those taken into the confidence of the plotters, and fully informed as to their plans. No sooner was Ortega in possession of this information than he hastened to disclose the plot to Vallejo, with the result that on March 16, 1835, Híjar and Padrés were arrested and deported back to Mexico. This piece of treachery was the beginning of Ortega's career of sculduggery in California and, incidentally of his connection with the beginning of the story of the Blue Wing Hotel. The betrayal of his erstwhile leaders was promptly rewarded by his being made a sergeant in Vallejo's company, and from that day onward Ortega was a pliant and unscrupulous tool in the hands of his benefactor and protector.[3]

With the transfer of authority from the Church to the State, and the induction of the involuntary colonists, it became necessary to set up a municipal organization to administer civil affairs and to provide closer military control of what until then had been a frontier mission and detached army post. To this end Vallejo (who by that time was a full lieutenant) was appointed Military Commandant and Director of Colonization of the Northern Frontier, and ordered to transfer his company to the ex-mission, where he was instructed to found a town. About the middle of 1835 he set about complying with these orders, and with the assistance of Captain William A. Richardson (who a year later was to found the village of Yerba Buena) he laid out the new settlement about what is today the city's *plaza*, and by late summer of the same year the place was established under the Indian name of Sonoma, or the Valley of the Moon. With this the stage was set for the practical prosecution of the business of secularization, and as by then Vallejo was well assured that Ortega could be relied upon to see that this was conducted in a profitable fashion, he named his henchman *mayordomo*, or foreman, to officiate at the melon cutting. And, not so incidentally, to see to it that Vallejo's own interests were not neglected.[4]

For some time thereafter Commandant Vallejo's time was taken up by the conduct of a number of punitive expeditions against the hostile

Indians to the north of Sonoma, and while his appointment of Ortega, who was assisted by Vallejo's younger brother Salvador, may in some measure have been dictated by military necessity, the choice of deputies was an unfortunate one in so far as the interests of both Church and State were concerned. Apart from his already proved infidelity, Ortega was uneducated, coarse and licentious, while Salvador Vallejo was an inexperienced youth with an overpowering lust for authority. The characters of these men were such that only trouble could have been expected, and even before the church property had been turned over to the government they had quarreled with and grossly insulted elderly Padre José Lorenzano de la Concepción Quijas, the last Franciscan custodian of the mission. Whatever Padre Quijas' shortcomings may have been, he was still much that Ortega and Salvador Vallejo were not, and the inevitable conflict of personalities had flared into an acrimonious issue that was made of the amount of space occupied by the father as living quarters. That this was purely an excuse to discredit Padre Quijas is proved by the fact that most of the mission's rooms were at the time unoccupied and closed, and as far as Ortega's own requirements went, he was in all probability occupying quarters that were responsible for the story of the Blue Wing now beginning to take definite shape.[5]

At the time San Solano was taken over by the Mexican government the activities of the establishment required the supervision of a mission *mayordomo*, and this official's residence must of necessity have been located where he could at all times keep a watchful eye on the somewhat more than less irresponsible Indian neophytes. The site of San Solano's *rancheria*, where the Indians dwelt, disappeared long ago, but the ground plans of other and contemporary Franciscan missions give a definite clue as to where it was located. There is little doubt but what it occupied the area that is today bounded by Spain, Berreyessa, United States and East First streets, the north side of this quadrangle having been parallel to the front of the mission buildings, and just across the road from Napa, that is now Spain Street. Again based on the evidence furnished by other missions, the *mayordomo's* house can be expected to have stood at about the center of the north side of the *rancheria*, facing the *padres'* dwelling, and an architectural survey of Sonoma's early buildings tends to prove that this is exactly where the place was located. Furthermore, it is probable that the central part of the ground floor of the Blue Wing Hotel is what is left of this selfsame building.[6]

There is no definite evidence to prove that when Antonio Ortega was appointed government foreman to supervise the secularization of San Solano he moved into the house formerly occupied by the Franciscans' *mayordomo* but just a year later he certainly was in possession of the premises. When the town of Sonoma was laid out in blocks of four 100 x 100 *vara* lots the lot forming the northwest quarter of the block just described was designated as Lot No. 35, and on July 11, 1836, Vallejo made a memorandum of the fact that Ortega was on that date granted a *solar*, or parcel of ground, in this lot. The grant included the site of the premises under discussion, and as such *pueblo* grants were almost always based on previous occupancy, it follows that Ortega had in all probability been living there prior to receiving title to the property.[7]

Emboldened by the fact that Vallejo had done nothing about his persecution of Padre Quijas, Ortega proceeded to give himself up to unbridled licentiousness. By July of 1835 he brazenly boasted that he had "made the rounds of every woman in San Solano, and expected not to miss a single one," and he was now publicly accused of having debauched the ex-missions' Indian neophytes by teaching them all the assorted vices which he himself possessed. There is litte question but what this catalogue included hard drinking, and it is not unreasonable to suppose that Ortega profited on this score by turning his house into Sonoma's first *pulperia*, or a low sort of saloon. Not to describe the place by a harder name. That this is more than supposition is borne out by the fact that in August of 1848 he was arrested for selling liquor to the Indians of the town, and his acquittal of the charge is suspected to have been due to the influence of his protector, Mariano Guadalupe Vallejo, who at the time was United States District Indian Agent.[8]

Ortega's behavior now became so openly scandalous that Padre Quijas gave up the struggle to protect those that were left of his Indian flock and withdrew to San Rafael, from where he announced his refusal to return to Sonoma unless the man was removed from his post as *mayordomo*. Despite the fact that the father's accusations, and those of others, were supported by the testimony of numerous witnesses about the outrageous conduct of his protege, Vallejo still did nothing and Ortega was left unpunished.[9]

Before proceeding with the story of the Blue Wing it will be interesting to return briefly to the bronze tablet's claim that General Vallejo built the place about 1840, for the accommodation of emigrants and others, who it is to be presumed are supposed to have been Americans. By the spring of 1835 most of the Híjar-Padrés party, Sonoma's original "settlers," had abandoned the place, and down to 1840 only some twenty-five families had gone to live in and about the village. Of these the heads of no more than five families were foreigners by birth, and as some of these men were already naturalized Mexican citizens, and all of them had been living elsewhere in California before moving to Sonoma, none of them can by any stretch of the imagination be called "emigrants," either historically or grammatically.[10] As a matter of fact, it was not until November of 1841 that the first Americans can be said to have immigrated to Sonoma, when General Vallejo sent five of the newly arrived Bartleson party from San José to settle there.[11] As was said earlier, the tide of immigration did not set strongly into California until about 1843, and it was not until the latter half of 1846 that the newcomers began to make Sonoma their home. So few, indeed, were the American settlers before that time that a little grist mill in the village stood idle, because "there was not a Yankee about who could attend to it."[12] From the foregoing it is evident that there could not have been an immigrants' housing problem in Sonoma in 1840, for the simple reason that at the time there were no immigrants there to be housed. Furthermore, the construction details of the ground floor of the original part of the Blue Wing building strongly suggest that this part of the house was erected earlier than 1840.

Returning to Antonio Ortega, it is not known what he did to occupy his time after having completed the rounds of the more complaisant ladies of Sonoma, but whatever his activities were, early in 1837 he was caught with his fingers in San Solano's till. This time the scandal was an official one that could not be overlooked, and his services as the ex-mission's *mayordomo* were per force dispensed with.[13] If Ortega's *adobe* had not already been turned into some sort of a public house, this may well have happened immediately after July 14th of 1846, when Ezekiel Merritt and his crew of bemused liberators captured Sonoma and, with the raising of the Bear Flag, turned the village into the capital of the Republic of California.[14] The amazing thirst that seems to go hand-in-hand with any enterprise that is aimed at upsetting established public order must have made a public drinking place a military necessity to top priority, and it is perfectly safe to say that some far-sighted California patriot noted the deficiency and did his duty. Furthermore, from what is known of the local citizens of that day it is equally safe to say that there was no one thereabouts better qualified to have undertaken this than Antonio Ortega. In April of 1947, Company C, First Regiment of New York Volunteers, was ordered to garrison duty at Sonoma, and with all due respect to the military, it is a cast-iron historical fact that where there are soldiers there is bound to be a place thereabouts where hard liquor can be come by.[15]

As far as the Blue Wing's antecedents are concerned, we now find ourselves on historical ground, even though at first this is a bit shaky in spots.

James C. Cooper (or Couper, as the name was spelled originally) was the red-headed Scot mate of an English vessel that is said to have arrived on the coast of California in 1845. According to a family tradition, he and the ship's carpenter, an Englishman named Thomas Spriggs, thereupon jumped ship and established themselves in Yerba Buena, where they opened a saloon. Cooper was born in Janetstown, Caithness, Scotland, and the same tradition claims that he named the tavern the "Blue Wing," after the public house in his home village.[16] The place does not seem to have achieved either fame or fortune, and Cooper became disgusted with what he described as "a hopeless village." The spectacular success of the "Bears" in June of 1846 confirmed him in his belief that Yerba Buena had no future, and that Sonoma was destined to become the metropolis of the San Francisco bay region, and early in 1847 he moved to what had been the capital of the short-lived "Republic of California."[17]

There are two accounts of what happened immediately thereafter. According to one story, Cooper traded his Yerba Buena interests for a house in Sonoma where he established his second California venture, while the other version claims that he bought the place from John Cameron, the man who was later elected the town's first mayor.[18]

Neither of these stories can be confirmed, and what seems to have happened is that shortly after Cooper moved to Sonoma he and Jesse L. Beasley, a pioneer of 1843, went into partnership and opened a saloon, billiard room and store, that shortly thereafter was expanded into Sonoma's first hotel. This American-Scotch establishment evidently eclipsed whatever it was that Antonio Ortega had been doing in the line of a Mexican saloon in his old house, and as the continuity of the story now hinges on the relationship of these two places, before proceeding with the fortunes of the Blue Wing it will be necessary to back-track and sketch the history of the house in which Beasley and Cooper were established at this time.

Some time between July, 1835, when Lieutenant Vallejo laid out the town of Sonoma, and July, 1836, a small *adobe* house was built just across the Napa road from the mission church, on the southeast corner of what are today Spain and East First streets. As on the latter date the property was granted to Antonio Peña he was presumably the builder, and in any event, as Vallejo and his friends used the place as a billiard room it was thereafter known as the "*casa del billar*."[19] As was stated earlier, on the same date Antonio Ortega was granted the lot that is today partly occupied by the Blue Wing building, and that adjoined Peña's grant on the east. From this point onward for the following decade and a half the annals of the two properties are so confusing that it is sometimes difficult to distinguish which of them is referred to in the surviving records of those days.

On February 1, 1848, the firm of Beasley & Cooper opened an account book that contains a number of references to an earlier book, so it may safely be concluded that their business was started either in 1847 or, at latest, by February 1, 1848.[20] While the earlier entries in this book are exclusively liquor sales, it is certain that by the end of February Beasley and Cooper were operating a store in connection with their saloon,[21] and a month or two later their establishment had been expanded to include a hotel. Thus far there is no hint as to where this place was located, and heretofore it has been assumed that it was in the Blue Wing building. That this was not the case is proved by "California's Pioneer Philosopher," Charles Edward Pickett, who, writing of the spring of 1848, says:

"General Vallejo and myself had been playing billards one Sunday morning at the Beasley & Cooper Hotel at that little burg (Sonoma) situated opposite the old Mission buildings. On coming out we heard someone preaching in the church. It being an unusual occurrence, I asked the General what it meant, suggesting that we go in for curiosity. 'Diablo,' he responded, 'it is that little Indian rascal, Santillan, and I would sooner call the dogs and run him out of town.' I stepped to the door and looked in, when there was the little padre preaching away to one solitary listener—old Berreyessa—and he so drunk as to lean against the wall for support, it not being the custom then to have seats in these old churches."[22]

Philosopher Pickett does not refer to the house by name, it is true, but there can be no question but that he meant Peña's "casa del billar," as at the time this was the only building opposite the mission church. Ortega's house was standing about one hundred fifty feet southeast of the church, it is equally true, but for several additional reasons this could not have been where Pickett and Vallejo were playing billiards. First, because the distance from the entrance to this building would have been too great for Pickett to have heard preaching in the church when he and the General stepped into the street. Second, because there is no mention anywhere of a billiard table in the Blue Wing, and the obvious place for one would have been in the "casa del billar," that had been built for this purpose. Third, photographs of the latter building, taken in the late '60s or early '70s, show a double door at the north end of the old "casa del billar" that was evidently the entrance to the place, and just across the street from the church.[23] Fourth, and finally, as a firm, Beasley and Cooper never had anything to do with the building that later became the Blue Wing.

While on the subject, it may be interesting to know that the "little Indian rascal," of whom General Vallejo so strongly disapproved, was Padre José Prudencio Santillan, a Mexican Indian, and the same priest who two years later attempted to get possession of the Sonoma mission lands through a fraudulent claim. His congregation on that Sunday morning was his *tocayo*, or namesake, José de los Santos Berreyesa, who was the *padre's* star witness in the latter's attempted land-grab.[24] Berreyesa also had the questionable distinction of being one of the last debtors appearing on Beasley & Cooper's account book, when he seems to have wound up a ten days' drunk, that lasted from January 4th to 14th, 1849, by persuading his hosts to sell him on credit a thirty dollar coat, that he did not pay for until August 6, 1850.

From the foregoing it is now evident that Sonoma's first hostelry was the "Beasley & Cooper Hotel," that was located in Peña's old "casa del billar" on the southeast corner of Spain and East First streets, and this establishment was opened in 1847 or early in 1848. Hitherto this honor has, in default of other claimants, been awarded to the Blue Wing, but as will be seen presently, far from having been the town's first hotel this establishment was the third in order of seniority. As in the case of the Washington at Monterey, that for so long has been called "California's first hotel," it seems almost sacreligious to grub out an old tradition that has become so firmly rooted, but history and sentimentalism have nothing in common.

Beasley and Cooper's hotel and tavern did a thriving business that reached its peak in May of 1848, when news of the gold discovery at Sutter's mill reached Sonoma. A stampede to the diggings followed, with an immediate decline in trade,[25] and it must have been at this time that "the only hotel keeper in the town sold his kettles and pans, closed his house, and departed" for the mines.[26] This innkeeper turned gold miner must have been either Beasley or Cooper, or perhaps both of them, and it was not until August that the saloon business picked up with the return of lucky and gold laden miners,[27] while the hotel part of the establishment remained closed until the latter part of October.[28] This situation called for a redistribution of wealth, and it was plain to everyone that a deck of cards was the easiest and fastest way of accomplishing this. That gambling was this early one, if not the principal source of the hotel's income is to be gathered from an entry in its proprietors' account book, dated August 23, 1848, when one of their patrons was charged $50 for $30 worth of gold dust. It will be recalled that it was precisely at this time that John Henry Brown was selling currency to the gamblers in the City Hotel, at San Francisco, at the rate of six or eight dollars per ounce of dust, and the foregoing transaction suggests that Beasley and Cooper were doing exactly the same thing in Sonoma. As, for that matter, was everyone else in California.

How long Beasley and Cooper continued to operate Sonoma's first hotel is not quite clear, but as the last current debit entry in their account book is dated January 14, 1849, it seems safe to conclude from this (and what follows) that their partnership in the place was dissolved some time between this date and August of the same year. By this time Sonoma had become one of the recognized points of departure for the diggings, and with the rapidly increasing two-way traffic the little single-story saloon, billiard room and hotel (that all together could not have contained much more than about 30 x 100 feet of floor space) [29] must have been far too small to meet the requirements of the day. That, as has been seen, now called for additional room to accommodate gambling tables.

About the middle of 1847 Cooper had married Sarah Bigelow Flint, and with this he appears to have rented Ortega's house. Whatever may have been its former social status, the place now entered upon a season of eminent respectability, and there the Cooper's two sons were born, Thomas Spriggs Cooper, on January 6, 1848, and John Rose Cooper, on September 15, 1849.[30] At the time the house consisted of only the ground floor of the central portion of the present building, with the original fireplace in the east wall, and it may be that the first or eastern extension to the house was built when the Coopers moved in, as a new fireplace was built in the east wall of the addition and this part of the house was thereafter used as a dining room and kitchen.[31]

Thomas Spriggs, Cooper's partner in the Yerba Buena saloon was already in Sonoma, and about the middle of 1849 the two men decided to open a new hotel in the premises the Coopers were occupying, and to this end renewed their earlier partnership under the firm name of Cooper & Spriggs. On August 15, 1849, Antonio Ortega sold them for the sum of one dollar the lot granted him in 1836, and while the deed does not mention a house there is no question but what the place just described stood on the property at the time of its transfer.[32] When the determination was reached to open a new hotel Cooper and Spriggs evidently required larger quarters than those available in the old "casa del billar," that, as has been said, could not have contained much more than 3,000 square feet of floor space. At the time they purchased Ortega's house this measured about 35 x 65 feet over-all, and therefore represented less floor space than Beasley and Cooper had been operating in, and it is probable therefore, that the western or second addition was made to the building, and the second story added at that time.

This again brings us back to the bronze plaque's statement that the Blue Wing was built by General Vallejo about 1840. Local tradition, aided and abetted by this brazen claim, insists that the General built the place and later turned his interest over to Cooper and Spriggs, and it is possible that this much of the story is true.[33] Antonio Ortega, the General's erstwhile henchman, sold out for one dollar, but as Vallejo was a witness to the deed of sale it is also possible that a certain amount of persuasion was brought to bear to induce him to be so accommodating. If the foregoing was the case, the General financed the remodeling and not the building of the house that a couple of years later became the Blue Wing Hotel, and this was in the fall of 1849. The story is intriguing, but there is not one scrap of evidence in General Vallejo's papers to show that he was ever in any way connected with the place.

As has been said, Cooper and Spriggs bought Ortega's house on August 15th of 1849, but in view of the fact that the Cooper's second son was born there just a month later, it seems doubtful if the new hotel would have been inaugurated while this happy event was in the immediate offing. By October, however, the place was a going concern, and from the fact that the saloon was at first located in the old central part of the building, from where it was moved to the new western addition, it appears that the remodeling work had not been completed at the time of the opening. The dining room and kitchen were in the addition at the east end of the house, that may have been made when the Coopers moved in two years earlier, and the central part of the ground floor, vacated by the saloon, was turned into a gambling room. This was strategically located between the bar and the dining room, so that the gamblers would not have to waste valuable time in going too far afield to drink and eat. This department of the hotel was equipped with square deal tables, about the size of modern card tables, and two settees stood against the walls for the accommodation of onlookers (if there were any), or for the refreshment of such of the gambling fraternity as might have been temporarily overcome by their labors. The saloon seems also to have been the hotel's office, and in addition to the customary rough and ready drinking paraphernalia of those days it contained a pair of gold scales and a small iron strong box, that is still to be seen in the State Museum, just across the street. The bedrooms were on the second floor, but all that is known of them is that they were furnished with poster beds made of maple, or some other light colored wood. When completed the building no doubt looked much the same as it does today. That is to say, a low two-story house about ninety-five feet in length by thirty-five in width, with thick *adobe* walls pierced by doors and windows, that on the ground floor opened directly onto the street, and on the second floor onto narrow wooden verandas running the full length of the house, front and back.[34] The original roof over the second story was doubtless of shakes or shingles, and while there is no known record of the place having boasted a signboard, there is no question about its having been called the "Sonoma House."[35]

It must have been about the time the Sonoma House was opened that the price of drinks in Sonoma went up from twelve and one-half cents (a *real*, or a "bit") to "Twenty-five cents the horn,"[36] and with this Ortega's little one-bit *pulperia* became a part of those golden bonanza days, with the usual pinch of dust paying for the usual drink at the bar. At the height of the gold excitement the returning miners were so free with both pinches and drinks that the womenfolk of the establishment are said to have swept up enough gold during their daily cleaning of the place to keep them in pin-money. Two or three years after the Sonoma House was opened, the Coopers' sons, Thomas and John, reached the age when, in common with other little boys of that time, they wore aprons, and the prodigal miners used to delight in having them hold these up to catch nuggets and coins tossed to them. A form of indoor sport at which both youngsters doubtless grew to be exceedingly proficient.[37]

Apart from their other profits, Cooper and Spriggs now did even better than John Henry Brown in trading for gold, as they would only accept dust and nuggets at from four to five dollars an ounce. Minted money was in the same demand in Sonoma for gambling as it was in San Francisco, and Mexican *pesos*, smuggled into California from Mazatlán and San Blas, were the smallest coins in circulation. To remedy this, as well as to increase the receipts of their gambling room, the hotel's proprietors hired a blacksmith named Guy Freeman Fling, whose shop was just across the street in one of the old mission buildings, to cut *pesos* into halves and quarters, and this supplied the town with its first fractional currency.[38]

During Sonoma's garrison days, and notably after the summer of 1849, when General Persifer F. Smith, military governor of California, moved his headquarters there from San Francisco, a number of young army officers who later won world-wide fame during the Civil War were either stationed at or on temporary duty in the town. At one time or another, the Sonoma House (under the purely literary alias of the Blue Wing) is said to have entertained Lieutenant-Colonel Joseph ("Fighting Joe") Hooker, Major Philip Kearney, Captains Ulysses S. Grant, William T. Sherman, John C. Frémont, Nathaniel Lyon, Charles P. Stone and Alfred Gibbs, and Lieutenants George Stoneman and George H. Derby, the latter having been the "Squibob" of literary fame of those days. The annals of Sonoma are discreetly silent respecting the following, but it does not require much imagination to credit the Sonoma House with having served these and other officers with many a horn of the "fighting whiskey" that later on President Lincoln wished all his generals would acquire a taste for, if it would inspire them to win such victories as those of General Grant.

While all the stories about Cooper and Spriggs' hotel refer to the place as the "Blue Wing," as far as the legal records are concerned this name does not appear until July 16, 1853.[39] In all probability, however, the name, as applied to Sonoma's hotel, antedates this by a couple of years, as it was about the middle of 1851 that there is reason to believe that it replaced the name "Sonoma House."

Thomas Spriggs, for whom the Cooper's first son was named, died in the Sonoma House on May 30, 1851,[40] and the loss of his oldest friend and partner may well have led Cooper to change the name of the hotel at that time. While as the family tradition claims, he may have renamed the place after his and Spriggs saloon in Yerba Buena, that is said to have been called after the old tavern in Cooper's birthplace, the following seems a more likely explanation. At the time of Sprigg's death, San Francisco's most popular saloon was the "Blue Wing," at 138 Montgomery Street, where its proprietor, James T. Jones, dispensed no less than one hundred different varieties of distilled, fermented and malt liquors to a clientele that ran down the social scale from the Governor of California and Judges of the Supreme and Superior courts, to the strap-hangers on the outer fringes of political circles.[41] Cooper always had an eye to business, and it is not impossible that he decided to capitalize on the popularity of the San Francisco gathering place of the politicos and other influential men of the day by adopting the name of their resort. However this may have been, the Blue Wing of Sonoma now began to be referred to as the most pretentious hotel north of San Francisco, and entered upon the heyday of its career.

Sonoma was the county seat as well as the headquarters of the military command of California, but politicians and army officers were not the only celebrities the Blue Wing knew at that time. If local tradition can be credited, California's most widely publicised bandit, Joaquin Murieta (whose real name was Carrillo[42]), and his equally bloodthirsty lieutenant Manuel García, better known as "Three Fingered Jack," were wont to frequent the hotel, in between murders and robberies. On such occasions these gentry are said to have mingled freely with the townfolk, and under the safeguard of their deadly reputations to have drunk and gambled without fear of being denounced to the authorities. At any rate, without fear on the part of anyone but those who were unfortunate enough to recognize the outlaws, and these citizens prudently kept the knowledge to themselves. The usual version of this story is that while engaged in these social relaxations Murieta and García lived in a cave somewhere near Sonoma, but unfortunately for the tale, habitable caves are at a premium thereabouts. A San Francisco newspaper went the story one better in describing the Blue Wing, by stating that "the notorious Joaquin Murietta (sic) had a secret hideout in the hotel." The reader can believe this or not, as suits his fancy, but it is only fair to point out out that the architecture of the place is such that it would be difficult to conceal a cat anywhere about the premises. A mature cat, at any rate. It is a fascinating yarn, admittedly, but even more open to suspicion than the one set forth on the bronze plaque. Of happier memory, and more historical reliability, the famous actress Lotta Crabtree, then a child of six years, and her mother are said to have stopped at the Blue Wing Hotel in 1853, when the little girl was being taken to Petaluma to make her stage debut.[43]

These stories, and many others of well known characters who were guests at the Blue Wing, have completely overshadowed Antonio Ortega, the man who was so largely responsible for the early history of the inn. Perhaps the rapidly increasing female population of Sonoma led California's version of Don Juan Tenorio to revise his original program, or he may prudently have concluded that the quick tempers and quicker trigger-fingers of the *Americanos* were not to be trifled with. If neither of these considerations induced him to change his way of life, then it must have been that he felt it high time to be thinking of his soul's welfare—and in the meantime of providing himself with a regular and adequate supply of beans and beef. Whatever the true reason for his reform, Sr. Ortega's first step in the matter was to marry Juan Miranda's daughter, Francisca. This young lady was no doubt an expert at cooking beans and beef, but over and above this there was a weightier consideration. In 1838 Francisca's father had settled a couple of miles outside the present city of Petaluma, and on October 8, 1844, Governor Micheltorena ordered that he be issued title to the three square leagues of land that formed the Rancho Arroyo de San Antonio. The grant was to include all the country between Petaluma and San Antonio creeks, lying south of Captain Juan Nepomuceno Padilla's ranch Roblar de la Miseria, that, it will be remembered, at one time formed part of the land scheme in which Captain Jean Jacques Vioget was interested.[44] It was at this time that Micheltorena was ousted from office by Juan Bautista Alvarado, and in the ensuing scramble for political booty Juan Miranda's title was forgotten, an oversight that Antonio Ortega was not slow in turning to his advantage.

On the strength of having visited his father-in-law at various times (when he doubtless lived on the latter's beef and beans), Ortega persuaded the new governor that *he* was the real settler of the land in question, and in the end succeeded in wangling a grant to the *rancho* that, to make assurance doubly sure, was given a fictitious date of August 10, 1840. General Vallejo's protégé then hurriedly disposed of his spurious title to Charles White, of San José, and while this has nothing to do with the story of the Blue Wing, it is comforting to know that after a long series of claims and counter claims the alleged grant was disallowed by the Supreme Court of the United States in 1863.[45] The returns from this last piece of rascality no doubt took care of Ortega's more pressing corporal needs, and he then turned his attention to the matter of the hereafter. To this end, and after having disposed of his Sonoma property to Cooper and Spriggs, by October of 1849 he settled down in Antonio Peña's old "casa del billar," where Lilburn W. Boggs ran the post-office. There he devoted himself to furbishing his soul's prospects by becoming the official bell-ringer of the little Catholic chapel just across the street, all that was left of the mission of San Francisco Solano, that but a few years earlier he had helped to rob. By way of additional insurance, Ortega from time to time visited the *padres* at some of the northern missions, and while it is reasonable to assume that on these occasions he helped consume the good father's scanty store of beef and beans, it is more than reasonable to believe that Padre Quijas was *not* one of these who contributed to his entertainment. Antonio Ortega died in San Francisco about 1868, and his departure from this life does not seem to have been unduly lamented by anyone, unless it was his creditors.[46]

At about the time of Sprigg's death Cooper moved his family to a ranch located just west of Sonoma Creek, that he had bought from General Vallejo and where he was building what was for the time and place a pretentious home, that is still known as the "Cooper house." For the next five years Cooper divided his time between the ranch and the hotel, and in one way or another was by then reckoned the richest man in Sonoma, after General Vallejo.[47] It seems that it was at this time that gambling in the Blue Wing was at its height, and the following anecdote, as told by his granddaughter, may give a clue to how some of Cooper's wealth was acquired. "One day a lady whose husband had been playing cards with Mr. Cooper the night before, stopped to tell him he would be better off helping his wife to raise the children than wasting his time playing cards. My grandfather drew himself up and said: 'Madam, I married a woman who has sense enough to be able to manage her family: it is too bad your husband was not so fortunate'."[48] Apart from the obvious question as to whether or not Cooper had wasted his time at this particular game, the anecdote, together with the fact that he was a red-headed Scot, lends color to his having been described as strong-minded, overbearing, and even quarrelsome.[49] Furthermore, this sketch tends to throw some light on the mysterious circumstances surrounding Cooper's violent end.

Martin E. Cooke, who in 1850-51 had been State Senator from the Eleventh Senatorial District, was a lawyer who was practicing in Sonoma, and after Spriggs' death he became Cooper's attorney and so close and trusted a friend that all of the latter's legal affairs were left in his hands to be taken care of. What the two men's business relations were apart from this is not clear, but on May 26, 1856, Cooper sold him the Blue Wing property, acting as executor of Spriggs' estate.[50] It is certain, however, that he and Cooke had an office in the hotel, but apart from one incident in which this place figures, the sale of the property seems to have been Cooper's last connection with the Blue Wing. Unless gambling was still being carried on there, which is far from improbable.

When the Coopers moved from the Blue Wing to the ranch their two boys went to a nearby school, where D. M. Graham was the teacher. Graham was a quiet and retiring man, but he was also a strict disciplinarian, and one day the Cooper youngsters did something that caused him to give them a severe whipping. Their father was furious when he heard of this, and threatened to thrash Graham if he ever again dared to whip the boys. The following day, September 5, 1856, the two men met at the school on Syd Tate's ranch, and the argument was resumed. Graham was of exceptionally small stature, whereas Cooper was a large and powerful man, and the general opinion seems to have been that the latter either struck the teacher or attempted to do so, when Graham drew a knife and stabbed him so severely that he died a few minutes later from the effects of the wound. Word of Cooper having been stabbed was brought by Mrs. Tate, who a few minutes later ran into the Cooper home crying hysterically "I knew it was to be today!" This, together with the fact that Cooper was a constant gambler at the Blue Wing and that his success was thought to have made him a number of bitterly resentful enemies, in the light of what is said to have followed led Mrs. Cooper and the rest of the family to conclude that her husband's killing had been premeditated.[51]

The following events are said to have transpired shortly after Cooper's death, and are derived from what his widow told her children and grandchildren in later years. While the accuracy of some of her statements may be open to question, the nature of others is such that they appear to have been factual recitals of what actually occurred. Generally speaking, it is unsafe to place too much reliance on family traditions that have their origin in events of emotional or controversial nature, but as in this case Mrs. Cooper's stories may contain at least hints at hitherto unrecorded happenings of those days, they are, with the foregoing reservations, offered at their face value.

A few days before his death Cooper sold a lot of cattle for which he was paid $2,500 in gold, and this money was left in his and Cooke's office in the Blue Wing Hotel. Mrs. Cooper knew of the transaction, and shortly after her husband was killed she went to the hotel to collect the money, but it had disappeared and was never found. According to Mrs. Cooper's story, she subsequently heard that the day after her husband's funeral General Vallejo was seen leaving the Blue Wing and carrying two money bags, that he put in his buggy and drove off. It appears that Mrs. Cooper was not at all reticent about her suspicions, and a short time thereafter she was fired at while in the front yard of her home, the shot passing so close to her face that she heard the whistle of the ball.[52]

At the time of his death Cooper was said to have been worth $100,000 in cash and real estate, the latter being represented by some 3,000 acres of land, much of which he had purchased from Vallejo. The deeds to most of this property had been entrusted to Cooke for registration, but when an attempt was made to settle the estate no record could be found of the transfers of these titles, nor, according to Mrs. Cooper, could either General Vallejo or Cooke remember anything about the transactions. The matter was in the courts for years, and in the end all that Mrs. Cooper had left was the half-section on which her home stood. In the meantime General Vallejo appointed Cooke his attorney, and the two became such close friends that Cooper's one-time confident went to live at Lachryma Montis, the General's home on the northern outskirts of Sonoma, where he died and was buried in Vallejo's yard.[53]

Martin Cooke was especially active and vindictive in pressing a charge of murder against Graham, but when the first witness for the prosecution was cross-examined at the preliminary hearing the case collapsed, and Graham was cleared of the charge.[54] At the time of his death Cooper was Master of Sonoma's Masonic Temple Lodge No. 14, having succeeded his friend Cooke in that office, as well as a member of the local Independent Order of Odd Fellows' Lodge No. 28, and if Mrs. Cooper's statements are correct, it is to be noted that, apart from Cooke's activities, neither order appears to have done anything toward the prosecution of the alleged murderer of their late member.[55]

It is doubtful if the Blue Wing building was used as a hotel after Cooper's death, as thereafter Mrs. Coleman Smith, Mrs. Cooper's twin sister, and her family lived in the place and on their departure took with them such of the furniture as they wished to remove. About this time, however, the hotel's old barroom was used as a saloon, and about 1888 a man named Monferdini had a grocery store in the place, and after 1895 the premises were used to store wine.[56]

On November 13, 1858, Theodore G. Hahman, Public Administrator of the estate of Martin E. Cooke, sold the Blue Wing property to Harold L. DeKamp, who ten days later sold to Patrick Hayne. Hayne operated the place as the "Blue Wing Tavern" until April 6, 1863, when he and his wife Julia sold to Margaret Hayne, who subsequently married David Sheerin. On April 20, 1867, the Sheerins sold to John Tivnen, and on his death the estate passed to Eva Rideout (nee Sydnor) on December 5, 1892. On February 4, 1895, Mrs. Rideout sold to Agostino Pinelli, and on his death the property was inherited by his widow, Rosa Pinelli, on March 27, 1925. On September 15, 1941, Mrs. Pinelli sold the place to Elmer M. and his wife, Alma de Bretteville Spreckels Awl, and on October 13, 1943, Mrs. Awl deeded her interest to her husband. Prior to this the offices of the Sonoma Chamber of Commerce were located in the building, and when the Awls purchased the property it was repaired and a certain amount of restoration undertaken with the idea of turning it into the headquarters of a local horsemen's club, but nothing much seems to have come of this plan. On September 18, 1945, Awl sold the place to Walter L. and Celeste G. Murphy, who retained possession of the property until May 15, 1948, when they sold to the present owners, William Henry and Eleanora Bosworth Black.[57] Appreciating to the fullest the historical and sentimental value of the place, Mr. and Mrs. Black have carefully and painstakingly restored the old building until today the Blue Wing is essentially the same as it was at the height of its career, a century ago.

Chapter 14. Sutter's Fort

A GOOD DEAL of ink has been spilled over the story of John Augustus Sutter, and he has been portrayed as either a sort of California patriarch, all complete with halo and wings, or a bumbling, lecherous old drunkard who did not have sense enough to feather his own fortunes, let alone those of his adopted country. Both descriptions are highly exaggerated, and from an unbiased study of Sutter's life it will be found that he was neither a saint nor a sinner, but just an average sort of man with more than average vision and enterprise, whose warm-hearted generosity more than outweighed his very human failings. That he possessed the latter not even his warmest supporters gainsay, but it must be remembered that as soon as gold was discovered he was surrounded by a gang of opportunists who played upon his weaknesses to further their own ends.

Much of what has been ascribed to weakness in Captain Sutter's character was in reality no more than his custom of judging others by his own standards of honesty, and the fact that this trustfulness in the end led to his financial ruin should not be held against the man. History bears out the fact that as long as it was humanly possible his one aim was to hold together the little empire of New Helvetia that he had carved single-handed out of a hostile wilderness, and he only gave up the struggle when the mad rush for gold swept away the last lingering hope of his colony succeeding.

At one time or another all of this and much more has been said of Sutter, but what no one has told about him is that if he was not the architect of American California (which he was very far from being) he certainly was the builder of the only hospice in the country that provided shelter and comfort for many of the American immigrants who struggled across the plains and the Sierra Nevada between 1845 and 1846. When these pioneers of the great westward migration at last reached the haven of his fort, most of them were sick from exhaustion, and so destitute that they had little left beyond the clothes

157

they stood in, some of their wagons, and what had survived of their gaunt and foot sore stock. Many of them were in no condition to do more than try to recuperate from the unbelievable hardships they had endured, and the accommodations that John A. Sutter provided for their reception and paid for out of his own pocket, were, to say the least, contributing factors to the story of California's American colonization. In so far as is known, this is a hitherto unpublished bit of the state's history, and apart from the additional light that it throws on those days of empire building it is high time that Captain Sutter be given credit for an outstanding act of kindly philanthropy that he must have thought so natural that it called for no comment on his part, and that goes far toward writing off most of the harsh things that have been said of him.

In some respects Sutter was like his friend and countryman, Jean Jacques Vioget. Neither of them were inn keepers, and like Vioget at Yerba Buena, in all probability Sutter had not the faintest idea that he was to become the earliest pioneer of Sacramento's hotel industry. But the facts speak for themselves.

By the end of 1840 he was settled on the Sacramento River, his fort had been built, and the first phase of his plan to form a colony of foreigners at New Helvetia was beginning to take form. The second phase required colonists, and he could only look to the United States for pioneer men and women to make his dream come true. Some American settlers had already reached California, but it was not until three years later that the flood of immigration began, and in 1845 over four hundred arrived, most of whom made the Fort their rendezvous. These were of the type that Captain Sutter was looking for, but as has been said, on their arrival they were physically unfit for anything but rest, and he has left a vivid picture of the situation as it was in those days:

"Sometimes my houses were full of emigrants, so much so that I could scarcely find a place to sleep myself. My farm houses and out-houses were filled every winter, during those emigration times, with wet, poor, and hungry emigrants, men, women and children. They arrived usually in a destitute condition. Very few had more than their teams when they arrived, and some lost everything."[1]

Writing some three years later, but referring to this same time, M. Moerenhout, Consul of France at Monterey, not only confirms the foregoing in his report to the French Minister of Foreign Affairs, but gives Captain Sutter the credit that he himself never claimed:

"His establishment ... attracted a great number of foreigners, especially Americans, who ... lived there generally at the expense of M. Sutter until they were able to look over the country and settle there ..."2

It is true that Sutter was anxious to see Americans settle in California, and especially on his own lands, and from this point of view his hospitable reception of needy immigrants may not have been prompted by pure altruism. Nevertheless, he was the one man in what was then a foreign and somewhat more than hostile country to whom the new arrivals could turn in their need, and whatever his motives, Captain Sutter did not fail them. At first there was no definite provision for taking care of the newcomers, and they were housed and provided for wherever space was available. But as their number increased this haphazard arrangement proved inadequate, and toward the latter part of 1845 Sutter decided to organize his hospitality on a basis that savored less of charity and more of social service. To this end he gave orders that a large house be built just east of the Fort, and at the point where the emigrants were wont to camp after reaching his establishment. The first intimation of this is the following entry made on October 13, 1845, by Captain Sutter's clerk, William F. Swasey, in the diary that was kept at the Fort and in which the most important events occurring from day to day were entered:

"... have also laid the foundation of new house before the East gate of the Fort ..."3

This is all; and nowhere in all the written records left by John A. Sutter does he so much as refer to what he planned. Were it not for William R. Grimshaw's narrative of events at the Fort, this laconic entry of Swasey's would probably have continued to be passed over as a statement of no especial importance, but thanks to the unpublished manuscript of the former pioneer writer the story is brought into sharp focus as of November, 1848:

"... at that time ... The firm of S. Brannan & Co. was composed of Henry Mellus, W. D. M. Howard, Talbot H. Green, Samuel Brannan and William Stout. Their store was an old adobe building of one story about 100 feet long by 30 wide situated about 50 yards East of the Fort. There was a loft filled with hides and other relics of trade before the mines were discovered. The building had been erected by Capt. Sutter for the use of emigrants who were without shelter; and somehow acquired the name of the 'old penitentiary.' The only other building outside the Fort was a small adobe house not far from the South gate. It bore the legend 'Retail Store S. Norris' and had formerly been used as a shelter for Sutter's vaqueros."[4]

This description of Sutter's Fort refers to the place as Grimshaw first saw it in November of 1848, and while the following, set down by Heinrich Lienhard in his diary probably two years later, refers to the same building that Grimshaw describes, it does not convey as clear an idea of what Captain Sutter had in mind when he built the place:

"East of the Fort Sutter owned a commodious adobe house where several families usually lived until they could find more suitable quarters."[5]

Neither of these tantalizing glimpses of the place give any hint of the episode in its history that alone more than repaid the fine and generous thought that led to its creation. But Eliza Donner's grateful recollections record that a year and a half after its foundations were laid the house was the refuge and home of the grief-stricken and bewildered survivors of the tragedy that overtook the Donner party in the terrible winter of '46 and '47. And what she says of Captain Sutter is a touching tribute to his warm-hearted sympathy for George and Tamsen Donner's little orphaned daughter, who his far-sighted planning sheltered in the hour of her greatest need:

"The room ... when we arrived at Sutter's Fort was part of a long, low, single-story adobe building outside the fortification walls, and like others that were occupied by belated travellers, was the barest and crudest structure imaginable ... We little ones were oblivious to discomfort, however ... We had rested, been washed, combed, and fed, and we believed that father and mother would soon come to us. Everything was beautiful to our eyes ... We watched the mothers sitting on the door sills or on chairs near them laughing as they talked and sewed, and it seemed good to see the little children at play and hear them singing their dolls to sleep ... Capt. John A. Sutter ... was he who had first sent food to the starving travellers in the Sierra Nevada Mountains. It was he who laid his hand on my head, when a forlorn little waif at the Fort, tenderly saying, Poor little girl, I wish I could give back what you have lost!"[6]

Eliza Donner does not speak of the building by name, it is true, but as at the time there was only one large *adobe* outside the Fort there is no question but that she describes Captain Sutter's immigrants' stopping place. The house stood fifty yards east of the Fort's eastern gate, and was about one hundred feet long by thirty wide, with a large loft

Old Adobe House, Sutter's Fort

over the living rooms. It was located on ground that was somewhat lower than that on which the Fort was built, and its length ran east and west. Both ends were gabled, and a masonry chimney was built against the western end of the house.[7] The roof was originally thatched, but between August 18th and 21st, 1847, this was renewed by two Mormon carpenters,[8] who probably replaced it with a shingle roof similar to the one over the two-story building in the Fort.[9] Masonry or *adobe* partitions divided the place into probably a dozen or more rooms,[10] and a porch was eventually built along the north side of the house and a lean-to shed against its western end.[11] Entrance was through batten doors along the sides of the building, and as late as February of 1847 the windows were no more than openings in the *adobe* walls, and the floor was of hard packed earth. The place was surrounded by a low wall that also enclosed a plantation of trees that stood to the east of the house.[12]

Captain Sutter's plans to attract overland immigrants to his colony were abruptly terminated on July 1, 1846, when the American flag was raised over the Fort and the place taken over by the United States forces, and with this ends the story of the only immigrants' hostel in California and the first travelers' stopping place in Sacramento. That is to say, if the overland immigrants are considered to have been travelers. But if the history of the building as a hostelry has been lost, its subsequent story has fortunately been preserved in sufficient detail to permit rounding out the record.

In his description of the building Grimshaw says that it somehow acquired the name of the "old penitentiary," and Captain Sutter confirms this statement in the following entry made in the Fort's diary on June 7, 1847:

"Breaking the partition walls of the penitentiary down to make a granary out of it."[13]

From this, and earlier references to the incarceration of the Fort's Indian malefactors, it appears that some part of the building was used as a jail until the New Helvetia harvest of wheat was large enough to require a special storage place. The masonry work of remodeling the building continued until July 5th,[14] and as has been seen, a new roof was put on during the latter part of August. This is the last that is heard of the place for the next nine months, and to preserve the cronology of the story it now becomes necessary to deal with another tough old legend that, like the yarns about the Washington at Monterey having been "California's first hotel," and the Blue Wing at Sonoma having been the first hotel in that place, has long been due for upsetting.

Heretofore when the question as to which was Sacramento's first hotel has come up it has been customary to follow the line of least resistance by saying, "Kyburz's, in the two-story house in Sutter's Fort." And then, by way of playing safe, to add "of course," under the breath. As a matter of fact, in this case the assumption is scarcely open to criticism, as it has been based on Captain Sutter's own statement of an event that occurred in 1848:

"May 21. Saml. Kyburz erected or established the first hotel in the fort in the large building."[15]

This misleading statement appears in a so-called diary, that is really a collection of memoranda, jotted down by Sutter in 1856 (mostly from memory) and published in 1878. At the time he wrote, Captain Sutter's recollections of what occurred were somewhat hazy, as will appear a little later. In this "diary" and referring to 1847, he says:

"October 12. A small store was established by S'l Brannan & Smith in one of the houses near the fort."[16]

This statement is vague, but in his entry in the Fort's diary for the same date Sutter is specific about the house involved, when he says: "Mr. Smith has opened his store in the Baquero house."[17] It may be wondered what this house has to do with the story, and the reason for bringing it in will appear shortly.

The Samuel Brannan referred to was the elder and leader of the Mormons who arrived at Yerba Buena on July 31, 1846, in the ship *Brooklyn*. It will be recalled that the idea had been to found a Mormon colony in what was then Mexican Alta California, but when it was found that the country had been annexed by the United States the scheme fell through, and Salt Lake City became the successor of the Latter Day Saints' headquarters at Nauvoo, Illinois. For three years after his arrival Brannan continued to exercise considerable power as president of the Mormon Mission to California and presiding elder of the local Brethren, and apart from this he entered upon a diversified business career that in the fall of 1847 centered at Sutter's Fort. A little earlier in the same year an overland immigrant had arrived at the Fort and announced himself as Charles C. Smith and a relative of the late Joseph Smith, founder of the Mormon Church but neglected to add that he was also a member of the firm of Jackson, Heaton and Bonney, who had conducted a counterfeiting business at Nauvoo until Brigham Young caught up with them.

When Elder Brannan arrived on the scene young Smith was installed in Sutter's old *vaqueros'* house, and the elder saw at a glance that the opportunity of capitalizing on the magic name of Smith was too golden a one to be missed. Without loss of itme, and without his name appearing in the picture, he organized the firm of "C. C. Smith & Company" as dealers in general merchandise and groceries. At first the place was jocularly known as "Brannan's Shirt Tail Store," but the elder no doubt saw to it that word got out among the Brethren to the effect that it was being operated under the ghostly patronage of the Prophet, and the undignified nickname was quickly dropped.[18]

At this point occurs the first mention of Sam Kyburz in connection with anything like a public stopping place at Sutter's Fort, or Sacramento. In his entry in the New Helvetia diary on January 17, 1848, Captain Sutter says:

"On this day Chs. Burch is no longer boarding at Mr. Kyburz."[19]

Samuel E. Kyburz was also a Swiss, from Aargau, whom Captain Sutter employed at different times as general overseer at New Helvetia, and the fact that he and his wife were taking in boarders this early is interesting, as this was probably what gave him the idea of the boarding house that he opened five months later. This statement is made categorically and despite the fact that (going Captain Sutter one better) it has been claimed that immediately after 1846 Kyburz took charge of the hotel in the Fort, in what was later called the "Kyburz Annex."[20] But as its author quotes no authority for this statement, it can be put down to still another embellishment of what has already been referred to as no more than another tough old yarn.

That the main building in the Fort was not being used as a hotel down to this time is proved by Sutter's following statements, the first being his entry in the Fort's diary and the second quoted from his *Reminiscences:*

"January 28, 1848. Mr. Marshall arrived from the Mountains on very important business."[21]

"One rainy afternoon in January 1848 Marshall, dripping with water, entered my office next to the guard house in a hurried excited manner, and asked to see me alone in the 'big house' where was my private office, and the clerks office."[22]

Apart from its bearing on Sacramento's earliest hotel, the first of these quotations is of more than passing interest, as it is the first documentary reference to the finding of gold a few days earlier at the sawmill that Marshall and Sutter were building at what later came to be called Coloma.[23] As has been seen, Captain Sutter attempted to keep the discovery a secret until he could try to secure from Governor Mason an exclusive concession to the mining rights, but a little over a fortnight later his diary entry for February 14, 1848, acknowledges that the fat was in the fire:

"Wittmer returned with the two wagons from the Mountains, and told everybody of the Gold mines there and brought a few samples with him."[24]

Just two months later, the following diary entry records the first appreciable amount of gold to reach the Fort, and after this the fat was not only in the fire but blazing furiously:

"April 14th 1848. S. Willis and Jesse Martin arrived from the Mountains with a good deal of Gold which they have brought to the Store."[25]

These men were Sidney Willis and Jesse B. Martin, two of a party of seven Mormons who had struck gold a few days earlier at Mormon Island,[26] and this was the first time in the history of California that gold dust had been exchanged over the counter for store goods.[27] The transaction also marked the beginning of Sam Brannan's fortunes, that in a few years made him the richest man in the state. Furthermore, the arrival of this gold brought the immigrants' stopping place back into the picture, and finally, it was doubtless responsible for Kyburz's decision to open a boarding house, as may be concluded from Captain Sutter's diary entries for May 17th and 21st, of the same year:

"Cleaned and whte (sic) washed the Magasin (penitentiary) and rented the whole to C. C. Smith & Co. for a store."[28] C. C. Smith & Co. moved the store in the large Granary to make Room for Mr. Kyburz to establish a Boarding House."[29]

The foregoing definitely eliminates any possible misunderstanding as to which building Grimshaw referred to as having been built for an immigrants' hostelry, and it also settles any argument as to where Brannan's store was located, first and last. The gold that Willis and Martin traded unquestionably helped, but this (together with other dust and nuggets taken into stock that all together amounted to $36,000[30]) was not entirely responsible for the sudden prosperity that warranted the firm's moving into larger quarters. As has been said, Smith was related to the late Prophet (or so he claimed), while Brannan was still the presiding Mormon elder in California, and according to Sutter, who may have been somewhat biased:

"Now that God had given the church gold the church must build a temple. Brannan and Smith rallied the hosts of heaven, and levied an assessment on all their increase of thirty percent, afterward reduced to ten percent, with which to build a temple to the Lord...Brannan was to furnish the Mormons goods and the Mormons were to dig gold which was to be divided between Brannan, the diggers and the Lord, but Brannan, who held the keys to the whiskey locker, got the chief share."[31]

According to General William T. Sherman (who, as a captain and Governor Mason's aide, was an eye-witness), what actually happened was that no sooner had Brannan and Smith's coreligionists struck it rich at Mormon Island than "Sam Brannan was on hand as high priest, collecting the tithes."[32] Both Sutter and Sherman concur in what was commonly believed at the time; that is, that whereas these tithes were supposed to be dedicated to the general welfare of the Mormon Church they were in reality diverted to the personal welfare of Sam Brannan. So well founded was this belief, indeed, that on April 5, 1849, President Brigham Young wrote Brannan from Salt Lake City demanding the return of these selfsame tithes—a demand that it is almost needless to say was never complied with.[33] This one-sided arrangement continued in effect for about three months, but when Governor Mason arrived at Mormon Island on a tour of the gold diggings it was abruptly terminated. The denouement of this sanctimonious shakedown is amusing enough to be recounted in General Sherman's own words:

"The next day (July 5, 1848) we resumed our journey and reached Mormon Island...We found about three hundred of them there at work. Sam Brannan was on hand as high priest, collecting the tithes. Clark, of Clark's Point, one of the elders...inquired, 'Governor, what business has Sam Brannan to collect the tithes here?' Colonel Mason answered, 'Brannan has a perfect right to collect the tax, if you Mormons are fools enough to pay it.'...'Then,' said Clark, 'I for one won't pay it any longer.'...I understood afterwards, that for that time the payment of tithes ceased, but Brannan had already collected enough money wherewith to hire Sutter's hospital, and to open a store there, in which he made more money than any other merchant in California."[34]

What with this and that contributing to Brannan's own "increase," about the time the store was moved he was in position to buy out his partner for a round $50,000, and shortly thereafter his receipts were averaging $5,000 a day.[35] In February of '49 Brannan began building a one-story frame store on the southeast corner of what became Sacramento's Front and J Streets, and between April and May he vacated Sutter's old building, when both he and Brother Smith step out of the story.[36]

Returning to the question as to who opened Sacramento's first hotel, and where this was located, the following entry in the New Helvetia diary, in Captain Sutter's own handwriting, settles the long-standing belief for which he himself was later responsible, that is, that Kyburz was the man and the present two-story building in the Fort the place:

"May 22, 1848. Mr. Kyburz left my Services and established a boarding house in the old Baquero house."[37]

As has been seen, this was the place where Brannan opened his store, in the small one-story *abobe*, that stood a short distance southwest of the Fort's south gate. The door was on the west side, and the north and south ends of the building were gabled, with a masonry chimney built against the former. The roof was probably shingled, and under this was a low attic that was lighted by a small window high up in the south gable.[38] This was the place where Kyburz opened his boarding house, *not* the two-story building inside the Fort, and while it cannot be termed a hostelry in the present sense of the word, it was what may be called the grandfather of Sacramento's first hotel. Apart from this, and if for no other reason than the fact that five weeks before Kyburz began taking in boarders the place was the scene of the first bartering of California gold for merchandise, it is entitled to more than passing notice. Down to this time there was no other transients' stopping place at the Fort, as is proved by the following extract from a letter written to the editor of the San Francisco *Californian*, and dated New Helvetia, June 30, 1848:

"About three miles from the fort, on the east bank of the Sacramento, the town of Sutterville is laid out...A hotel is building for the accommodation of the traveling public, who are now obliged to impose on the kind hospitality of Capt. Sutter."[39]

The short lived town of Sutterville had been laid out in 1846,[40] but what this hotel was and who was supposed to be putting it up does not appear. If such a place really was built at that time it was probably no more than another such shack as those that sprang up at Sacramento City six months or so later.

Referring to the first 4th of July celebration held at the Fort under the American flag, another of Captain Sutter's statements adds to the confusion about Kyburz and his supposed hotel. In his so-called diary he says:

"As we wanted to celebrate the 4th of July we invited the Governor and his suit to remain with us, and ... Kyburz gave us a good dinner."[41]

From this it has heretofore been concluded that the affair was held in Kyburz's establishment, but the following from Sutter's *Reminiscences* proves that this was not the case. Furthermore, as in his more detailed account of the celebration Sutter makes no mention of Kyburz, it may safely be assumed that the latter's only connection with the affair was in the capacity of a sort of *maitre d'hotel*, who oversaw the arrangements but had nothing to do with either the locals or the food and drink that were served:

"On the 4th of July 1848 I gave a great dinner ... There were quite a number of women there, about four, who were good cooks, Mrs. Montgomery was one so was Mrs. Lehigh, Mrs. McDowell and another. The table was laid in my old armory hall ... I had recently had a chance to purchase from a French vessel a supply of good Sauterne, brandy and other things ... We had beef, game, fowl and all the substantials and luxuries of frontier life."[42]

Describing his visit to the Fort at that time as a member of Colonel Mason's staff, General Sherman in his *Memoirs* confirms this statement as to where the celebration was held:

"There was not a sign of a habitation there or thereabouts, except the fort, and an old adobe-house, east of the fort, known as the hospital ... Inside there was a large house, with a good shingle-roof, used as a storehouse ... We found preparations in progress for celebrating the Fourth of July ... and we agreed to remain over ... the tables were laid in the large room inside the storehouse of the fort."[43]

This also effectually clears up any possible misapprehension as to the two-story building inside the Fort having been turned into a hotel prior to that time, and the following extract from Colonel Mason's report to General Jones, describing his stay at Captain Sutter's estab-

lishment between July 2nd and 5th, 1848, makes it perfectly plain
when this happened:

> "Merchants paid him (Sutter) a monthly rent of one hundred dollars per room,
> and while I was there, a two-story house in the fort was rented as a hotel for five
> hundred dollars a month."[44]

On July 30th, less than three weeks later, M. Moerenhout arrived
on a tour of the diggings and has left what is not only a vivid description of the chaotic conditions that, following the discovery of gold,
attended the dissolution of Captain Sutter's empire at New Helvetia,
but also positive confirmation of Colonel Mason's statement to the
effect that the hotel in the Fort was opened at that time:

> "It was noon when I reached the fort, and although forewarned, I was aston-
> ished at the confusion that reigned there—men on foot and on horseback; wagons
> going in and out, some bringing goods from the Sacramento landing, others taking
> them to the different mining regions. Within, the square was filled with casks,
> boxes, bales and workmen, and there was such a crowd and such a stir that one
> would have thought himself either in a Turkish bazaar or in one of the most
> frequented markets in Europe. M. Sutter was not in his quarters and I had a great
> deal of trouble finding him in the midst of all the crowd and the tumult, but when
> he was informed of my arrival he soon came and received me with his usual
> affability. As he had kept only one small room for his own use, however, he could
> no longer afford the hospitality that formerly one was sure to find there. He came
> with me to the hotel into which the old armory had been converted. All was in
> frightful confusion. It was full and I had to wait for an American and his wife
> who were leaving that day to move out before I could get a room. This room
> had no other furniture than two old chairs, and cost two dollars a day. (Author's
> note: The room cost two and the food three-five a day. But their expenses were
> enormous. The house, which had only four rooms, a dining room, a kitchen, and
> a pantry, rented for five hundred a month. The cook drew one hundred and fifty
> dollars a month, and did not care to stay at those wages. And besides the high
> price of provisions, the least servant, the worst scullion, had to be paid from three
> to four dollars a day). The fort is all occupied and rented for gold; the armory as
> I have already said, for five hundred dollars a month; the other rooms and apart-
> ments at one hundred and fifty and two hundred dollars, the total rent, accord-
> ing to what M. Sutter told me, came to eighteen hundred dollars a month, not
> including some houses outside, one of which was used as a hospital. The whole
> establishment soon would bring him he hoped, from two to three thousand dollars
> a month."[45]

Colonel Mason's and Consul Moerenhout's accounts are of additional historical interest as they show clearly that by the end of July
Captain Sutter had rented practically all of the Fort, in contradiction

to the statement that has been made to the effect that this did not take place until March of 1849, nine months later.[46] There is now no question as to when and where the first hotel in Sacramento was established, but no one seems to have thought it worth while to say who it was that opened the place. However, in view of what has been said, together with the facts that by November of 1848 the old *vaqueros'* shelter, where Kyburz established his boarding house four or five months earlier, was being used as a store by Samuel Norris,[47] and that thereafter nothing more is heard of Kyburz or his place, Grimshaw's following description of the situation at the Fort as it was in that month makes it almost certain that Rufus Hitchcock was the man who rented the old armory from Captain Sutter on or about July 4th of '48, and opened the hotel:

"In the center of the inside of the fort was a two story adobe building ... the lower portion of which was used as a bar room with a monte table or two in it."

"This bar was crowded with customers night and day and never closed from one month to the other. The upper story was rented by Rufus Hitchcock and wife for a boarding house. Board was $40 per week; meals $2 each. The fare was plain and simple. We had plenty of fresh beef, beans and bread (mostly in the form of 'biscuit') tea and coffee: no milk. The few potatoes and onions that came into the market were sent to the mines as a cure and preventive of scurvy and brought such enormous prices ($1.00 each) as placed them entirely out of reach as an article of food ... The Hitchcock family consisted of Rufus Hitchcock, his wife one son and two daughters."[48]

Referring to the winter of 1848-49, the following description (while a few years posterior to Grimshaw's) confirms and amplifies the foregoing, and is therefore worthy of being quoted:

"At this time (1849) the building inside Sutter's Fort was occupied by Rufus Hitchcock, the upper story being used as a boarding house. The front room below was used for drinking and gambling purposes. The bar was kept open night and day. If a customer had any coin, which was not often, the price of a drink was fifty cents; but in most cases he opened his purse and the bar-keeper took a pinch of dust, the extent of the pinch being regulated by the quality and quantity of the liquor consumed. In those times hardly anyone ever drank alone. The cost of board in this establishment was $40 per week."[49]

Rufus Hitchcock and his family were overland immigrants who arrived at the Fort in the first half of 1848, and shortly thereafter he closed the deal for Captain Sutter's building and opened his hotel.[50] As has been seen, he was still running the place in November of the same year, but by that time business was beginning to move away from the Fort to the site of the future city on the river, and that fall Frederick Whittle told the pioneer writer, William Redmond Ryan (to whom we are indebted for so much colorful material about those days) that a "magnificent hotel" was being built at Sacramento.[51] This statement is another of those that are open to serious question, as in that same month of November two other pioneer writers say that the only buildings thereabouts were a board shanty store at "Sutter's Slough," (or Sutterville), that was also used as a dwelling by the proprietors, George McDougal and Judge William Blackburn, and an old storeship.[52] As these men were there at the time, it is safe to put this story down as another of the effervescent yarns of those days, and continue the story of Hitchcock's establishment. From what Moerenhout says the operating costs were high, and four or five months later his place may have gone on the rocks, or at least so Grimshaw suggests:

"Early in the Spring Mr. Brannan came to our rescue in a dietetic sense. He erected a shanty alongside the store and, for our benefit hired a cook, Ch's Lewis colored afterward succeeded by Louis Keeseberg & wife."[53]

Whatever his reasons, by the latter part of March, or early in April of '49, Hitchcock departed for the Stanislaus diggings. From there he returned to the American River, where he kept a hotel, and later moved to Green Springs, in El Dorado County, where he acquired a ranch of the same name and opened another hotel. There, at the age of forty-five, he died of smallpox on April 8, 1851, his wife succumbing to the same disease.[54]

On Hitchcock's departure from the Fort he was succeeded by Michael T. McClellan, who with his wife and daughter had also immigrated in 1848. By April of the following year he had purchased Sutter's two-story building and was continuing the hotel business, and perhaps due to the fact that he owned a number of fine milch cows and was thus able to offer the rare luxury of fresh milk in addition to the orthodox menu of beef, beans and biscuits, he seems for a time to have been somewhat more successful than his predecessor.[55] But by August New Helvetia had lost all of its earlier importance, and while the hotel and a few small stores were still holding out in the Fort, the rest of the community had shifted to the new settlement on the river front that John A. Sutter, Jr., had laid out during the past winter.[56]

By the first of the same month, the falling off of business brought the rates for board down from $40.00 to $21.00 a week, although a dollar was charged for a cup of coffee and three small cakes by an old negro in the Fort.[57] While in the fall of '49 the "big house" was still being run as a hotel, it is not known whether or not McClellan was operating it,[58] but in 1860 he moved to Sonoma County, where he was farming near Fisherman's Bay as late as 1877.[59] The last that is heard of Sacramento's first hotel is in March of 1852, when (according to his granddaughter) Abraham Keefer, a hotel man and a good cook from Massilon, Ohio, was keeping the place.[60] As far as its immediate successors at Sacramento city are concerned, the following contemporary description gives an excellent idea of what they amounted to, and shows that in the piping days of '49 Sacramento's hostelries were no improvement over those of San Francisco:

"There were no hotels; but in lieu of them there were boarding-houses, where your bare meals cost you twenty five dollars per week, attached to each of which there was a large apartment, littered over with hay, where you paid one dollar for the privilege of lying on the ground in your own blanket. If you remained over one night you rolled your blanket up on the spot you lay and left it there; but as all did not come to bed at the same time, or in the same trim, you were subject to having your snoring interrupted by the iron-heel of a huge boot on your nose, or the knee of a staggering emigrant in search of his nest on the pit of your stomach; nor was it unusual in the morning to find a congealed tobacco spittle on your cheek, or like a big soot-drop on your blanket."[61]

To conclude the story of the building that Captain Sutter designed for an immigrants' hostelry, it will be recalled that in July of 1848 both Sherman and Moerenhout refer to the place as a hospital. Dr. Frank Bates, the Fort's physician, may have been using a part of the house for this purpose, but it is certain that by that time Brannan and Smith had moved their store into the building. These references are given color by the fact that by August 4, 1849, two or three months after Brannan vacated the premises, Dr. Charles Hartwell Cragin, of Washington, D. C., and Alexander G. Abell (who had arrived two years before from Honolulu) had turned the place into Sacramento's first private hospital. Some degree of comfort was provided for their patients, it is true, but as they charged anywhere from $16.00 to $50.00 a day for medical attendance and board, the establishment can scarcely be said to have carried out Captain Sutter's original plan for a philanthropic institution. The place was used as a hospital as late as October 7 the same year,[62] and thereafter it was turned into a brewery by M. Yager, the last vestige of the old building disappearing in the flood of January, 1862.

Chapter 15. Gold Era Roads

THE STORY of California's earliest hostelries has been told, and it remains to sketch the amazing expansion of these pioneer stopping places, that took place between 1849 and 1869. As has been seen, before 1849 there were less than a score of so-called "hotels" scattered among the principal communities of the state, and, at the time there was no reason to suppose that their number would be increased by other than the normal requirements of immigration. However, when in February of that year the steamer *California* dropped her anchor in the bay of San Francisco and landed the first contingent of Forty-Niners, the great Gold Rush was off to a flying start. And hard in its wake came the multitude of hostelries of that fabulous era, which two years later led Dame Shirley to call California "the Hotel State."

With San Francisco as their starting point, these primitive establishments sprang up along the trails to the diggings as fast as the latter were opened, and it is no exaggeration to say that the speed with which they made their appearance rivaled that of the proverbial jackrabbit. And, it may be added, the speed with which many of them disappeared. From first to last, the number of these places was literally legion, and their story must be reserved for another time. In the meantime it is necessary to know something of the roads of those days, which, after the mines themselves, were responsible for this bewildering array of wayside stopping places.

As holds true elsewhere in the world, the aboriginal Indians of California seem to have gotten about to most places that were worth while going to by the shortest and most practical trails, and the State's present-day system of highways owes its inception to this, and to three subsequent factors. First, Spanish exploration and colonization; second, American immigration; third, the discovery of gold. It would be fascinating to tell the story of all the roads and trails that saw the unrolling of this drama, but like the inns that dotted their waysides, they grew into such an amazing network that we can do no more than make passing mention of the principal early arterial highways.

The dean of California's roads was, of course, the *Camino Real* of Spanish days, and while there were no early inns along this route, it was the first white man's highway in all the vast region of northwest America. For this reason, if for no other, it should not be passed by with the brief statement that there was such a road. A good deal of romantic nonsense has been written about what is popularily believed to have been the royal highway of the kings of Spain, but when this so-called "road" was being traveled the kings of Spain probably knew nothing about the existence of what was, as its name clearly implies, no more than the recognized route from one place to another. Furthermore, it is certain that not one of the Spanish kings spent a single *maravidí* on its maintenance, at that time or at any other. Along this "Royal Highway" is supposed to have rolled the shining steel and gilded magnificence that typified the power and majesty of Spain, but it is equally certain that neither this pomp and circumstance or anything else rolled along the *Camino Real* for three-quarters of a century. As a matter of fact, the storied *Camino Real* was an institution rather than a road, and it took the sturdy wagons of the American immigrants to prove that it could be negotiated by wheeled transportation. The route crossed the Colorado River at the mouth of the Gila, and after swinging southward into what is now Lower California, it eventually reached the presidio of San Francisco, by way of San Gabriel, San Luís Obispo and Monterey. While it had been pioneered by Lieutenant-Colonel Juan Bautista Anza in 1774, the route saw little traffic until 1849, when American miners and immigrants began to arrive over it by the thousands. From this point of view the *Camino Real* might be considered to have been the first of California's gold era roads, but as it stopped far short of the mines it was really only a way of getting as close as possible to the "diggings." That there were no early inns along this road is not to be wondered at, as the Americans were far too anxious to reach the land of promise in the central part of the country to stop along the way any longer than was absolutely necessary, and where there are no lingering wayfarers there are no wayside stopping places.

The first of what may properly be called California's golden highways, and along which the wayside inns first appeared, were the routes across the Sierra Nevada, which the Americans began pioneering as early as 1827. While a little over ten years later the western portions of some of these routes developed into roads to the mines, before 1849 they were used almost exclusively by immigrants, and as was the case with the *Camino Real*, as no one lingered along them before that year, there were no wayside stopping places that were worthy of being described as inns. There were at least a dozen of these trails that later on became transmountain roads, and as with their Pacific littoral ramifications, these eventually developed into two score or more road systems, it is necessary to select a typical example for the purpose of this sketch.

By far the most important of these routes, and the one that can without exaggeration be called California's great bullion highway, was without question the road that led from Sacramento to Nevada, via Placerville and Johnson Pass, or Echo Summit, and that is today followed by United States Highway 50. In so far as is known, the section of this road between Placerville (or Hangtown, as the place was then called) and Genoa (or Mormon Station), in the Carson Valley, was first used by John Calhoun (Jack, or "Cock-eyed") Johnson in 1848, when he made several trips carrying mail between the two places. While Johnson is credited with having discovered the route, it is probably that he, like other trail-breakers through the Sierra Nevada, followed tracks which the Indians had used from time immemorial, and there is therefore no telling how old the route really is.

At first it was only a more or less vague track, that wound its way among the pines and clambered up, over and around huge granite boulders, to follow ridge tops that happened to be pointed in the right direction, and when a jumping off place was encountered the road literally slid down from the roof of California. Gullies and streams were forded, often at the expense of long detours, and the only bridge on the route's entire one hundred thirty miles was Bartlett's, across the South Fork of the American River, eighteen miles east of Placerville. As traffic increased from an occasional pack-train to the lumbering ox-drawn wagons of the immigrants, and finally to the dashing six-horse Concords of the Pioneer Stage Company, and the treasure laden stages of Wells Fargo, the road was relocated time after time to improve the grades, and wherever possible to straighten out the alignment. Bridges and culverts were constructed at all the stream crossings, and where the gorge of the American River was entered no less than five paralled roads were built, so that the slow moving twelve-horse freight outfits would not delay the mail, express and passenger coaches. By 1869, the high-water mark of the road's importance, traffic was so heavy that its dustiest portions were sprinkled daily, and maintenance gangs were constantly at work keeping it up, even to the removal of small stones that might lodge in the horses' hooves. At the time it was said to have been the best highway in the country, but at the beginning of the Washoe silver excitement some ten years earlier, J. Ross Browne wrote: "The road is five feet deep by 130 miles long, and is composed chiefly of mountains, snow, and mud."[1]

This was the grand trunk road of the golden era of 1849 to 1869, that at different times was known by a variety of names, such as Johnson's cut-off, the Johnson road, the Placerville-Carson or Nevada road, or more generally as the Overland, and at the height of the Nevada silver excitement it was known far and wide as the Washoe Road. Along it passed a vast company of immigrants, miners and other travelers, and over it were carried untold millions of dollars worth of gold from California and silver from Nevada's fantastically rich Golconda, at Virginia City.

In common with most of the other roads leading into California, the first stopping places along this route were a few so-called trading posts, which were located at points where the immigrants generally halted for the night. But as no accommodations of any kind were offered by these places, and all that they had to trade for was a little flour, bacon and beans, and, of course, whiskey, they can be dismissed with the statement that there were such establishments, and that they generally consisted of no more than a small brush shack, or at best a little tent. With the discovery of gold in 1848 the situation changed rapidly, and a year later wayside stopping places were springing up as if by magic. And as has been said, disappearing with equal rapidity, as the centers of mining activity shifted from one locality to another.

Along this road the first typical wayside inns of the Gold Rush days appeared at Dry Diggings (Hangtown, or Placerville) to cater to the needs of the local miners, and as tents were by that time at a premium,

Mormon Tavern on "Hangtown & City" road

Hotel California, Mud Springs

Brockliss Bridge

Ohio House at Sicard Flat, Yuba County

177

and it took too long to build brush shacks, these places were hurriedly run up with pole frames covered with the cheapest available material, which was either plain or elaborately printed calico. As an improvement over what their predecessors, the trading-posts, had to offer, these establishments were prepared to supply their customers with whiskey, gambling, bacon and beans, and with sleeping accommodations which consisted of the bare ground and the guest's own blankets. This was about the middle of 1848,[2] and by the end of that year there was scarcely a gulch or a ravine on the western portion of the route where some sort of a stopping place was not being built.[3]

Chapter 16. The Overland Road

T̲HE ORIGINAL ROUTE of the Overland road between Sacramento and Placerville followed the Carson Pass immigrant road, and first began to be traveled between 1848 and 1849. Leaving Sacramento, the road ran eastward to about the present village of Manlove, and thence northeastward through White Rock, Clarksville, Shingle Springs, Mud Springs (now El Dorado), and Diamond Springs, to Placerville, and is today followed partly by a county road and partly by the old State Highway 50.

Between Placerville and the summit of the Sierra Nevada, or Johnson Pass (now called Echo Summit) Johnson's road, or cut-off, ran eastward to William Bartlett's bridge, on the South Fork of the American River. Thence it climbed north and east, up and along Peavine Ridge, to the present location of United States Highway 50, a short distance east of Georgetown Junction, and from there along the north bank of the river to the summit. From this point Johnson's route plunged down the abrupt eastern escarpment of the Sierra to the Upper Truckee River, and thence northeast through Lake Valley to the southeast corner of Mountain Lake (now Lake Tahoe). From there it skirted the east shore of the lake as far as the present Glenbrook, in Nevada, where it turned east to cross the "Eastern Summit," in the Carson Range, at Spooner's Summit, and thence northeast down King's Canyon to the site of Carson City, where it joined what shortly thereafter became the Immigrant Road, which continued southward to Carson Pass.

After Johnson pioneered his cut-off in 1848 the route was used by pack outfits and a few immigrant wagon trains, but the bulk of traffic was by way of the Carson Pass road, that began to be heavily traveled in the summer of 1849. Early in 1851 a new route began to be used by Absalom Woodward and George Chorpenning, mail contractors, that turned south at the Upper Truckee River and followed up the west bank of this stream for a couple of miles to again cross the Sierra at

179

what later came to be known as Luther Pass, and join the Carson road at the head of Big or Rocky Canyon (West Carson Canyon). But due to the almost prohibitive grade from Johnson Pass down to the Truckee River this road was unpopular with the immigrants, and it was not until 1855, when Asa Hershal Hawley built his grade down the eastern escarpment of the Sierra, that the route came into general use.

By 1853-54 traffic over the Carson Pass road had become so heavy that a new route was being sought, not only to shorten the distance from Carson Valley to the California gold diggings, but also to avoid the animal killing grades involved in crossing the "Western Summit" at Carson Pass and Round Top Mountain and farther along the route at the Iron Mountain grade. In February of 1854 a bill was introduced in the California legislature granting Johnson a concession to build and operate a wagon toll road from Placerville to the Utah state line, but before anything was done Hawley built his grade, and with this the eastern end of Johnson's route, from Carson City to the foot of the eastern escarpment and thence up to Johnson Pass, was virtually abandoned for the next five years.[1]

Thus far there does not seem to have been any concerted movement toward opening a regular stage road from California to "the States." The first suggestion of this nature was put forward by the *Sacramento Union* about November of 1854. That paper recommended that such a road be built from Placerville to Carson, thinking, at the time, that when the line between California and Utah was surveyed Carson valley would be in California. Acting on this suggestion, Adams & Company, of San Francisco banking fame, in December of the same year sent a representative to Salt Lake City via Los Angeles and San Bernardino, to open a branch at Salt Lake and to examine that route for a stage road, it being believed that the grades across the Sierra Nevada, via Johnson Pass, were too steep for stage travel. This threat of a southern route galvanized Placerville into action, and on January 25, 1855, a mass meeting resolution was passed calling for a survey of the Johnson route, and the first reconnaissance of this was begun on January 30th.[2] On April 28th of the same year an act was approved by the California legislature providing for the survey and construction of a wagon road across the Sierra Nevada, and a couple of months later Sherman Day, whose services had been retained by S. H. Marlette, the surveyor-general of California, departed from Sacramento to begin the field work.[3]

On the strength of Day's survey, the California Board of Wagon Road Commissioners in September, 1855, reported favorably on the Johnson route as far as Johnson Pass, and thence via Luther Pass to connect with the Carson Pass road at the head of Hope Valley (the top of West Carson Cañyon). On October 16th they advertised for bids, but as far as California was concerned no further action was taken for the next two years.[4] Until this time there was no more than a trail from Placerville across the Sierra, but private individuals now began to improve the worst parts of the route and turned this into a loosely connected series of toll roads. With this the route began to settle down to approximately the final location of the Overland road.

Bartlett's bridge was washed out in 1855, and shortly thereafter Anthony Richard Brockliss built a new bridge about a mile and three quarters up the river, at the site recommended in Sherman Day's

BROCKLISS' NEW STATION!

Mile beyond Pete's Ranch.

FOUNTAIN HOUSE

TWENTY-THREE MILES FROM PLACERVILLE.

I would inform the Public that my house, on the Placerville and Carson Valley Road, is twenty three miles from Placerville, eleven miles from Sportsman's Hall, five miles from the Fresh Pond House, three miles from Brockliss' Bridge, and half-a-mile beyond Pete's Ranch.

I have HAY, BARLEY, a GOOD STABLE, and STOCK CORRALS; plenty to eat and drink, good beds, also, good rooms for Families.

MRS. E. BROCKLISS, Proprietress.

April 10, 1860.

Mountain Democrat Print.

report, and from this structure a new road was opened to connect with the Johnson cut-off, or immigrant road, some two and a half miles north, up Peavine Ridge. With the construction of Hawley's grade traffic became so congested that in 1857 El Dorado, Sacramento and Yolo counties between them got together $50,000 wherewith to further improve the road, and on July 11th of the same year the *Mountain Democrat*, of Placerville, announced the route open for traffic from Placerville to Salt Lake, via Genoa.

The foregoing is the general picture of the original route that a few years later came to be known as the Overland road, but before its final alignment was established there were numerous divergences and re-alignments, all of which will be described in the following chapters. Apart from the great volume of traffic that it carried as the principal arterial highway linking California with the eastern states, there were several other factors which contributed to, or were vitally interrelated with the development of this great highway.

On June 11th, just a month before the road was announced as having been opened, J. B. Crandall, one of the pioneer stage men of the Pacific Coast, took one of his six-horse Concord stages from Placerville over the Sierra Nevada to Genoa, and thereafter inaugurated the Pioneer Stage Line's weekly service between these places. At Genoa the Pioneer Line connected with George W. Chorpenning's line from Salt Lake City, and on July 19, 1858, the first through mail from the east arrived at Placerville.[5]

Early in 1861 the activities of Southern Confederates forced the abandonment of David A. Butterfield's southern Overland Mail service. His equipment and personnel were transferred to the central route, and on July 18, 1861, the first daily Overland Mail arrived in Sacramento, having been brought from Folsom by the Sacramento Valley Railroad, where the stagecoach connected with the terminus of this line, the Pioneer Line forming the last link in the service between Carson City and Folsom. Daily stagecoach service over the Overland road was maintained for the next eight years, and when in 1869 the western railhead of the Central Pacific Railroad arrived at Cisco (today a station on the Southern Pacific's Overland Route and a few miles west of Donner or Truckee Pass) the stages were rerouted from this point to Nevada.[6] During this time the fastest trip on record was made by one of the Larue Line stages, when on June 20, 1864, the run between Virginia City and Sacramento was made in twelve hours and twenty-three minutes,[7] a distance of one hundred sixty-five miles at an average speed of some thirteen miles per hour.

The California section of what became the transcontinental telegraph line was another factor that contributed to the development of the Overland road. The Alta California Telegraph Company began construction work in the fall of 1852, and by the latter part of 1853 had completed its line from Sacramento to Nevada City, California, via Mormon Island, Diamond Springs, Placerville, Coloma, Auburn, and Grass Valley, and a little later the line was extended from Diamond Springs to Stockton, Oakland, and San Francisco. The Placerville, Humboldt & Salt Lake Telegraph Company was organized at Placerville in May of 1858, and their line from Placerville to Genoa was completed in the fall of the same year. Service was opened to Carson City in the spring of 1859, and the line was completed to Salt Lake City in 1861, when on October 22nd transcontinental service was inaugurated.[8]

The railway lines running eastward from Sacramento were another of the above factors. Work on the Sacramento Valley Railroad (now the Placerville branch of the Southern Pacific) was begun in 1855, and the line between Sacramento and Folsom was opened on February 3, 1856. Construction work on an extension to Placerville was started in January, 1860, and the line was completed to Shingle Springs by the middle of June, 1865, where, due to financial difficulties and litigation, the railhead rested and rusted for years before the line was finally completed.[9]

The Central Pacific Railroad (now part of the Southern Pacific's main line) was incorporated on June 28, 1861, and before construction work was begun most of the engineers and surveyors of that day favored the Johnson Pass route as the best crossing of the Sierra Nevada. This line would probably have been followed but for the attitude of the owners of the various sections of toll roads referred to earlier. These concessions covered the proposed railway route, and their owners insisted on receiving a controlling interest in the railway in exchange for their toll rights. When it was found impossible to induce them to modify their demands, nogtiations were broken off and the railway was built from Sacramento to Roseville, and thence across the Sierra by way of Donner or Truckee Pass.[10]

In the meantime the famous Overland Pony Express was still another factor that had a bearing on the history of the Overland road. This service was inaugurated on April 3, 1860, simultaneously from San Francisco and St. Joseph, Missouri, and was designed to provide a fast semi-weekly mail between California and the eastern states. St. Joseph was the western railway terminus at the time, and the Pony Express operated from that point to San Francisco, via Salt Lake City, Carson, Placerville, Folsom and Sacramento, whence it proceeded to its destination by river steamers. The Overland Mail's running time, by railway and stagecoach from New York to Sacramento, was twenty-one days, and when the Pony Express cut this down to nine days it was hailed as the greatest achievement in rapid communication that the world had ever known. But the service was short-lived, for as has been said, the transcontinental telegraph line began operating in 1861, and with this the Pony Express was discontinued on October 25th, after only eighteen months of colorful but non-profitable life.[11]

No road in all the nation is more storied than is the Overland, and tales which have grown into traditions cluster about it like bees around a honey-pot. Many of these stories are about famous or notorious characters of those days, and others have to do with the road itself.

In the first category, what is easily the most outstanding is the aptly titled modern version of the "Fabulous Feats of 'Snowshoe' Thompson." According to this story, Thompson was the originator of the idea of using snowshoes, or their equivalent, to carry mail between Hangtown and Carson City, and he is said to have made his first trip in the winter of 1848, loaded down with one hundred pounds of mail.[12] As a matter of historical fact, Carson City was not founded until ten years later;[13] Thompson did not arrive in California until 1851, and it was not until January of 1856 that he made his first trip across the Sierra.[14] Nor was he the first to use snowshoes to carry the mail, as he was anticipated in this by Fred Bishop and Dritt, who in the early spring of 1853 started using Canadian snowshoes—and these pioneers had been succeeded by George Pierce, using the same equipment, before Thompson came along with his ten foot Norwegian skis.[15]

The memory of that famous old stage driver, Hank Monk, has been kept perennially green by the periodic recrudescence of that moth-eaten old story about the wild ride he gave Horace Greeley from Carson City to Placerville, to enable his distinguished passenger to arrive in time to deliver his scheduled address at the latter place, when he bounced Greeley about so violently that at last his head shot up through the roof of the stagecoach. Hank Monk was unquestionably one of the Overland's most distinguished whips, and he was also one of the road's most distinguished drinkers. In all probability he dreamed up the yarn on one of those occasions when he was so befuddled that he gave his team a drink of whiskey and watered himself,[16] but he made such a good story out of it that it had become current along the road as early as 1865, five years after the episode is alleged to have happened.[17] And it has continued to be current to the present day, despite the fact that in 1872 Mark Twain emphatically denied its authenticity.[18] As far as can be ascertained, the only true part of the story is that Monk drove Greeley from Carson City over the Sierra Nevada, but it was in one of the Salt Lake Mail wagons, not in a stage-coach. Furthermore, the trip was not to Placerville but to the Eight Mile House, where a committee met the traveler and transferred him to one of the California Stage Company's coaches, and thus, behind six gray horses, he was conveyed in triumph to the Cary House, in Placer-ville.[19] Whether the story is true or not, Horace Greeley, like Queen Victoria, was not amused, and the yarn may have contributed to his defeat for the presidency in 1872. Before the election Monk is said to have written Greeley reminding his one-time passenger of their famous ride, and suggesting that as a token of appreciation he be given some not too onerous but well paid government post. To this Greeley replied as follows:

"I would rather see you ten thousand fathoms in hell than give you even a crust of bread. For you are the only man who ever had it in his power to put me in a ridiculous light before the American people, and you villainously exercised that power."[20]

This story is so well entrenched as one of those hoary old traditional frauds referred to earlier, that no reference to Horace Greeley's trip to California would be considered complete without some mention of it being made. But another of Hank's alleged feats does not seem to have been so well publicized.

Back in 1861 the judges who followed Governor James W. Nye to

Nevada are said to have been so open minded in their decisions that it is quite understandable why the bailiff announced the opening of the Territorial Supreme Court in this wise: "Oyez, oyez, oyez. The Honorable the Supreme Court of the Territory of Nevada is now in session. God help the people of the Territory of Nevada!"[21] One night Hank Monk was carrying one of these judicial luminaries, and being behind time (and no doubt full of local tarantula juice) he was pouring the leather into his six-horse team, and snaking the stage on two wheels around hairpin mountain turns in the pitch-dark in a way that not only ruffled the dignity of his passenger but also frightened him out of his boots. Expostulations proving in vain, the judge finally shouted out asking if the driver did not know who he was carrying, and threatened to have him discharged for endangering his life. Hank replied with another volley of whip cracks, and yelled back over his shoulder: "Sure I know who you are, but I'm going to take this coach into Carson City on time if it kills every one-horse judge in the Territory!"[22]

One of the choicest tales about the Overland road is that it was completed to provide a highway over which troops of the Confederate States of America could march to capture California. At the outbreak of the Civil War General Albert Sidney Johnston was in command of the United States forces on the Pacific Coast, and the fact that he was a Southerner, together with the similarity of names, seems to have given rise to this interesting story. According to this, General Johnston used Northern troops to hurry the completion of the grade up the eastern escarpment of the Sierra Nevada, intending to use the road to move Confederate artillery across the mountains to seize California and turn it into a Southern state. Needless to say, there is no shadow of truth in the fantastic tale, that was doubtless bred of the uncertainties and fears of the early days of the war. Even if General Johnston had wished to do this, it is difficult to imagine his marching Southern troops all the way across the United States, and this entirely apart from the fact that the Confederacy had no troops available for any such hair-brained scheme. General Johnston was an ideal soldier and a gentleman in the fullest sense of the word, and as long as he held his commission in the United States Army no act of his could in any way be construed as even hinting at disloyalty to the flag he served.

An interesting sidelight on the development of the road is that in

1854 it was in all seriousness proposed to use camels as means of rapid transportation, and when six years later the Pony Express was inaugurated it was the outgrowth of this original idea. On the strength of an appropriation made in that year by the United States Congress for the purchase of camels for military transportation, William N. Walton petitioned the legislature of California for a concession to operate a transcontinental mail and express service into the state, and asked for title to five quarter sections of public land to be used for stations on the proposed route. He guaranteed that within twelve months of the granting of the concession he would establish terminal stations on the Atlantic and Pacific seaboards, and have in operation a regularly scheduled line of camels and dromedaries all the way across the continent. His memorial was accompanied by many citations of the speed and endurance of camels used in desert countries in other parts of the world for like purposes, but nothing was said about how the unfortunate beasts' foot-pads were supposed to adapt themselves to the rocky trail across the Sierra Nevada. Or, for that matter, the equally rocky trails leading to that point. In 1858 the United States government actually tried camels on the southern route to California, and in 1861 dromedaries were used for a while in Nevada to transport salt from the marshes on Walker River to the mills at Virginia City, but both experiments resulted in failure.[23]

The recital of such stories could be continued almost indefinitely, but the foregoing will suffice to give an idea of the colorful tales which are part of the road.

"And now, for a more intimate picture of the route, let us make a trip over the great Overland as far as Placerville, at the time that saw its greatest activity, and stop at the many inns which lined that part of its wayside. Actually, this activity began in 1849 and all but ended in 1869, and during these two decades stopping places appeared and vanished, and their places were taken by new inns, none of which have survived. The scene covers twenty years, and to view it both in retrospect and in the future, let us select a median date for our trip, say at the end of July, 1859. By that time the highway was open throughout its length, the stages were running regularly, the Pony Express was preparing to gallop across the plains in eight days, and the Washoe silver excitement was approaching its climax."

DINNER AT STRAWBERRY

188

Chapter 17.[1] Sacramento to Placerville*

O UR TRIP over the great bullion highway will be at the time when stagecoach service was settling down to schedules which compared not unfavorably to modern railway timetables. We propose looking both backward and forward as we proceed on our way. Before our departure from Sacramento it will be interesting to see what the transportation situation was some seven years earlier, when the service was beginning to take shape. No better picture of this exists than the account written by J. D. Borthwick, an English traveler and gold miner, of the beginning of his trip from Sacramento to Hangtown early in the spring of 1852:[2]

"My stay in Sacramento on this occasion was limited to a few hours. I went to a large hotel, which was also the great staging-house,[3] and here I snoozed till about five o'clock, when, it being still quite dark, the whole house woke up into active life. About a hundred of us breakfasted by candlelight, and, going out into the barroom while the day was just dawning, we found, turned out in front of the hotel, about four-and-twenty four-horse coaches, all bound for different places in the mines. The street was completely blocked up with them, and crowds of men were taking their seats, while others were fortifying themselves for their journey at the bar.

"The coaches were of various kinds. Some were light-spring-wagons—mere oblong boxes, with four or five seats placed across them; others were of the same build, but better finished, and covered by an awning; and there were also numbers of regular American stage-coaches, huge high-hung things which carry nine inside upon three seats, the middle one of which is between the two doors.

"The place which I had intended should be the scene of my first mining exploit, was ... Hangtown ... I soon found the stage for that place—it happened to be one of the oblong boxes—and, pitching in my roll of blankets, I took my seat and lighted my pipe that I might the more fully enjoy the scene around me ...

"The teams were all headed the same way, and with their stages, four or five abreast, occupied the whole of the wide street for a distance of sixty or seventy yards. The horses were restive, and pawing, and snorting, and kicking; and passengers were trying to navigate to their proper stages through the labyrinth of wheels and horses, and frequently climbing over half-a-dozen wagons to shorten their journey. Grooms were standing at the leaders' heads, trying to keep them

---

*via the White Rock Road

quiet, and the drivers were sitting on their boxes, or seats rather, for they scorn a high seat, and were swearing at each other in a very shocking manner, as wheels got locked, and wagons were backed into the teams behind them, to the discomfiture of the passengers on the back-seats, who found horses' heads knocking the pipes out of their mouths. In the intervals of their little private battles, the drivers were shouting to the crowds of passengers who loitered about the front of the hotel ... before resigning all control over their motions, and charging with their precious persons a coach or a train, on full cock, and ready to go off, and shoot them out upon some remote part of creation.

"On each wagon was painted the name of the place to which it ran; the drivers were also bellowing it out to the crowd, and even among such a confusion of coaches a man could have no difficulty in finding the one he wanted ... but in this go-ahead country, people who had to go were not allowed to remain inert till the spirit moved them to go; they had to be 'hurried up'; and of the whole crowd of men who were standing about the hotel, or struggling through the maze of wagons, only one half were passengers, the rest were 'runners' for the various stages, who were exhausting all their persuasive eloquence in entreating the passengers to take their seats and go. They were all mixed up with the crowd, and each was exerting his lungs to the utmost. 'Now then, gentlemen,' shouts one of them, 'all aboard for Nevada City! Who's agoin? only three seats left—the last chance to-day for Nevada City—take you there in five hours. Who's there for Nevada City?' Then catching sight of some man who betrays the very slightest appearance of helplessness, or of not knowing what he is about, he pounces upon him, saying 'Nevada City, sir?—this way—just in time,' and seizing him by the arm, he drags him into the crowd of stages, and almost has him bundled into that for Nevada City before the poor devil can make it understood that it is Caloma he wants to go to, and not Nevada City. His captor then calls out to some one of his brother runners who is collecting passengers for Caloma—'Oh Bill! oh Bill! where the - - - - are you?' 'Hullo!' says Bill from the other end of the crowd. 'Here's a man for Caloma!' shouts the other, still holding on to his prize in case he should escape before Bill comes up to take charge of him.

"This sort of thing was going on all the time. It was very ridiculous. Apparently, if a hundred men wanted to go anywhere, it required a hundred more to dispatch them. There was certainly no danger of any one being left behind; on the contrary, the probability was, that any weak-minded man who happened to be passing, would be shipped off to parts unknown before he could collect his ideas ...

"However, I was not thinking of this while sitting on the Hangtown stage. I had too much to look at, and some of my neighbors also took up my attention. I found seated around me a varied assortment of human nature. A New Yorker, a Yankee, and an English Jack-tar were my immediate neighbors, and a general conversation helped to beguile the time till the 'runners' had succeeded in placing a passenger upon every available spot of every wagon. There was no trouble about luggage—that is an article not much known in California. Some stray individuals might have had a small carpet-bag — almost every man had his blankets — and the western men were further encumbered with their long rifles, the barrels poking into everybody's eyes, and the butts in the way of everybody's toes.

"At last the solid mass of four-horse coaches began to dissolve. The drivers gathered up their reins and settled themselves down in their seats, cracked their whips, and swore at their horses; the grooms cleared out the best way they could; the passengers shouted and hurraed; the teams in front set off at a gallop; the rest followed them as soon as they got room to start, and chevied them up the street, all in a body, for about half a mile, when, as soon as we got out of town, we spread out in all directions to every point of a semi-circle, and in a few minutes I found myself one of a small isolated community, with which four splendid horses were galloping over the plains like mad. No hedges, no ditches, no houses, no road in fact — it was all a vast open plain, as smooth as a calm ocean. We might have been steering by compass, and it was like going to sea; for we emerged from the city as from a landlocked harbour, and followed our own course over the wide wide world . . .

"We made a straight course of it across the plains, for about thirty miles, changing horses occasionally at some of the numerous wayside inns, and passing numbers of wagons drawn by teams of six or eight mules or oxen, and laden with supplies for the mines . . .

"The road, which, though in some places very narrow, for the most part spread out to two or three times the width of an ordinary road, was covered with stumps and large rocks; it was full of deep ruts and hollows, and roots of trees spread all over it.

"To anyone not used to such roads or to such driving, an upset would have seemed inevitable. If there was safety in speed, however, we were safe enough, and all sense of danger was lost in admiration of the coolness and dexterity of the driver as he circumvented every obstacle, but without going one inch farther than necessary out of his way to save us from perdition. He went through extraordinary bodily contortion, which would have shocked an English coachman out of his propriety; but, at the same time, he performed such feats as no one would have dared to attempt who had never been used to anything worse than an English road. With his right foot he managed a break, and, clawing at the reins with both hands, he swayed his body from side to side to preserve his equilibrium, as now on the right pair of wheels, now on the left, he cut the 'outside edge' round a stump or a rock; and when coming to a spot where he was going to execute a difficult maneuver on a piece of road which slanted violently down to one side, he trimmed the wagon as one would a small boat in a squall, and made us all crowd up to the weather side to prevent a capsize."[4]

Our own departure from Sacramento will be on July 30th of 1859, and it will not be attended by quite so much commotion as marked the beginning of Borthwick's trip to Hangtown, seven years earlier. At the time of our trip there were thirty-eight hotels in the city,[5] but we will refer to only two of these. The Orleans Hotel, the successor of the Crescent City as Sacramento's staging center, had been closed three months earlier, and the stage companies' offices moved next door to the Union Hotel, that in 1854 had been rebuilt on the site of the old Verandah, on 2nd Street between J and K.[6]

After an early breakfast at the Union we take our places in the Pioneer Stage Line's four-horse Concord stage that is standing in front of the hotel, and at about half-past six we are off at a brisk trot, swinging around the corner of 2nd into J Street. In 1853 this street had been planked to 12th, from where the celebrated "Plank Road," paved with three and one-half inch Oregon fir planks by The Sacramento Plank Road and Turnpike Company in the same year, continues eastward along the south bank of the American River to Patterson's as part of the later location of the Coloma road.[7]

At mile 2.25 we pass on the right the ruins of Sutter's Fort and on the left, Travelers Rest Hotel established by Mark Stewart as a cloth house in 1849. This is at the end of the immigrant trail on the south bank of the American River about a mile from Sutter's Fort. Stewart's great grandson, Edward A. Sprague, tells us that the tent was replaced by a building constructed with the boards from Sutter's tanning vats. A short distance from this we come to the Oak Tree House. All that is known about the place is that a few years earlier its proprietor (who was also a jeweler) was twice assaulted and robbed by drunken miscreants.[8]

At 5:25 on the afternoon of April 13, 1860, Sutter's Fort (or to be more exact, a block north of the ruins, and on J Street) was the scene of Sacramento's reception of Russell, Majors & Company's first westbound Pony Express, that had galloped out of St. Joseph, Missouri, ten days earlier. The rider was Sam Hamilton, who on April 4th had ridden the first westbound Pony from Sacramento to Placerville in three hours fifty-five minutes, his westbound trip being accomplished in twenty-five minutes less time.[9]

A word of explanation is now in order regarding the distances from Sacramento by which many of the inns and stopping places were known.* As has been said, the Overland road saw many changes of

---

*The distances between points were later verified by the use of an automobile speedometer.

alignment before it settled down to its final location, and before this happened distances from place to place were either guessed at or roughly measured along its earlier locations. Later on, when the latter were either shortened or lengthened, many of the stopping places had become so well known by their original designations, such as the so-and-so mile house, that these names were retained, regardless of the fact that in many cases the new alignment of the road altered the distances from Sacramento by as much as two miles or so, plus or minus. An example of this occurs at the very beginning of our trip. It appears that at first distances east of Sacramento were reckoned from Sutter's Fort, and later on from the city's staging center on 2nd Street, between J and K, or from the *Embarcadero*, on the river front. The Fort is about two miles east of the river, and consequently the stopping places which retained their original mileage designations, such as the Eight Mile House on the Coloma road, were actually some two miles farther east than their names indicated. On our trip the old names will be used, and in each case the approximately correct mileage will be given along the road followed, as this was located in or about 1859.

At the Fort the road we have followed thus far forked, the right-hand branch being a continuation of Sutter's original road from the *Embarcadero* to his headquarters. In a general way this road followed Sacramento's present L Street, which is, therefore, the city's oldest thoroughfare. At the Fort this route became the western end of the original road that Sutter built in 1847 to the sawmill Marshall was constructing for him at Coloma, on the South Fork of the American River. To avoid the flood waters, the old road bore off south and northeast from the Fort for about 5.00 miles, and the first 3.25 miles of its alignment is now closely followed by United States Highway 50. At mile 5.00 it crossed the present Southern Pacific Railroad at about Manlove, and continued northeast for another 6.50 miles as the original location of the old Placerville road, and in so far as is known there were no roadhouses along this portion of the route. By 1859 a levee had been built along the south bank of the American River, and with this the original western end of the Coloma and Placerville road was relocated, and we will now follow this route.

Continuing past the Fort, and along the extension of J Street, at mile 4.00 we pass the Marion ranch, and on the left the abandoned site of

Norristown, or Hoboken. This settlement was laid out by Samuel Norris in February of 1850, on the high ground which forms the south bank of the American River at this point, when despite its founder's having hopefully advertised the place as "New Sacramento," the only building put up at the time was the Four Mile House. The great floods of 1852 and 1853 cut off all communication between Sacramento and the interior, and as river steamers were then able to navigate as far as Norristown, the merchants of the former city established temporary stores at that settlement, when the place was rechristened Hoboken.[10] By 1853 two other inns had been opened, the Hoboken House and the Saline House,[11] but by the time of our arrival these places had disappeared, together with all other signs of the settlement's ephemeral importance as the one-time distributing point for all the towns and mines east of Sacramento.

From Hoboken we continue along the river bank, and our next stop is at the Magnolia or Five Mile House, where some sort of a stopping place is said to have been opened as early as 1849.[12] In 1856 A. B. Gilbert purchased the Magnolia property, including the Five Mile House, and on April 13, 1860, Sam Hamilton, the rider of the first westbound Pony Express, made his last change of horses here before galloping into Sacramento.[13] On June 14, 1863, the place burned down. It was rebuilt, only to be destroyed by a second fire on July 31st of the same year that ended its existence.[14]

Our road now swings northeast, around a bend in the river, and at about mile 5.50 we pass through the original site of Brighton, that was named after Brighton, England.[15] The place was founded in 1849 by a group of Sacramento speculators, the principal of whom appears to have been a Volcano mine owner and sportsman, who, while he is referred to simply as "Colonel D," may have been an Englishman named Charles Denman, as will be seen presently.[16]

The first stopping place in Brighton was a willow pole and canvas shelter put up in 1849 by Lewis B. Meyers, where he served meals and drinks.[17] By June, 1851, "Colonel D" appears to have been the owner of the town, where, apart from a race track and one or two stables, little development had been done.[18] About this time, or perhaps a little earlier, the founders of Brighton built the Pavilion Hotel at a cost of over $30,000, and at the time this was described as being "one of the handsomest and most commodious hotels in this section of the state, and until recently the 'Burnham's' of Sacramento."[19] On the Fourth of July, 1850, the Pavilion was the scene of a public dinner and ball, which were attended by California's first governor, Peter H. Burnett, Captain Sutter, and all the other outstanding personages of Sacramento. During the dinner the fun waxed so fast and furious, and the diners became so full of alcoholic patriotism, that there were several near fist-fights before the celebration was concluded, but this eventually ended with a general amnesty and in good-fellowship.[20] In 1852 the Pavilion was being operated by the Charles Denman referred to earlier, and on October 13th of that year the place was totally destroyed by fire, together with the stables and other outbuildings and appurtenances.[21]

When the Pavilion burned John and George Berry built a new place in Brighton that was also known as the Five Mile House, but this was closed in 1856, as in 1852 defective land titles caused the settlement to be abandoned, and it was not until 1861 that the present town of the same name was established on the Sacramento Valley Railroad.[22]

During this time there was another stopping place in Brighton that is worthy of mention. This was a tavern kept by James Allen[23] a short distance east of the Pavilion, that was the scene of the bloody culmination of Sacramento's "Squatters' Riot." On August 15, 1850, Sheriff Joseph McKinney learned that several individuals said to have been implicated in the rioting on the 14th were in Brighton. In the evening the sheriff and a posse of some twenty men galloped out to the Five Mile House, but failing to find any squatters they proceeded toward the Pavilion, and en route were told that the men they were looking for were at Allen's. McKinney entered the bar alone, and seeing eight or ten men in an adjoining room ordered them to lay down their arms and surrender. His demand was met by a fusillade of shots, when the posse rushed into the bar and a general melee ensued. The sheriff, who was standing in the door, was mortally wounded by a discharge of buckshot, when his murderer was instantly killed by one of the posse. Two other squatters, Kelly and Henshaw, who were firing from behind the bar, were also killed, and Allen, the proprietor, was wounded but managed to make his escape. Four prisoners were taken, and with this the rioting ended.[24]

Just east of Brighton, we pass the site of a roadhouse that in June,

1851, was being operated by a man named Crockett[25] and his wife, and Frank Marryat's description of this place and its host cannot be improved on:

"We stopped for breakfast at a house of entertainment kept by one Crockett, who had a very pretty wife; but the possession of this luxury, so far from humanizing Crockett, appeared to keep him in a constant fever of irritation; for he was jealous, poor fellow! and used to worry himself because there was ever a dozen or two of hairy miners gazing in a bewildered manner at Mrs. C.; but, if report speaks truly, the bonnet and boot of a 'female' had been successfully exhibited in this region at a dollar a head (a glimpse of them being thought cheap even at that price), surely, therefore, Crockett might have excused the poor miners for regarding attentively the original article when presented gratis in the shape of a pretty woman.

"Crockett carried a revolver of disproportunate size, he not being a large man, and this instrument he occasionally used upon provocation. A great number of miners had looked at Mrs. Crockett on the morning of our arrival, and her husband had not quite finished foaming at the mouth in consequence, when we entered the house. It was some time before he condescended to be civil; but having at length informed us that was 'so riled that his skin cracked,' he added that he was a 'devilish good fellow when he was *right side up*, and commanded us to drink with him. After this he procured us a most excellent breakfast, and, on the strength of our respectable appearance, allowed Mrs. Crockett to preside at this repast, which she did in a nervous manner, as if momentarily under the expectation of being shot."[26]

Continuing northeast, our road now converges toward the track of the Sacramento Valley Railroad, and at about mile 8.00 we come to the St. Louis House. All that is known about this place is that on September 27, 1852, the Whigs of Brighton Precinct met there and elected their delegates, and on February 21, 1853, Mr. D. Williamson, a guest at the house, was robbed of $2,100, the money being extracted from under his pillow.[27]

At mile 9.25 we stop at the Nine Mile House, that is said to have been built in 1850 by Nathan J. Stevens, and conducted by him until his death in 1875.[28] But as the same authority states elsewhere that this (or perhaps another Nine Mile House) was built in the same year by Israel Luce,[29] and again, that the place was kept by Charles Malby,[30] it is difficult to arrive at the truth of the matter. However this may have been, according to local report, in 1910 a two-story Nine Mile House stood on the south side of the road, with its large barn across the road. The barn collapsed during the winter of 1937–38.[31] Early in 1853 the earth used to fill and grade the streets of Sacramento was dug hereabouts and hauled nine miles into the city,[32] a civic undertaking that may or may not have had some connection with what follows.

Three-quarters of a mile farther on we reach the end of the Plank Road (at what is today the northern end of the modern Bradshaw Road), and Arnold D. Patterson's ranch and Ten Mile House. Here in December of 1849 Patterson put up a cloth-covered pole shelter that he called the American Fork House. This quickly became so well patronized as a stopping place that in the following year he replaced his original tent by a frame building that is said to have cost $40,000, the high price of labor involved in its construction having been due to an epidemic of cholera then raging in Sacramento.[33] In 1852 Patterson was elected sheriff of Sacramento County, and as has been said, immediately thereafter the Plank Road was built to his place, when this at once became the popular roadside resort for the people of Sacramento.[34] During the flood of 1852 Patterson's place achieved the distinction of being the highest point on the American River ever reached by a steamship, when Captain Albert Foster, of the Steam Navigation Company, piloted a small steamer (that may have been the *Cleopatra*) that far up the river.[35] Patterson continued to live on his ranch until 1856, when he moved to Folsom and operated the Patterson House there. In 1868 he returned to his ranch and built a house on the railway, due south of his ranch and three-quarters of a mile south of Routier Station. This place burned in the fall of 1870, and in the following winter Patterson moved to Routier, where he built a new place.[36]

In 1846 William A. Leidesdorff, of Yerba Buena, built an *adobe* house on his land grant in this locality and about a quarter of a mile east of what later came to be known as Routier Station. This still remained a stopping place after Leidesdorff's death on May 18, 1848. In November, 1849, William G. Johnson says that he was there served the worst meal he remembers ever having eaten, the repast consisting of cold victuals and cold tea, the evening being colder and wetter than what he was served.[37] In June, 1853, Joseph Routier settled there in the old *adobe*, and in 1880 he was still using this as a kitchen.[38] Today no trace is to be found of any of these places, and the foregoing will explain the various references to Leidesdorff's, the American Fork House, or Hotel, and the Halfway House (between Sacramento and Folsom), that otherwise are somewhat more than confusing.

At about mile 11.00 the road again forks. The left-hand branch continues up the river as Sutter's old Coloma road, that we will later follow through Folsom to Placerville, and the right-hand branch turns due east to cross the railway at what was originally known as Hangtown Crossing, and is today Mills Station.[39] The relocation of the old Placerville road represented by this crossing was put in operation after the construction of the railway and subsequent to 1854,[40] when it superseded that portion of the original alignment described earlier, and we will continue our trip along this route.

On the east side of the track at Hangtown Crossing a two-story roadhouse was kept by Louis Lepetit,[41] and were we to return a century later we would find the same house on the *west* side of the track, as well established and sedate as if it had always stood there. Lepetit must have operated his place in the late 50's or early 60's, and local tradition has it that the house was moved across the track sometime in the 80's. An artistic bronze plaque, set in a granite monument in front of the building as it stands today, bears the following inscription:

"To the Memory of the Riders of the Pony Express
— 1860-1861 — the First Relay out of Sutter's Fort."

The Pony Express was discontinued on October 25, 1861,[42] and, therefore, the above refers to the building as it stood originally, on the east side of the track. But as will be seen, the first (and only) rider relay station in California was forty-five miles east of Hangtown Crossing, and the first remount station was at the Five Mile House, so the historical accuracy of the foregoing statement is open to question. Furthermore, it was only a short time after the inauguration of the service when the Pony route west of Placerville was changed to the Green Valley–Mormon Island road, and thereafter Folsom was the Pony riders' terminus, from where the express was carried to Sacramento by the Sacramento Valley Railroad. This brings up the subject of the number of Pony Express stations which appear to have broken out like a rash between Sacramento and Genoa, in Nevada.

To begin with, there were two types of stations: remount, and rider relay stations. Of the latter there was but one in California, and this was at Sportsman's Hall,[43] twelve miles east of Placerville and fifty-six miles from Sacramento, and this was not changed during the life of the Pony Express. Remount stations, however, were changed from time to time as the schedule of the service settled down, as well as when the route followed by the Pony shifted from one location of the Overland road to another. This accounts for the otherwise puzzling number and location of these stations, and as we proceed on our trip we will pass some of them, when the situation will be made clearer.

At Hangtown Crossing we begin the gradual ascent from the river valley, and at this point an excellent idea could be obtained of the immense amount of traffic the Overland carried when this activity was at its height. The road is visible as far as the Prairie House, some nine miles to the east, and at the time referred to an almost continuous line of vehicles of every nature could be seen, from light two-horse wagons to great prairie schooners, drawn by a dozen or more yoke of oxen or teams of mules. So continuous was the stream of traffic that it was not unusual for the freighting outfits to follow each other so closely that the noses of the leading teams bumped against the tailboards of the preceding wagons, and where the road was narrow, if a teamster was forced to pull off to one side it might be a whole day before an opening in the line permitted him to return to the road. In addition to this, there were numberless pack trains of from twenty mules upward, carrying loads to the mines, and the travelers afoot and on horseback were literally legion.[44] What the tonnage of freight totaled, and how many passengers passed back and forth over the road, there is no means of telling. With wagons carrying up to 16,000 pounds and mules packing 300 pounds apiece, together with the fact that in 1852 there were no less than 67,000 new arrivals by sea at San Francisco alone, and that most of these were bound for the mines, the figures would be amazing.[45]

We are now on what was known as "the prairie," and for the next thirty miles our route follows the general line of the old Carson Pass immigrant road. At mile 13.50 we pass the point where the original Placerville road branches off to the southwest, and half a mile farther on reach George Hanlon's stock ranch and farm, where his two-story place was the first roadhouse east of Hangtown Crossing. From this point for the next six miles the prairie sweeps gradually upward in long, low undulations of undisturbed land, and our vista is unobstructed for at least that distance. This is in 1859, but today the road at this point enters the mouth of what almost amounts to a canyon, whose walls are composed of water-worn boulders, stones and gravel, heaped up on both sides to a height of twenty or thirty feet by the huge dredging machines that are still grunting and rumbling high above the level of the road, as they bring up the gold-bearing gravel from the bed of the great Tertiary river channel that in Eocene or Miocene times spread out here after emerging from the mountainous country to the eastward. George Hanlon's place, together with all but one of the other old stopping places as far as the Prairie House, was long ago engulfed under this man-made mountain of worked-over material, and the only landmarks of a century ago that are to be seen today are the occasional moldering ruins of the foundations of what at the time of our trip were thriving roadside establishments.

Our next stop is at the Fifteen Mile House, that we reach at almost exactly mile 15.00. The house stands on the south side of the road, and in 1855 it was being operated by A. M. Plummer.[46] In 1857 the house and land were purchased by Henry Frederick William Deterding, who

FifTEEN MiLE HousE owned by H. F. W. Deterding

improved and enlarged the place to make it one of the popular inns between Sacramento and Placerville. The Fifteen Mile House was typical of the larger roadside stopping places, and was a two-story building. On the ground floor was a large dining room, kitchen, parlor, bar, and dance hall, and there were eight or nine bedrooms upstairs. Two of the stage companies had barns here where they kept their horses, and this was the second Pony Express remount station during the early days of the service. It was not customary for either the stages or freighting outfits to stop here overnight, and when they did beds cost fifty cents a night, and meals fifty cents each.[47] Deterding ran the Fifteen Mile House until his death in 1875, and thereafter his son, Charles William, kept it open until as late as 1890.[48] The site of the old roadhouse is in a small level space between towering piles of dredged-out boulders, and no sign of the place is to be seen today.

A quarter of a mile farther on we come to the Missouri House, where many of the freighting outfits were wont to spend the night.[49] The place stood on the north side of the road, and today its site is marked by a slight depression in the ground, that was the inn's cellar.

PLEASANT GROVE HOUSE of George K. and John Ney

At about mile 15.50 we pass the second Oak Tree House, standing on the south side of the road. This place was bought in 1854 by Vincent Hatch, who owned it until 1861, renting to James M. Enos during part of this time, when as many as one hundred teams stopped there over-night. The inn took its name from a white oak standing in front of the house and on the north side of the road,[50] and today the gaunt old tree is all that marks its site.

We next stop at George K. and John Ney's ranch known as the Pleasant Grove House, on the north side of the road, at mile 18.00. This was later the site of the Pleasant Grove School,[51] and is today covered by a mountain of dredging debris, a few eucalyptus trees being the only evidence left of either place.

Half a mile beyond we come to a roadhouse and dairy owned by Pete Haase, who was known as "Six-toed Pete" because of an extra toe on one of his feet. Apart from cattle and sheep ranching, Haase worked a placer mine right on his home place, and where a hundred years ago his sluice boxes were recovering a modest amount of gold,[52] today one of the dredges of The Capital Dredging Company is operating high above the level where he worked. His old two-story house is still standing on the south side of the road and is now the field office of the dredging company.

At about mile 19.00 we reach the Western House, standing on the south side of the road. This place was owned by George Sherman, and later passed into the hands of his nephew, Benjamin Franklin Briggs, who was formerly a conductor on the Sacramento Valley Railroad.[53] In January of 1852 a twenty-two-pound "prairie salmon" was caught in a streamlet draining into the American River and crossed by our road at this point, an occurrence that was so unusual that it was com-mented on by the *Sacramento Daily Union* of January 26th. In the following year placer gold was found in such quantities about the Western House that several hundred miners were shortly at work there. One experienced miner stated that the diggings would not be worked out for fifty years, a forecast that began to be borne out a few years later, when the Prairie or Western Ditch Company built a ditch (portions of which are still to be seen) from Deer and Carson creeks to the Western House,[54] and is today confirmed by the dredging oper-ations being carried on as far east as this point.

LODGINGS about 1855

204

Chapter 18. Sacramento to Placerville*

At The Western House our road begins to ascend the rolling foothills which gradually blend into the increasingly mountainous country to the east, and here end the immense piles of dredger debris which today hem in the route we are traveling.

Our next stop, at mile 20.50, is at the Prairie House. It stands on the south side of the road on a high knoll some three hundred yards east of the intersection of the road from Folsom to Michigan Bar and Jackson. The location is a beautiful one that commands sweeping vistas to the south and west and is, moreover, a very practical site for a roadhouse. The Sacramento road can be seen for miles, and the dust clouds raised by approaching vehicles enable the innkeeper to calculate the approximate number of guests he will be called on to serve. This, by the way, is the reason why so many roadhouses of those days were located on hilltops, at the summit of grades.

In 1851 the Prairie House was operated by Lucius Ripley Beckley,[1] and thereafter, until 1858, it was managed by Almon Vedder, who then returned to his home in Deerfield, Illinois.[2] Late in July of 1852 the place was the scene of an abortive robbery, when a man named Ibbiddesher stopped there on his way to Sacramento for dinner, and was trusting enough to leave $1,600 in his wagon. On his return the money was missing, and for some reason one Joseph Sweet was suspected of being the thief. The accused vehemently protested his innocence until threatened with an immediate application of Judge Lynch's drastic law, when he broke down and showed where he had buried the money in a wood close to the inn.[3] Today the only evidences of the Prairie House are a few half-obliterated foundations, a gnarled old fig tree, and half a dozen decaying locust trees.

At mile 21.00 we reach the What Cheer House standing on the south side of the road. About the time of our arrival it was being run by Mrs. Elizabeth Manning. The place was later occupied by Joseph Tom-

---

*via the White Rock Road, continued

linson, or old "Uncle Joe," as he was familiarly called by his neigh-bors,[4] and today a depression that was the cellar, and four old trees, are all that mark the site.

A mile farther on is one of the oldest inns on our route, the Welling-ton House, twenty-two miles east of Sacramento.[5] This two-story house also stands on the south side of the road, and opposite are the barns, corrals, and quarters for the hired hands. It is a favorite stopping place for teamsters, as according to their calculations it is just halfway between Sacramento and Placerville. As a matter of fact they are only in error by a quarter of a mile! Due to this, the name of the place was later changed to the Halfway House, and in the fall of 1863 the prop-erty was purchased by John E. Butler.[6] The house where we stop was burned in 1936, and the present building was erected thereafter.[7] To day the only vestige of the old roadhouse is a slight depression where the cellar was located, west of the entrance road to the new building.

After crossing the site of the 1864 track of the Sacramento & Placer-ville Railroad, and at mile 23.25, we come to White Rock Springs, a name derived from a small, isolated cropping of white "bull-quartz" on the hillside, a short distance north of the road, and a spring enclosed by a small stone house on the south side. A few rods beyond the spring on the north side of the road, we stop at the White Rock Springs Ranch Hotel that, together with the ranch, was purchased by William Chapman in the fall of 1850, and at the time of our arrival was being run by Mrs. Chapman's second husband, M. J. Wilkinson. In 1871 Mrs. Wilkinson won a $20,000 prize in the Mercantile Library Lottery, of San Francisco, when she and her family moved to Sacramento, and sometime after 1880 she sold the property to Samuel Euer. The first stopping place at White Rock is said to have been a canvas tent, where miners on their way to the diggings used to put up for the night, and from this humble beginning the place grew to be one of the favorite taverns on the old Overland.[8]

At mile 24.00 we come to the site of the Aldridge Ravine House, on the south side of the road, that in about 1857 was being run by James Douglas,[9] and where a few cottonwoods on the north side of the road mark its site. Half a mile beyond we pass the Bar E ranch, that was known as the Dennis Phillip Bence property, and in 1864 was acquired by Samuel Euer.[10] This is still a thriving cattle ranch, and is being oper-ated by Robert S. Euer.

The Carson River House is our next stop, at mile 25.50. The place is on the north side of the road and on the bank of Carson Creek, a tributary of the Cosumnes River. In 1854 its proprietor was a man named Paris. Beyond this nothing is known of its history.[11] Here begins the transition zone between the low, rolling foothills and the mountain country, and our road now winds through ravines and over grades that lead upward to the increasingly rugged western ascent of the Sierra Nevada.

At this point the public road we have been following swings north and east from the present highway, that continues along the location of James Tong's old toll road, whose tollhouse is in Clarksville. This is the beginning of the series of toll roads mentioned earlier, and altogether there were fifteen or more of these between Sacramento and the Nevada state line. They paralleled the public roads at varying distances, often crossing these back and forth, and while they were generally a little longer than the latter, their grades were somewhat less steep and they were better maintained. These toll roads were operated as private enterprises for a matter of forty years, and it was not until 1889 that they were declared public highways.[12]

At about mile 26.00 we reach the Mormon Tavern, another of the oldest stopping places on our route. In 1848 or 1849 a Mormon named Morgan is said to have opened a place here, and in the latter year John Ingalls wrote the following description of his overnight experiences at this establishment:

"We started [from Sacramento] on the 18th [of December, 1849] ... & came on the way ten miles. It was so muddy that we were obliged to come very slow with our packed mules. The next day it commenced raining at about noon but we succeeded in getting 18 miles farther on our journey & stopped for the night at Mormon tavern. O how it rained that night. If we had had a tight roof I should have cared nothing for it but truly a respectable rail-fence would have made a splendid roof compared to the one we had. We bought barley for our mules for the low price of one dollar a quart & a little cold tea for ourselves for two dollars each & then as we could not get within a rod of the fire we made up our minds to turn in & get warm. There was such a crowd in the house, the berths were all taken up so we had to spread our blankets on the ground, I should say in the mud for the mud was nearly ankle deep on the ground. We were obliged to cover up our heads as well as our bodies for the rain came down in torrents. I had just got into the house when a man stepped square on my head in getting into his berth. I should have thought that rather rough treatment at home but we don't mind such little things in California. We got our shins stepped on several times with remarkably heavy boots containing a pair of feet not *very light* but aside from these *little* inconveniences we got through the night very well. The next morning it rained equally hard but at about nine A.M. we packed up for I was determined not to pass another night in that house."[13]

About 1851 the place seems to have been remodeled and enlarged,[14] when it was kept by John Beaver and later by Franklin F. Winchell, who owned the tavern for many years, and is its host at the time of our arrival. The dining room is about one hundred feet in length, and it is not unusual for all its tables to be occupied by teamsters, while still more wait for a second and even third serving.[15] Sometime in the early 70's the Mormon Tavern was the scene of a dance and general celebration, whose tragic ending was the result of a practical joke played by James K. Page. He was one of those present who had celebrated far too well, and in the course of the evening it occurred to him that it would be a rare jest to put croton oil in the coffee. This resulted in the deaths of three men, and Charles W. Deterding (to whom we owe many of the reminiscences of those days) almost died from the effects of the "joke."[16] Page seems to have progressed from practical jokes to grim earnestness, and was finally hanged at Placerville on August 10, 1883, for the murder of an unknown man in New York Ravine, near Folsom.[17] The tavern was a stage station, and the year after our visit it became the third remount station for the Pony Express riders at the beginning of this service. At a later date it came into the possession of Joseph Joerger, Sr., and is today operated as a cattle ranch by his son, Joseph Joerger, Jr.

Our road now drops down a hillside, and at mile 26.50 we pull up at Clarksville, named after the ranch owned by Harry Clark and his brother.[18] Here we are entertained at Mrs. Margaret Tong's Railroad House, that owes its name to the hoped-for arrival of the Sacramento & Placerville Railroad, but was left three miles to the northeast when the line was built five years later. This place is only half a mile from the Mormon Tavern, it is true, but the traffic on the road is so heavy that it too is a well-patronized stopping place. Its bar is always crowded, and its seventy-foot-long dining room is as congested as the Mormon Tavern's, while in the evenings the dance hall is generally well filled.[19] The original inn is said to have been a place of somewhat questionable character, run by the Clark brothers,[20] and the following events may have had something to do with its having acquired this reputation. In

July of 1854 a party of travelers were aroused in the middle of the night by an attempt to steal their horses from the barn of the Railroad House, and the landlord was only just in time to prevent the theft.[21] Mickey Free, a small-time highwayman and ruffian, is said to have lived at the Tong's place, presumably while carrying on his business as a "road agent" at the junction of the road from Folsom to Placerville and the Coloma road,[22] eight miles to the northeast of Clarksville. Mr. Free was hanged at Coloma on October 26, 1855, for the murder of a man named Howe, and entertained himself and his audience by eating peanuts and dancing a jig on the trap of the scaffold while waiting his turn to be executed.[23] On September 21, 1856, the notorious gang leader, cattle rustler, highwayman, and killer Tom Bell (whose real name was Thomas J. Hodges) stopped for dinner at the Railroad House, and thereafter took his ease while his horse was resting. He is described as being over six feet in height, and, apart from a badly broken nose, a fine-looking man. He was armed with two heavy revolvers and a bowie knife, and wore a "coat of mail," or breastplate. That he was well known at the Tong's place is proven by the fact that after his departure a Mexican who lived there stated openly that this was the badly wanted bandit, Tom Bell.[24] Mr. Bell met his well-deserved end less than a month later, when on October 4, 1856, he was captured near Knight's Ferry and hanged without benefit of trial.

Tom Bell's criminal activities have hitherto been supposed to have developed in and been confined to California, between the years 1854 or 1855, and 1856. As a matter of fact his career of banditry dates back at least five or six years earlier, and the Mexican state of Sonora was the scene of his first recorded robbery and outrage. In June, 1849, he and a gang of followers, that included Charley Johnson, who was later killed by Williams, another of the gang, appeared in northern Sonora, ostensibly to buy horses. Instead of pursuing this enterprise they attacked and robbed a little mining camp, and concluded the foray by stringing up the aged priest and raping and carrying off his sister.[25]

The Railroad House was eventually destroyed by fire, and today a gas and service station is being operated on the site of this once-famous roadhouse.[26]

After leaving Clarksville we pass Samuel Freeman's place and the Atlantic House, the latter probably having stood at the junction of the road to Bass Lake, now the Diamond Ridge Water Company's reservoir, and at about mile 29.00. Nothing more is known of either place.

At mile 29.50 we come to the Ohio House, on the north side of the road and just west of Deer Creek. In 1849 a log cabin stood here, and at this point the old Carson immigrant road (whose alignment we are still following) crossed the creek, that during the rainy season carries so much water that it is dangerous attempting to ford.[27] In 1858 Sebastian Zimmerman purchased the property and erected several buildings, where he opened a hotel. Before the railway was constructed to Shingle Springs as many as eighty teams were wont to pass the night here.[28] Today the place is part of a ranch, but all that remains of the old roadhouse are the ruins of some stone foundations.

At about mile 30.50 we pass the Deer Creek Hotel, operated by Daniel Hate Holdridge.[29]

At mile 31.00 we stop at the DuRoc House, where Johnson's tollhouse was located.[30] This place stands at the top of a hill and on the south side of the road, and today all that marks the site of what was at one time an important stopping place is a caved-in well, the remains of a few rock foundations, and half a dozen old oaks, cedars, and cottonwoods.

The earliest record owners of this property were Lewis Holdridge and Sarah Ann, his wife, in 1857 and 1858. In their deed to E. S. Hanshett and Maria, his wife, the property was mentioned as being the "DuRoc house and ranch." Eventually it was acquired by Theron Foster and Mary, his wife, whose address in August, 1860, was DuRoc Post Office in White Oak Township, El Dorado County. Foster at one time was a member of the California Assembly.

Frederick Gustavus Crawford was born in Groton, Tompkins County, New York, October 28, 1831. The first fourteen years of his life were spent in his native state, when he moved with his parents to Dundee, Illinois, where he received a common school education. In 1852 he set out for California on horseback with an ox team caravan, arriving at Placerville October 28, 1852, his twenty-first birthday. He still carried the bag of red peppers his mother had given him to use as a preventive of cholera. It was to be administered in soup form. His traveling chum contracted cholera and his life was saved by the use of this remedy. So it is told as family lore. He engaged in mining for one week, panning out $1.08, and paid out $36 for board. He then turned his attention to teaming to and from the mines, frequently stopping at the DuRoc House. In the course of time, Crawford met Mary Lanette Foster, the daughter of the household, and they were married at the DuRoc House on November 20, 1860. In 1867 he assumed the operation of the DuRoc House with Mr. Foster but continued teaming until about 1868. At that time they planted a large vineyard. In the fall of that year he went to Davisville and built a hotel and conducted that business for twelve years. On October 18, 1880, he moved to Willows, Glenn County, and rented the old Willows Hotel which was destroyed by fire May 30, 1882. On the ruins, after purchasing the lots, he built the Crawford House, which was one of the best-appointed hotels in Northern California. He was the father of Dr. R. Tracy Crawford, noted astronomer of Berkeley, California.

Up to this point we have passed increasingly numerous signs of mining activity, and for the next ten miles or so we will be in the midst of the intensive placer diggings that scar the countryside in every direction.

At mile 33.25 we reach the little town of Shingle Springs, that owes its name to a horse-powered shingle-making machine erected here in 1849 by a group of immigrants, among whom were Henry and Edward Bartlett. In 1850 one of the Bartlett brothers built the first hotel, the Shingle Springs House, on a hill at the west end of the town, and on the south side of the road. The lumber used in the construction of this place is said to have come around Cape Horn and up the river to Sacramento by sailing ship, and thence by ox-drawn wagons to Shingle Springs. Bartlett sold the place to Humphrey Taylor, who in turn sold to Daniel Tompkins Hall, and in 1856 it was rented for a year by Allen T. Gray. The original timbers of the house are still intact, and after passing through various ownerships the place was remodeled and is today known as Mary's Inn.[31]

A few rods east of the Shingle Springs House was a log cabin called the Missouri House, built by R. S. Wakefield in 1851.[32] In 1852 he built the famous old Planters' House on the same site, and this became the stage station where we stop for a few minutes for refreshment. Wakefield continued to run the place until 1863, when it burned down but was rebuilt on the still-hot ashes of the original place. He operated the new house until his death from smallpox, when his widow married

Hall, who ran it for some years. Thereafter the place came into the possession of John Russi, who was the proprietor until 1933, when the hotel burned for the last time.[33]

About mile 34.25 we pass the mining camp of Buckeye Flat, christened by men from Ohio, and where a hotel was kept by Peter King Rockwell, a Salt Lake City man.[34] At mile 35.00 we stop at the Forty Mile House. This is a large place on the south side of the road, with the barns standing a few rods to the east, and its name is derived from the fact that it is located just north of the head of Forty Mile Creek, that drains southward into the Cosumnes River. The records of the place are very meager, but it was a going concern by 1853, and at one time may have been run by Thomas Davidson, the owner of the nearby toll road.[35] The following is one of the stories about the Forty Mile House that has survived. A teamster had slept in a little cabin near the barns, and next morning a poke, filled with $50 gold slugs, was missing from beneath his pillow. A great to-do was raised but to no effect, and some time later it was found that a packrat had been carrying articles from the cabin to a hole under a nearby oak tree. For some reason or other this clue was never followed up, and the gold may still be hidden among the roots of the tree, that is still standing.[36] The old roadhouse eventually burned down and the barns were demolished, and today the property is E. B. Livingston's Forty Mile Ranch.

Here we have an excellent example of the many different alignments of a given section of road. About a quarter of a mile south of Mr. Livingston's home is the still well-marked track of the 1848–1849 Carson immigrant road, that crossed the head of Forty Mile Creek, and here is a pathetic reminder of the trials and sorrows that were borne by so many of our pioneers during the great westward American migration. A hundred yards west of the point where the Carson road crosses the county road to Latrobe is the grave of a girl, who died less than forty miles from Sutter's Fort, the end of her parents' long overland journey. A few years ago a brush fire destroyed the fence and headboard that marked the child's resting place, and today this is only preserved by those who still cherish the memories of those days. A hundred feet north of the Carson road is the original location of the present county highway, and here, on a granite boulder, is the "40 mile" stone. As has been said, the 1859 Overland road passed directly north of the old roadhouse, and the present county road is located some fifty feet north of this. Finally, a quarter of a mile farther north is Johnson's, and in 1864 Davidson's old toll road, where the latter's tollhouse was located.[37] Thus, in a distance of half a mile, we have five different roads, each of which has its own background of stories and traditions.

Leaving the Forty Mile House, at mile 35.75 we reach the Mountain House, that stood at Greenstone, the intersection of the above road to Latrobe. This was the eastern end of Johnson's or Davidson's toll road, and beyond the possibility that the latter may have run the roadhouse,[38] nothing further is known of its history.

At mile 36.50 we reach the Kingsville House, where in the spring of 1853 the proprietors were said to be "erecting the largest building in the state."[39] This description of the size of the house is to be accepted with somewhat more than the proverbial grain of salt, but the following advertisement, appearing in the June 23, 1864, issue of the *Folsom Telegraph* and dated April 28, 1861, shows that the proprietor had broad ideas about his responsibilities to the traveling public:

"Kingsville House. This Eligible and commodious house situated on the Folsom and Placerville road, 18 miles from Folsom has been opened under the management of the undersigned, who is ready to entertain, refresh and recuperate the traveling and teaming community. L. Foster, Proprietor."

A quarter of a mile farther on our road turns northeast from the present route, and at mile 37.50 we reach the Lone Tree House, established by Young Gray in 1852.[40] This must have stood at the junction of an old crossroad to Placerville, but nothing remains of the place. Half a mile to the southeast we rejoin today's highway, and a quarter of a mile beyond this point, and on the south side of the road, pass the site of a house that James Askew built in 1861, and that later became the headquarters of his famous stock ranch and dairy farm.[41] Still later the place was run as a roadhouse by Jeremiah Nichols, and until some fifteen years ago part of the building was still standing.[42]

At mile 38.50 we reach the mining town of El Dorado, that until January 1, 1856, was known as Mud Springs. This name was coined by the immigrants to distinguish the place from Diamond Springs, two miles to the east, as here their stock and cattle turned the springs into mud wallows. The first stopping place at Mud Springs was the old Mud Springs House, built in the winter of 1849–50 by James Thomas, one of the earliest settlers, as a trading post and hotel.[43] The place consisted of three connected buildings with a frontage of some seventy-four feet, five log cabins, stables, and two large corrals.[44] In 1851 Mud Springs became a busy mining center, and many stores and hotels were built at that time and during the ensuing years.[45]

Among the earliest of these hostelries was the Nevada House, a two-story building standing on the south side of the road at the eastern end of the settlement. At one time this was a popular social gathering place, and on the 4th of July, 1855, "the ball of the season" was held here, when no less than one hundred ten ladies were present.[46] In 1860 the Nevada House was probably the fourth of the early Pony Express remount stations out of Sacramento, as by 1862 it was the station where the stagecoaches from Folsom to Nevada changed horses. By the latter year the managers were O. B. Westcott and Richard Atmore, and five years later the place was being run by an Irishman named Dennis Higgins.[47]

Another old place is the Oriental Hotel, a two-story frame house that was built about 1852. In 1862 its proprietor was Charles Boyd, and in 1867 the house was being operated by William Henry Pavey, an Englishman. In the 70's the place was managed by Mr. and Mrs. Harvey, and during this time the hotel was the scene of a weird attempt at arson and murder. Dr. Schultz, an elderly physician, was established in Mud Springs, where he had a monopoly of the medical business until a younger man, Dr. Proctor, arrived from the east and opened an office in the Oriental Hotel. Most of the patients then went to him, and Dr. Schultz, brooding over the loss of his business, attempted to readjust matters by setting fire to the hotel in the hope that his competitor would lose his life in the conflagration. The fire was extinguished, however, without injury to the younger physician, and Dr. Schultz was convicted of the crime and sentenced to a term in the State Prison at San Quentin. W. H. Pallet seems to have been the next proprietor, and on his death Richard Pitzer married his widow and changed the name of the hotel to the California House. The place then came into the possession of Seymour Hill, who in 1934 ran it as the Hill Hotel, and three years later it became Mr. Hill's private residence.[48]

Among the many other stopping places that flourished in Mud Springs during the mining camp's days of prosperity, the Temperance House is one that is worthy of mention, if for no other reason than that of a marriage which took place there on November 19, 1854. On that date Judge E. Ballenger, of Buckeye Flat, and Mrs. Zerelda E. Deering, of Diamond Springs, were united in matrimony after one hour's acquaintanceship. The united weight of the happy couple totaled five hundred pounds, and their collective ages ninety years.[49]

At the east end of town Michael O'Keefe's toll road turns due north, and the only stopping place on this route is William Madison Tanner's roadhouse, at about mile 41.50, some two miles west of Placerville, and where the slaughterhouse is now located.[50]

Continuing eastward via the Overland, the first inn after leaving El Dorado is "Doc" Bradford Hammill's roadhouse and stage station, at mile 39.50. The house and barns are on the south side of the road, and all that is known about the place is that Hammill was running it in 1869. Thereafter it is said to have been operated by a man called "Van Voss," who was probably William Voss.[51] Part of the old house was standing a few years ago, but today little remains to mark its site.

Mile 40.75 brings us to the bustling mining town of Diamond Springs, where the crystal-clear, sparkling spring water made the place a favorite camping ground for the immigrants. The first cabin was built in 1849.[52] The first stopping place of which there is a record was opened in September, 1850, by Andrew Carbly Bloom. He kept a hotel and bakery until March, 1855, when he sold out and moved away.[53] The house stood on the Carpenter place,[54] and under different managements continued to be operated until August 5, 1856, when the conflagration of that date swept it away, together with all but one of the other stopping places in the town.[55]

Gold was discovered around Diamond Springs in 1851, and from that time onward so many inns and hotels were established that it is impossible to do justice to any but the oldest of these places.

As far as can be ascertained, the second hotel was the California House, built in 1851 by John Reed, and, like Bartlett's hotel at Shingle Springs, the lumber used in its construction is said to have come around Cape Horn.[56] Another version is that the place was built by Louis Lepetit (the same man who subsequently ran the roadhouse at Hangtown Crossing, or Mills).[57] However this may have been, while the house was the only one to survive the fire in '56, its subsequent history is so involved that it is difficult to unscramble truth from fiction. About the time of the fire the place seems to have been owned by

Alexander Siesbuttel, when it was known as Siesbuttel's and was managed for some years by Peter Cook. By 1867 the property appears to have come into the possession of John Frederick David Illsohn, who, succeeded by his sons, ran the hotel for some sixty years, when it was called Illsohn's Hotel. About 1907 it burned down and was rebuilt; in 1925 it was purchased by Mr. and Mrs. Walter Ball, and in 1939 the place burned down for the last time.[58]

The Howard House (known also as Titus' Hotel) was a large place on the north side of the street, that was refitted in November, 1852, by Titus (probably Dr. Isaac Sutthen Titus) and Hughes (perhaps William Carson Hughes)[59] and thereafter the former sold out to Vining Barker and John S. Ellis, when the place was managed by Nathan Young.[60] The fire of 1856 broke out in the Howard House about 9

KOCH'S DIAMOND SPRINGS HOTEL

o'clock in the morning, and as the town was built of the most combustible material, it swept the place. Shortly after the fire Michael Rickert built a small cabin on the site of the Howard House, where he opened a boarding house, and in the same year John Bartholo Koch bought the place and turned it into a hotel.[61] In 1878 The Howard House was replaced by the Diamond Hotel. It was run by Koch until his death in the following year, and thereafter by his widow and two sons, Carl and Johann. The place was a two and a half story frame structure, and under the Kochs' management it is said to have been the best stopping place between Folsom and Placerville.[62] In 1884 the hotel was still being operated by Johann,[64] but thereafter nothing is known of its history. By 1925 a new Diamond Hotel had been built on the south side of the street and was under the management of Antone Meyers,[63] and in 1937 the same place was being operated by Carl Meyers.[64]

The Crescent City Hotel, on the south side of the street, was another of the early places burned in 1856, and the Golden West Hotel, built on its site in the same year, was being managed by Charles Green on July 19, 1937, when it too was destroyed by fire.[65] The stone walls of this place, with the date of its erection, 1856, carved on the keystone of the main doorway, are probably the oldest mementos of Diamond Springs' early hostelries.[66]

A few hundred yards east of the town is the Sacramento Hotel, run by John Schneider, Sr., a Frenchman, but beyond this nothing is known of the place. Just beyond this is East Diamond, or "Polliwog Settlement," as it is called locally because of the number of French settled there.[67]

At the eastern end of Diamond Springs we leave the Carson immigrant route (our road turning due north, while the latter continues eastward), and at mile 41.75 reach Webber Creek, where we stop at Smith Morrill's bridge tollhouse.[68] We are now well into the mountains, and from this point onward the Overland becomes increasingly winding and the grades steeper, as the giant peaks of the Sierra Nevada tower above us on either side.

Mile 42.75 brings us to Coon Hollow, that is really more of a canyon than a hollow. This is one of the richest mining camps in the region, where no less than $5,000,000 in gold was recovered from the Excelsior mine's five acres of ground.[69] The Champion Hotel was the camp's popular stopping place, but nothing of its history is known to have survived.[70]

Our road now drops into the gulch of Hangtown Creek, and after rattling down Placerville's Sacramento Street we swing around the corner to the right and at mile 43.75 pull up before the famous old Cary House. Our arrival is so well timed that at 5 o'clock in the afternoon we are able to witness the reception accorded Horace Greeley who, as has been said, was met at the Eight Mile House by a select committee and brought to town in one of the California Stage Company's six-horse coaches, and at 8 o'clock in the evening we form part of the "immense" audience which from the *Plaza* listen to his address delivered from the Cary House balcony.[71]

This is the end of our trip over the White Rock road, and we must now backtrack and describe the later Overland route to Placerville, via Folsom, Mormon Island, and Green Valley.

Chapter 19.   Sacramento to Placerville*

To COMPLETE the picture of the Overland road between Sacramento and Placerville we must now travel over the final location of the western end of the route. The first twenty-two miles of this trip will be by a Sacramento Valley Railroad train to Folsom.

In a general way, the railway follows the western half of Sutter's 1847 road from the Fort to his sawmill at Coloma, and for two or three years this was the most heavily traveled road in California. With the discovery of gold at Old Dry Diggings, Hangtown, or Placerville, the local importance of this road began to be shared by the Carson immigrant road, via White Rock, when the freighting outfits, and later the stages bound for the new diggings, started using the latter route. Sutter's old "sawmill road" continued to carry the traffic between Sacramento and the original placer ground at Coloma for the next eight years, until the completion of the railway to Folsom on February 3, 1856. A new road was then opened to Placerville from Green Valley, on the Coloma road and some fourteen miles east of Folsom, and with this the latter place became the stage terminus of the Overland route. Freight for Coloma was thereafter carried by wagons from Folsom, while many of the freighting outfits bound for Placerville continued to use the White Rock road.

We depart from Sacramento at 2:30 P.M., August 1, 1859, on the special train that carries a large reception committee to greet Horace Greeley at Folsom,[1] and a few minutes before three o'clock pass Mills station, or Hangtown Crossing, at mile 11.00. From this point the old Coloma road runs northeastward about halfway between the railway and the river, and the first stopping place is the Twelve Mile House, of which nothing is known except that there was such a place. At about mile 13.00 we pass the Pittsfield House, built by Joel Harvey in July, 1850, and run by him for the next three years.[2] The Fourteen Mile House is a large place that was opened in 1850 by a man named Rush,

---

*via the Green Valley Road

who in 1853 sold out to John Taylor. Taylor operated the roadhouse until 1858, when he devoted himself to farming, and the one-time inn became his home.[3] At about mile 15.00 we pass the Salsbury House, and at mile 16.00 the Natomas House, a mile west of Alder Creek, that is said to have been run by Freeman McComber in 1864.[4] The Monte Cristo House or Exchange, at mile 18.00, was opened sometime before 1852, when Lucius Ripley Beckley bought the place after leaving the Prairie House, on the White Rock road. Beckley ran the roadhouse until 1855, and in 1862 Robert Allen was the proprietor.[5] The Nineteen Mile House probably stood at the junction of the present road to Nimbus, and in 1851 it appears to have been managed by Joseph McKlintock.[6] The last roadside stopping place before reaching our destination is the Twenty Mile House, that in 1852 was run by Perry Reed.[7] In common with all the other places along this portion of our route, nothing remains today to mark its site.

At mile 21.75 and at 3:10 P.M. we reach Folsom, and as Greeley has not yet appeared, most of the reception committee wander off to inspect the various saloons before the arrival of the uncompromisingly teetotal visitor. At a quarter to four a carriage, drawn by a pair of roan ponies, rattles up to the station, and we are just in time to witness the distinguished journalist's unofficial greeting by the onlookers who are drawn to the station by the arrival of the special train. Greeley emerges from the carriage wearing his famous well-worn white coat (now travel-stained and dusty), one hand clutching a faded blue umbrella and the other a little glazed bag marked "H. Greeley, 154 Nassau street, New York, 1855." There are no official handshakers in sight, and he peers about uncertainly through his dusty spectacles, and fingers his scanty chin whiskers. The crowd instantly recognize him, and press about so closely, and with such vociferous and unparliamentary remarks of welcome, that he makes for the first open door in sight. This, unfortunately, happens to be the entrance to the barroom attached to the ticket office, and here a few minutes later the Sacramento committee find Greeley, turned resolutely away from the array of bottles behind the bar, the defiant stiffness of his back proclaiming his outraged feelings.[8]

The site of Folsom was originally known as Negro Bar, where several Negroes began placer mining in 1849. The present town was not laid out by Captain Joseph L. Folsom, U.S.A., until 1855. By January of the following year all the town lots had been sold at auction in Sacramento.[9]

The first stopping place at Negro Bar was the Meredith Hotel, opened by James L. Meredith in April, 1850. Six years later this was replaced by another house of the same name that was thirty feet wide by one hundred in length, and was erected expressly to accommodate the thousand guests who attended the celebration of the railway's completion in February, 1856.[10]

In the same year Arnold D. Patterson, of Patterson's Ten Mile House, and J. M. Waters opened Patterson and Water's Hotel, and ran the place until Waters' death in 1865. As Patterson's Hotel, the former continued operating it until 1868, when he leased to Charles H. Watts. The latter subleased to Mrs. H. B. Wadilove, and the last manager was M. Doll, who was in charge when the place burned in 1871.[11]

As was the case in most of the other mining towns of California, a considerable number of hotels, inns, and stopping places were erected in Folsom between 1849 and 1869, and the following are the earliest of these places.

The Olive Branch Hotel was built by a man named Heaton in 1856, and the Mansion House by J. Holmes in 1857, both of these buildings having been destroyed by fire within the next few years. In 1858 Captain Hughes built the Granite Hotel, and was succeeded by Martin Wetzlar, the house burning down in 1866. The Central Hotel was put up in 1859 by George Wellington (who may have been the first owner of the Wellington or Halfway House, on the White Rock road), and after several changes of management it burned on August 13, 1886, when a better building was erected on its site. In 1860 Mrs. Lucinda Smart built the Tremont House, and thereafter sold to Ira Rounds Sanders, who ran the place until it burned in 1868.[12]

The only remaining place of interest in Folsom is Wells, Fargo & Company's office, at the western end of the town, that a year after our visit became the western terminus of the Pony Express messengers' transcontinental ride. The building is typical of the more substantial constructions of those days, its thick masonry walls and stout iron doors being designed to withstand the devastating fires that from time to time destroyed most of these little towns.

In 1847, when Sutter opened the road to Coloma, there were no such places as Negro Bar, Folsom, or Mormon Island. At Alder Creek (mile

17.00 on our route) his "sawmill road" drew away from the later high-way and railway and continued almost due northeast, leaving the sites of these mining camps about a mile or two to the northwest. It was re-joined by the 1859 road that we are following, at about the present line between Sacramento and El Dorado counties. This was never part of the Overland road, but there were a couple of early stopping places along it that should be mentioned. At mile 19.25 the Lexington House stood on the south bank of Willow Creek and on the east side of the "Prairie" road leading from Negro Bar, or Folsom, to the Prairie House (on the White Rock road), and thence to Michigan Bar and Jackson. At mile 20.50 the Willow Springs House was located on the west side of the western headwaters branch of the same stream, and on the road from Folsom to White Rock. Both of these places were still being operated in 1854, and the latter was opened as early as 1849, when miners bound for the Mormon Island diggings used to stop there.[13] Unfortunately, nothing further is known of either place.

We will stop overnight in Folsom at the hotel above the freight de-pot, where Horace Greeley was taken for his official reception after being rescued from the barroom at the ticket office, and next day re-sume our trip by the California Stage Company's morning coach for Placerville.

The first stopping place east of Folsom is the Saratoga House, stand-ing on the north side of the road on Saratoga Hill. In its day this was a wild place, but now the remains of the cellar are all that mark its site.[14] At about mile 24.00 we stop at Captain George K. Ney's ranch and stage station, standing on the south side of the road and a short distance east of the old road to Folsom State Prison. The place was later purchased by Monroe, who sold to Joseph Perrazzo, both having been cattlemen. Like so many of the other old roadhouses, a slight de-pression in the ground that was its cellar is all that remains of the place today.[15]

About a quarter of a mile northeast of Ney's station we pass the point that within a short time will be the high-water mark of the Fol-som Dam empounding area. For the next three miles all the old road-houses and stopping places along the Overland road, including the town of Mormon Island, will be submerged, and their sites lost for all time.

At mile 25.00 we arrive at Mormon Island. After Coloma, this was

the most famous of the early mining camps of the gold rush days. It
owes its name to the discovery of gold at this point on the South Fork
of the American River by a party of Mormons. These were Sidney
Willis and Wilford Hudson, the original discoverers, Ira Willis, Jesse
B. Martin, Ephraim Green, Israel Evans and James Sly, all discharged
members of Colonel Stevenson's Mormon Battalion, who were on their
way to rejoin their co-religionists east of the Sierra Nevada. They were
camped some fifteen miles above Sutter's grist mill, where they improved their time by doing a little gold washing. Early in April, 1848,
they struck it rich. Shortly thereafter the river was diverted to the
south of the bar they were working, thus forming the island that bears
their name.[16]

At Mormon Island, as elsewhere along the Coloma road, "There
was no lack of houses of call ... for every hollow tree was the nucleus
of a grog-shop while in the neighborhood of every spring or stream,
a sort of Tavern sprung up as from the soil, 'like a rose-tree in full bearing embowered in blooming flowers of printed calico.'"[17] So true is
this statement that again we are forced to confine ourselves to the
earliest of these establishments.

As nearly as can be determined, the first stopping place at Mormon
Island was the Blue Tent, said to have been established by Samuel Rufus
Caldwell by December of 1849, the name being due to its covering,
which was blue denim or drilling. The following description of the
establishment and its proprietor, written at that time, is a classic:

"I took up my quarters at the hotel made of blue drilling, the polite landlord
,,, bowed me into my room, which consisted of ninety pine poles covered with
canvas and would accommodate forty persons, but contained only two pairs of
blankets. As soon as one fell asleep, the accommodating landlord would remove
the blankets from him for the next customer, and if they were slow to retire a glass
of '49 Bourbon soon compelled them to. After all were asleep, the landlord took
the blankets from his last patron and went to bed himself. Many inquiries were
made for the bedclothing, but the gentlemanly proprietor settled the muss by
another cocktail and a steerage cigar (cabin cigars at the time sold for fifty cents),
and all was peace.[18]

The floor of the Blue Tent was of earth, and while this held up well
enough, by the end of 1849 the denim roof had become so rotted that
it was decided to replace it with a heavier covering. As will have been
gathered, the proprietor was of a somewhat more than economical
turn of mind, and to defray the cost of the improvement the idea of a

Christmas dinner and public ball was hit upon. Large notices, written in blue pencil on brown wrapping paper, were posted in every direction, advertising the forthcoming event as the first ball to be held in Sacramento County. And lest the potential guests be under any misapprehension as to how public the affair was to be, they were further informed that tickets would cost $20.00 apiece.

At first it was proposed to lay down a board floor for the dancers, but this extravagance was vetoed when it was argued that the ladies' brogans would suffer less wear and tear shuffling around on the ground than they would on boards.

The question of the cost of food for the dinner was solved in an equally economical manner by inducing the miners to submit samples of their culinary art in competition with each other, for theoretical premiums for the best offerings, these awards to be half the price of admission. Needless to say, few premiums were awarded, and such food as was accepted was paid for at current prices, less deductions for extra-culinary art. As an example of this, one worthy submitted what he claimed was a prime ham. When it was found that this consisted of four inches of ham shank with a wooden peg driven into the bone, and a piece of shoulder impaled on this device, he was paid a dollar a pound for his efforts and charged $20.00 for a ticket.

The table consisted of boards from the diggings used to run wheelbarrows over, and the tablecloth was the old blue denim roof covering. No seats were provided, and the table was purposely built so high that the diners had to stand about the board, it being calculated that they would thus tire more quickly and eat less.

After the collation had been demolished the table was transformed into benches, and the final touch of elegance was added when the landlord brought out his two pairs of blankets and generously permitted the ladies to use them as cushions. The interior of the tent was tastefully decorated with miniature flags and evergreens, and "handsomely illuminated" by twelve candles stuck in the necks of porter bottles, which were wired to the poles supporting the roof of the structure. Music was provided by a fiddler, but when one of his fiddle strings broke he declared himself unable to play for any more fancy dances. What the pieces were after that calamity is not stated, but they must have been satisfactory as the ball continued until 4 o'clock in the morning, by which time only the bass string remained intact.[19]

Sunrise House, 1868

Walkershaw House

Sportsman's Hall, 1868

Rolling Hill House

Mr. Caldwell continued to guide the destinies of the Blue Tent until 1852 when it was moved to another part of the town and reopened as the Caldwell House. In 1854 the place was closed.[20]

During the '50s there were several other stopping places in Mormon Island, such as the Miners' Hotel, opened in 1851 by Alexander Dallas Kneas and burned in 1856;[21] the Union Hotel or Tavern that a Mr. Turle began operating about 1850 and that was closed in 1855;[22] J. P. Markham's hotel, that was running between 1850 and 1854;[23] Thomas Stephenson's Mansion House between 1853 and 1856;[24] John Flavel and Catherine Young's hotel, run by them from 1854 until 1859–60;[25] The Island House;[26] Samuel Ricker's House and James Hawn's Cincinnati House,[27] but beyond the fact that these places existed nothing is known of their history.

A mile east of Mormon Island we come to a crossroad leading to Clarksville, also known as the "prairie road," and here at mile 26.00 stop at Smith's old Exchange, standing on the north side of the road and just south of the Natoma Valley Ditch, where this is crossed by the Overland. When the place was built in 1853 it is said to have been the largest public house in Natoma Township. In 1855 it was purchased by Cox (perhaps Roger) and Hamilton. They were bought out in 1858 by William Jarvis, and at that time the name was changed to the Natoma Valley or simply the Valley House. Jarvis sold to a man who may have been Squire Lee, who was followed by Freeman McComber, who in the following year refitted the house and ran it until 1864. The place then became a popular resort, dances being held in a big barn that stood a short distance south of the Overland and on the west side of the "prairie road." This was known as the Red Barn. The ballroom was on the second floor, with music supplied by orchestras from Sacramento, and dinners served on the ground floor of the building.[28] On July 4, 1864, an Independence Ball was held there, when McComber advertised that he would be "happy to greet with a cordial welcome the public generally and the rest of mankind."[29] About this time the Natoma Valley House was the scene of a story of buried treasure that has persisted until the present. According to this a miner, who had struck it rich, decided to return to the "States," and went to the Valley House to await the Overland stage. The stage was delayed, and when night came on the man became fearful of being robbed. Under cover of darkness he slipped out and buried the treasure in gold dust he was carrying, somewhere near the house. During the night he was suddenly taken sick and died. So far as is known his gold was never recovered.[30] The last known record of the place is that it was owned by James Hoke, who sold to Wallace B. Plumb, who also seems to have owned Plumb's Hotel, just to the southwest on the east side of Sutter's old "sawmill road."[31]

Directly across the road from the Natoma Valley House stood Davies Darry's place, that later, under the management of Mr. and Mrs. Patrick Murray, was called the Valley Home. Today no vestige of these places remains, and a few yards to the north of their sites rises one of the great earth wing-dams of the Folsom Dam project. A short distance to the east we pass McFarrison's or Cohen's ranch on the south side of the road where Jean Baptiste Ferrazzo later had a garden, but so far as is known this was never a roadhouse.[32]

At mile 27.25 we pull up at the Leachman House, kept by Austin Taylor Leachman, a Kentuckian. Due to this it seems also to have been known as the Kentucky House. The place is on the south side of the Overland, at the junction of another crossroad to Clarksville, in a flat at the foot of Rolling Hill. Somewhat remodeled, it was being operated as late as 1867 by Frank Cirby, Leachman's son-in-law. Until some fourteen years ago all that remained of the old place was the wreckage of some timbers on the north side of the road, that marked the site of its barn.[33]

At mile 28.20 we come to the Rolling Hill House, standing on the north side of the road and about halfway up Rolling Hill. This place was conducted by Charles Post, and in its day was a notorious dancing resort. If the stories told of it are to be credited, the reputations of some of its patrons were not of the best.[34] It is a large two-story frame building with an extension or wing at the rear. Post sold to Wendel Leike, and Jacob Hyman eventually came into possession of the property.[35] This place was the scene of the tragic ending of a love match and an attempted elopement, but as the affair had its beginning at the New York House, a mile to the east, we will postpone further mention of the tragedy until we reach that stopping place. Across the road from the Rolling Hill House, and at the western end of a field, was Doc. Ebenezer Fairchild's blacksmith shop.[36] but today no remains of either place are to be seen.

Just to the east and about three-quarters of the way up Rolling Hill was Kaufman's Deadfall House or saloon, standing on the north side of the road. Despite its promising name, all that is known of the place is that it later came into the possession of James K. Page, who has been referred to in connection with the Mormon Tavern, on the White Rock road.[37]

At mile 28.50 we stop at the New York House, on the south side of the road and on a flat in the ravine of the New York Creek, between Twin Bridges. This place was kept by Constantine Hicks, a Vermont carpenter, who is said to have been a man of cruel disposition.[38] According to the surviving stories of his activities, he must have been exceptionally lawless, even for those days. Early in 1856 Hicks was one of the principals in an attempted election fraud aimed at making Coloma the seat of El Dorado County, and while the grand jury found a true bill against him, when the case was called for trial it was dismissed when the District Attorney moved to enter a nolle prosequi, which the court sustained.[39] In 1867 he made a squatters' or preemption claim to the section of land about the New York House, which involved him in an unsuccessful action with the Central Pacific Railroad.[40] Perhaps these frustrations conditioned him for the act of violence that was to follow.

According to the story, Hicks' daughter (who was the waitress at the New York House) fell in love with one of the hired hands, and that winter the couple attempted to elope. They had gotten as far as the Rolling Hill House, where the girl's father and a party of his friends overtook them. Hicks is said to have horsewhipped his daughter's lover to death, carried the young man's body back to the New York House, and buried his victim on a hill across the road from the hotel.[41]

No record of this alleged crime appears in the El Dorado County criminal annals, but the story is still current among the old-timers thereabouts. In 1880 the property was purchased by Jeptha Wilson, and after passing through the hands of various later owners it was bought by Royal Ray Campbell, the present proprietor. The old house burned down years ago and another was built on its foundations, where it stands today, looking almost as ancient and weather-beaten as if it were the original building. At the easternmost of Twin Bridges, and beyond the New York House, is the beginning of Hopkins' toll road that parallels the county road to a point a short distance east of the Wakasha House. This is better maintained than the public road, and in consequence is preferred by the heavy freighting outfits.[42]

Half a mile more brings us to the site of a little log cabin, standing on the north side of the road and close to where the Live Oak school-house was later built, where a Mrs. Powell kept a roadside "hotel," but no further record of her establishment is known to have survived.[43]

At mile 29.75 we reach the Wakasha or Walkershaw House, another of the Overland's well-known old hostelries. This is a large two-story frame building on the south side of the road, and if tradition can be credited is another of those old houses whose timbers were brought around Cape Horn. It is managed by Joseph Taylor and his wife, and during their regime many well-attended dances were held here.[44] While no derivation of the name has been found, it may be that it was bestowed by some member of that section of the Bennett-Arcane party known as the Sand Walking Company or the Jayhawkers, who, after their tragic experience in Death Valley, settled down in 1849 or 1850 to mine at Jayhawk, some six miles to the northwest of the road-house. Their ill-advised route to California is said to have been taken on the strength of information furnished by a Paiute chief called Waker-aw (better known as Chief Walker), and the name of the house may commemorate that of this Indian of unhappy memory.[45] The old building was razed years ago and a small cabin built on the site from some of its timbers by John Hughes, who still lives there. At the top of the hill, and a short distance east of the Wakasha House, is the toll-house where Joseph Taylor, and later his brother John, collected charges for the use of Hopkins' toll road.[46]

Mile 31.00 brings us to Green Springs, at the eastern end of Green Valley, so called from the thousand or more springs hereabouts. On the south side of the road, we stop at the Green Springs House. As stated earlier, this place was built by Rufus Hitchcock after he severed his connection with the Sutter's Fort Hotel, and was operated by him until his death from smallpox in 1851.[47] The property was later purchased by William Dormody, who managed it until his death in a runaway accident in 1876, and thereafter the business was conducted by his widow, Mrs. Sarah F. Dormody. The house was twice destroyed by fire, and in its palmy days was a favorite resort for wedding parties.[48]

Our next stop is at mile 31.50, where we pull up at the Pleasant Grove House that is operated by a man who may have been Ira Rounds Sanders, later a hotelkeeper at Folsom. This is a good-sized frame building standing on the north side of the road and is another popular roadhouse, whose importance was considerably increased the year after our arrival, when it became the first Pony Express remount station east of Folsom. The Express ponies were reshod here, and a large, old-fashioned blacksmith's bellows used in this connection is still to be seen in the yard. The place was purchased by William Wallace Rust in 1864, and was later managed by his son-in-law, John Fleming, whose widow, Mrs. Louisa Rust Fleming, still lives in the original house. While somewhat remodeled, it appears today much as it did in 1859.[49] In 1937 the Placerville Parlors of the Native Sons and Daughters of the Golden West erected an artistic monument in front of the old building, commemorating the Pony Express.

GREEN VALLEY RANCH of Fred Engesser

At mile 32.00 we pass the store and stopping place owned by Frederick Rohlfing, a Hanoverian, located at the top of the Rolling Hill grade and in the southeast angle of the crossroad to Bass Lake and Clarksville, at the southern end of which stands the Mormon Tavern.[50]

Mile 33.00 sees us at the Green Valley ranch, where in 1868 Frederick Engesser, a Wurtemburger, built the Green Valley House. This was another roadhouse that was very popular with the traveling public, and the original big two-story frame building, standing on the south side of the road, is today one of the best-preserved of the old hostelries. Albert Engesser, son of the founder, and his wife Lena are still living there, and their recollections of the old Overland are fresh in their memories.[51]

Our next stop is at mile 34.00, where toward the western end of White Oak Flat in early days George D. H. Meyers, a miner from Tennessee Creek, built a large red brick store on the south side of the road. Later on the place came into the possession of John Wing, one of El Dorado County's English pioneers, and for years after his death his widow Louisa conducted a roadhouse there in conjunction with the store. Another section of toll road parallels the county road at this point, and as James Wing's tollhouse is just across the road and a few yards east of the Wing House, many of the big freighting outfits were wont to stop at the latter place.[52]

At mile 35.00 the White Oak Springs Hotel stands on the north side of the road and opposite an old brick house that was originally owned by Constantine Hicks and later became the home of Aylmar Pelton. The White Oak Hotel was being operated as early as 1852, and in 1859 the property was purchased by Arthur Litten, who is the proprietor at the time of our arrival. In addition to this, all that is known about the place is that on the evening of April 28, 1852, an altercation took place there between James Hewlett, an employee of the hotel, and an Abner Spencer, and in the course of this Hewlett stabbed the latter so seriously that he died the next day. A citizens' committee tried and convicted the murderer on the spot, and he was hanged from a nearby tree one hour after the crime was committed.[53]

Beyond the White Oak Springs Hotel we pass the present settlement of Rescue, that in 1895 was named after a nearby mine owned by Andrew J. Hare,[54] and where today Mrs. Pearle Wing owns and manages the modern version of the original "Wings's Store."

Five or six hundred yards east of Rescue we cross Kelly Creek, the main tributary of White Oak Creek, where William Harriett conducted the Kelly Creek House. On his death in 1880 his widow Agnes married Frederick Riemer (who is said also to have been known as August Baring), and thereafter the couple carried on the business for some years. The place was located on the south side of the road and the east bank of the creek, a short distance west of where the Tennessee Schoolhouse was later built.[55]

At mile 36.00 the Rising Sun, Sunrise House, or Pelton's Hotel stands on the south side of the road, at the top of the hill between Kelly and Tennessee creeks, and in the southeast angle of the junction of the "upper road" to Gray's Flat and Shingle Springs. The place is a typical large, two-story New England farmhouse, that was built by Samuel B. Pelton shortly after 1854, and where he operated a roadhouse until about 1876. He is the host at the time of our arrival. The place was later acquired by John Carre, who opened a general store on the premises and was running the establishment as late as 1883.[56] This is still another of the early roadhouses whose timbers are said to have weathered the passage around Cape Horn, and from the number of these places one is warranted in wondering what space, if any, remained for the accommodation of other cargo in the sailing ships of the gold rush days; such, for instance, as immigrants.

At mile 36.50 we reach Rose Springs (so called because of the abundance of wild roses growing thereabouts), where the Rose Springs House is located on the south side of the Overland, and in the southeast angle of the junction of the "lower road" to Shingle Springs. The place was built by Thomas Wood as a stage station sometime before 1859, and by 1862 it was owned by John William Hodgkins, who added a general store to the establishment and operated the place as late as 1867. In 1863 it was purchased by Alfred P. Grainer, and in 1870 Jacob Eggers became the proprietor. In 1880 Eggers built the house that still stands across the road from the original place.[57] The old stage barn, or what is left of it, is all that marks the site of the Rose Springs House, and while this is said to have been a Pony Express stop there is no positive evidence to this effect.

We cross Tennessee Creek at mile 36.75, and here, on the south side of the road and on the east bank of the stream, stood the Tennesseee House, but nothing further is known about this place.[58]

Mile 37.00 finds us at the Dry Creek crossing, and "Hell-roaring Diggings." Judging from the name, this must have been a somewhat more than lively mining camp in the early days, but apart from the fact that a hotel once stood on the west side of the road, and in the middle of the creek's present channel, nothing is known about the place.[59]

At a point across the creek from "Hell-roaring Diggings" the old Coloma road turns north, while the Overland continues eastward for some eight miles to Placerville. It is almost certain that there were at least a couple more stopping places along this last portion of our route, but if so nothing is known about them.

As has been said, when the Central Pacific Railroad reached Cisco all but local stage service on the Overland road was diverted to that point, when it followed the old immigrant trail around the northern end of Lake Tahoe to the Washoe Valley. The tremendous tonnage of freight that was being hauled to and from the Nevada silver mines followed the stages, and it is no exaggeration to say that when on May 10, 1869, the golden spike that joined the eastern and western sections of the railroad was driven home at Promontory Bluff, Utah, the whistle of the first through train was the signal for all this feverish activity to cease as if by magic. Gone were the dashing and gaily painted stagecoaches of the Pioneer Line, the Overland Mail, Wells, Fargo & Company, and half a dozen other lines, and gone were the endless trains of lumbering and dust-coated freight wagons. Most of the inns and stopping places along the route closed their doors for the last time, and almost overnight the vibrant life of the great Overland road fell silent, and the golden dust settled for the last time.

Chapter 20. A Buggy Ride to Tahoe

O<small>N</small> S<small>EPTEMBER</small> 3, 1864,* Jesus Maria Estudillo, son of Jose Joaquin Estudillo of San Leandro, started on a journey with horses and carriage from San Leandro to Virginia City, Nevada, by the way of San Francisco, Sacramento by river boat and thence to Virginia City by the way of Folsom and Placerville. His diary on that trip has been preserved and, in an edited form, that portion covering the trip from San Leandro to Tahoe follows. The information contained therein pertinent to the subject of this narrative is included. It is interesting to note, as I have been informed, that the nickname of the diarist was "Chumaliá," the present name of one of the streets in San Leandro.

September 2, 1864, Friday. This indeed has been a busy day for me. Jose Antonio, my brother, said that we had to start today for the city and tomorrow for Virginia City. I sent the carriage to be fixed to have it ready for starting but it could not be finished in time to allow us to catch the last boat, and so we remained until tomorrow. I told Jose Antonio to go to the City this evening and engage staterooms and he left by the afternoon stage.

We received from Mr. Ward today for our trip to Virginia City five hundred dollars, two hundred of which was given to me of which I shall give account of all I pay out. This evening I was at the weekly meeting of the Lincoln and Johnson club but did not hear the orator, Mr. Blake from Oakland. I was too late.

September 3. Left San Leandro at 20 minutes of seven en route for Virginia City. In the carriage were Mr. & Mrs. Ward, Mrs. Nugent, child and servant and myself. Jose Antonio we were to meet in the city. I drove to Oakland. They got out at Alameda and there took the

---

*A<small>UTHOR</small>'<small>S</small> N<small>OTE</small>: The two following articles, written eighty-four years ago and ninety years ago, respectively, are included in the belief that they will be of interest to those readers who are travelers over the paved highways of today. It is hoped that their inclusion may result in preserving them many years for the enjoyment of interested readers.

cars. I passed over to the city on the ten o'clock boat (Ferry Creek Route between San Antonio and San Francisco—Halley 176). I left the horses at the Black Hawk stable and went to see Mrs. Nugent at the Russ House. During the time I got to the city till an hour before leaving for Sacramento I was very busy dispatching the baggage and other little things. At 4 o'clock we left for Sacramento on the fast and beautiful steamer Yosemite, Captain Pool. Mr. & Mrs. Ward with Johnnie, their son, came to accompany us as far as Sacramento. Mr. Rodgers returned to the City from Benicia. When we were out on the bay it became very rough and the steamer staggered along like a drunken man. Mrs. Ward was seasick. At six o'clock we came in aline with the house at the Ranch. With my field glass I looked at several objects around. At ten minutes of seven we got to Benicia. The first place we stopped after leaving Benicia was Collinsville, which we reached at nine o'clock. At Rio Vista we remained for one or two hours waiting for the tide to rise as the steamer was very heavily loaded, having, I heard, seven hundred tons on board. On this account the steamer travelled very slowly. I went to bed at ten or thereabouts. I had a very good berth in our stateroom.

Sept. 4. I was up at six o'clock and the steamer was still going. At Freeport we stopped. Here the passengers for Virginia City took the cars that go to Latrobe and there to Placerville and thence through to Virginia City. This newly established place presents a very busy aspect on the arrival of the boat. Men are seen hurrying to the cars, others busily taking out freight, but no looker-on appears or gentleman of leisure. We had to travel hours before getting to Sacramento and when we got there it was not until after nine that we could get the carriage out. We stopped at the Orleans Hotel. At 3 o'clock we left for Folsom, a distance from Sacramento twenty two miles. We travelled very slowly but soon found out that it was getting late and had to hurry. But such roads! Had I not been told before of the great quantity of dust, I would certainly have now exclaimed, "oh! for our own Alameda County roads." The dust was very thick but we managed to escape from it at least a little. We met several Washoe teams on the way. As I expected it became dark about five miles before getting to Folsom and we had to make the best we could. About eight o'clock we got to Folsom and stopped at Patterson's hotel.

September 5, Monday. Up at six. Folsom presents or, better, has presented a very lively appearance. Here the Sacramento Valley Rail-road passes through and has a depot. The town is built on several small hills. To the North of it the creek (American River) presents a most attractive appearance on account of a beautiful suspension bridge for the cars. All along this creek are to be seen the different mining claims, particularly those of the Chinese. I was very much pleased with Folsom. At 9 o'clock we left en route to Placerville a distance of 26 miles. We arrived at Mormon tavern at 11:12 A.M. Clarksville we passed after quarter of an hours drive from M.T. which we left on our right. At 20 m. of two, we passed the first toll house where I paid twenty five cents. At 20 m after twelve we arrived Cariboo house. Here we took lunch, watered the horses and started on our route. Passed Mountain House at 1:42 P.M. Shingle Springs at 2:42. Next Planters house to Buckeye House, Mountain House and then Kingville, where we stop to water the horses. Here I was accosted by a red eyed looking individual who said, as I took out my pocket book to pay the place, "Kingville is played out." He was Kingville himself. We left the live yankee alone in his glory, already agreeing with him that Kingville was played out.

We passed by Mud Springs about half past three. This little village presents a very strange appearance. It has one street. At the west end nothing but Chinamen reside but as we advanced some very respectable houses appeared, some nice gardens and plenty of fruit. The scenery here begins to be very beautiful, but for scenery so far the two creeks (Weber & ——) between this place and Placerville give one a rare chance to behold such fine scenery. Pine trees several hundred feet in height are to be met here. We paid four tolls before getting to Placerville. We arrived at this place at twenty minutes of six. Placerville is in El Dorado County. It is surrounded by hills and the principal street makes several zigzags. We stopped at the Cary house. I was surprised to meet such fine accommodations. This is a fine large brick building. I took a good shampoo before supper and a good wash.

September 6, Tuesday. We left Placerville this morning at five o'clock. After a short ride of two miles we passed a large mining town named Smith's Flat. Met two Pioneer Stages from Virginia City. At 20 minutes of seven we ascended the mountain. Ten minutes of 8 o'clock passed a sawing mill. As we proceeded on our route we passed the four, five and nine mile houses. Sportman's hall we passed at quarter of nine. A man on horseback caught up with us and gave us the news which had been received at Sportman's hall by telegraph and this was the blowing up of the opposition steamer Washoe. No particulars. Watts, deserted, formerly a mill. We arrived at Pacific House at half past ten A.M. Here we took breakfast and fed the horses. This is a small place. There is a sawing mill and a large stable of the Pioneer Stage line. At quarter after twelve we left this place and after fifteen minutes we passed the American River over a large bridge (Brockliss).

At 2 o'clock we reached 25 mile house. Cock's Station at 3 and White hall at 3½ P.M. All this while we had been travelling on a bad road, cut by the side of the hill and indeed very dangerous. At several places we got down and walked. We descended to the bed of the American River about half past five and soon reached Webster's. From this place we learned how far the next stopping place was. About half past six we reached River Side (Riverton). Here we stopped for the night. No better name could have been given to this place for part of the house is built on the very river and swishing waters pass below, making a terrific noise. There is but one house and this is in the one we stopped. If the supper was not of the best kind, I can say that we had better beds than at Placerville.

September 7, Wednesday. At 6½ we left River Side Hotel and the first house we came to in the road was Champlain house. At True's station we stopped to water the horses and were received by a jovial individual, who told us of the particulars of the accident several days ago near his house which was the upsetting of the opposition stage. We thanked him for his water and bade him adieu. We passed several houses of little importance until we reached Strawberry Valley, a distance of nine or ten miles from the place we started this morning. Here we took breakfast. The situation of this place is very nice, being on the very center of the Sierra Nevada. Mrs. Nugent received a dispatch from Mr. Nugent saying for us to remain two days at Lake Bigler (Tahoe), that he would try to join us there. As we left Strawberry, we began to travel through some of the finest scenary in this State. On our right stood a rock on the side of the mountain, thousands and thousands of feet high. All of granite. Sayle's Station we reached at twelve o'clock. At 1½ P.M. we came to the head of the American River, and soon reached the very summit of the Sierra Nevada and began the descent of this wonderful formation of nature. Through several months of the year all this part of the country is covered with snow. As we proceeded a little farther, I caught sight of the renowned Lake Bigler. Would that I had the Geoffry Crayon* to describe this wonderful lake. From where I saw it first it was about twelve miles distant but the position was so elevated that I had a fine view. So much have I heard of the scenary of this place that I can but say with those whose praises have been given to the world in the most flattering manner, that I can but agree with them. I can't say much of the house and vicinity, as we got here in the afternoon about dark.

September 8, Thursday. I have been able to have a better look of the place today, but this only from the house and when out in the water this morning, but the impression it has made on me will be as lasting as monumental brass. Such scenary and such beautiful water are enough to enchant the pleasure looking individual. There was a shooting match here today for a silver cup, won by the proprietor of the house, Mr. Dean. We will leave tomorrow and go to Glenbrook and then to Carson.

September 9, Friday. I was up this morning very early in order to go out fishing at a good hour. At 2 o'clock we left the Lake House en route for Glenbrook. Our route was along the Lake. At 25 minutes of three we passed the line that divides California from Nevada and found ourselves in the Territory of Nevada, soon about to be a state, I believe. We passed two nice places before reaching Glenbrook, namely, Fridays and Cephyr Cove. About five we reached Glenbrook. Here I met my friend from San Jose, A. S. Beaty, who of course, was very glad to see me, perhaps better my purse. Glenbrook is a beautiful situated place. I prefer it to the Lake house. The situation is on the side of a hill with a nice little brook on one side. The house has a fine view of the Lake and is about a quarter of a mile from it. About two or three hundred yards below the house there is a nice little valley or flat where some vegetables are raised. The house itself is very handsomely gotten up, furniture and rooms are of the best kind. I was astonished to meet with such good accomodation in this part of the country.

September 10, Saturday. Today Saturday and yet we are in the road. A week ago today we left San Leandro and San Francisco and yet have not reached our destination.

---

*A pseudonym of Washington Irving.

Chapter 21. Did it pay to visit Yo Semite?

LUNATICS HAD NOT YET reached such depth of imbecility as to ride of their own free will in California stages. —*Bret Harte in "The Luck of Roaring Camp," etc., p. 121.**

I can imagine with what a shout of derision my audacious question will be received by those valiant travellers who have never been to the celebrated Valley; but as I have just returned from my trip *de rigueur* to Yo Semite, and am now, thank fortune, comfortably quartered in a civilized hotel, I think it not unwise to tell a plain, unvarnished tale of what awaits the Yo Semite pilgrim; for of the dozens of persons who have written about Yo Semite, I have never known one who gave anything like an accurate description of the perils and tortures attendant upon the journey thither.

I have known Californians who went to New York, and returned home without seeing the Adirondacks; but wo betide the wandering Easterner if he seeks the Pacific without bringing a trip to Yo Semite back with him! All along the railroad westward he is badgered with inquiries as to the probable data of his journey to Yo Semite; and when, after the long ride across the continent, he is received at last within the hospitable walls of one of San Francisco's grand hotels, the first thing he receives is the card of the agent for Yo Semite, who encloses a small map showing the three different modes of reaching the same. The

*THIS STORY was originally published in the magazine *Galaxy* for October, 1870, and was published in the March, April and May, 1954, issues of *Yosemite Nature Notes*. The article is a remarkable narrative. The report here serves to remind the reader of the condition of the pioneer roads along which the inns were located. For twenty-three years after the discovery of Yosemite Valley in 1851 there was no way to enter it except by horse trail, and the visitor had to start his trip into the mountains by stagecoach ride over primitive roads. Today's traveler cannot appreciate the severity of such a trip. The article here appears in an edited form. (Credit to the Yosemite Natural History Association, Inc., for the source of this description is gratefully acknowledged.)

239

newspapers in chronicling your arrival speak of your intention of visiting Yo Semite, and the first question asked by persons to whom you have brought letters of introduction is—as the reader will naturally suppose—"When do you leave for Yo Semite?" It may cause you some surprise, perhaps, when you discover that they who live here have themselves never been to Yo Semite; but you naturally imagine that this is because they do not feel that great love for the beautiful which distinguishes your noble self; perhaps they have not the time, nor the money; in fact, you frame a thousand excuses for them, and it never once enters your head that it is because they don't care to go. Of the scores of people I met in San Francisco only two or three had been to Yo Semite. But then there must have been insuperable obstacles in the way of their going, or they certainly would all have rushed in a body. Thrice happier I! Thrice luckier I! Nothing stood in my way. Would something had!

I must confess it was rather apalling to discover that of the three roads leading to the Valley, even the shortest required two days of staging and one whole day on horseback—before reaching the Earthly Paradise. The Mariposa road is admitted to have fifty miles of horseback trail; the Coulterville twenty-five; that via Hardin's and Chinese Camp only eighteen. I chose the last.

I found that travellers cannot take baggage to Yo Semite. The stages are full of passengers, and have small accommodation for superfluous freight; and when you leave the stage and take horses, the transportation of baggage is next to impossible. Everything is carried into the Valley on pack-mules, and travellers are frankly told by the agent that a small hand-bag is all that can be taken. "What, no linen—no clean dress? Nothing in the world for two weeks in summer, but a comb and a tooth-brush?" Even so.

We arrived at Stockton in the evening, and strolled out for a walk. Stockton, you will observe, is the starting point for the Yo Semite. If you don't know that before you get there, you will soon discover it. The leading hotel is the Yo Semite House. Be very sure I stopped there. I was stricken with the Yo Semite fever. I was enthusiastic over the prospect of what was before me. I wanted to commune with Nature.

A short walk in the town revealed the fact that there was an Insane Asylum there. Can this have any connection with its being the return-

Yosemite tourists on trail at Union Point

Staging from Yo Semite (*Signal Peak*)

ing point for Yo Semite tourists? There were also a large number of runners for the different stage lines. These persons asked questions with an easy familiarity which was delightful; and recommended different routes with noise and persistency enough to disgust a New York hack-driver.

The stages all leaving at 6 o'clock, we were pounded awake at 4 and summoned to breakfast. What the flies left of the meal was very dirty and disgusting. Sick at the very outset, myself and the other idiots went outside. The air there was sweet and refreshing. While we waited, the rival stage drew up. It was already full of Chinese, Irish, Italians, and Mexicans, who were going—not to Yo Semite—but to different stations in the mountains—to mines, to fruit ranches, to vineyards, wine-shops, and other queer places up in the wonderful Sierras.

Our own stage comes rattling up a minute later. It is soon full of tourists—not a business person among us. Oh, what fun we are going to have! Here is a young couple from Chicago; a pretty girl is the young wife, with dreamy eyes and raven hair eked out with a monstrous chignon that begins at her very brow and ends somewhere between her shoulder-blades. She will have trouble with that before she gets to Yo Semite; even the least experienced of us can see that; but nothing can be serious with us. We are all youngish persons, gay, healthful, and bound for the Yo Semite Valley.

Pretty soon the sun's rays begin to fall heavily. There is not a breath of air stirring. The road is level as yet, but the dust is dreadful. I had heard of the dust of California roads, but this surpasses belief. It would be an impossibility for any road in an Eastern State to be so dusty, try as it might, for its soil is nowhere parched with a six months' drought. California ladies have told me that they have seen their husbands come home after stage rides so begrimed with dust that neither the wives of their bosoms nor the mothers who bore them could recognize the wanderers. I tried to talk to my companion in the stage; I was choked by the dust. Conversation was impossible. A fence six feet from the stage window was invisible behind the dust cloud. I put my head gasping out of the window to see the driver. He was gone; so were the horses. The crack of the whip was still heard, and some locomotive power was impelling us forward; but through the dust who should say what it was? The features of my companions grew indistinguishable through the layers upon layers which gathered upon their once ruddy faces; the jet-black waterfall of the Chicago bride miraculously turned white after the fashion of the prisoner of Chillon; and more than that—it began to wobble. But if the wobbling had been confined to waterfalls alone, never, oh never, should this plaint have been penned. The wobbling very soon became general, universal, annoying, painful, intolerable, maddening! We had left the few miles of level road which beguile the traveller on leaving Stockton, and were now ascending the foothills. And our troubles were but begun. At Chinese Camp some of our passengers got out to go by another route. We also got out, for here we changed stages. We left the decent coach which took us up at Stockton, and were now ensconced in a hard, lumbering, springless, unpainted fiend (I am satisfied this wagon was a thing of feeling, and chuckled in every one of its rusty bolts and creaked in all its ugly joints at the pain it caused us), and were thumped along at the pace of lunatics over the stony ascent.

We try our best to enjoy life. Along the road we stop at ranches and buy delicious fruit at moderate prices. The scenery is wild and grand; the air is pure and sweet; the fruit we buy is so ripe and juicy that it fairly melts in the mouth. Isn't this a delightful picture? This is what all tourists write about. Now the truth is, that the possession of these things—even no further than this on our journey—is scarcely noticed. After the Yo Semite trip is all over, and you try to find some excuse for yourself in having been such a ninny as to run sheep-like where the other sheep bells tinkled, then you remember that those ranches where the fruit was sold were luxuriant, the fruit was delicious, the view of the mountains grand. At present you are coated with dust, your eyes are smarting, your tongue is clogged, your hair is caked, your limbs are sore, your flesh is inflamed, you want to go home. And this is only the first day, over the best part of the road, and in the stage. What will it be when it comes to the "trail" and the "pack" and the "horseback" part of it?

At 10 o'clock on the night of the first day (having been jolted since 6 o'clock in the morning) we pulled up supperless at Garrote. Here, for the first time in the journey so far, we get food which is eatable, even palatable. The cook is a Chinaman, the landlady French, and the landlord a Boston man. "We must leave at 4 o'clock," the driver says, as we creep wearily and painfully to bed. "Oh, very well, just as you say; I'll get up at midnight if you desire it; *only* — I thought this was a pleasure trip."

We left Garrote a mile or so behind, and until we reached Big Gap the road was endurable enough. This was lucky, because we were so sore and stiff from the previous day's ride that a repetition so early the next morning would have probably killed us. The young bride's waterfall, too, had acted yesterday in a very undignified manner from the merciless jolting it received. It wobbled and wiggled and shot off hairpins, and finally settled, a sticky mass, somewhere in the region of her left ear. She giggled as it wiggled, and clapped her hand to her head and vowed that it was too bad! and that she was going to shave her head like the Chinese, you see if she didn't! But this was her honeymoon, you understand, when it is hard not to be looking one's prettiest. So out she came on the second morning still bearing the waterfall triumphant, though it flapped like a pendant flag through lack of the needful pins. Presently the road began to grow worse, then worse; then — "Oh, driver, stop! let me get out and walk! Oh, do go slowly!" — a chorus from inside. The brute, unmindful, tears madly on — jolting over rocks, goading his horses down the hollows only to run up the opposite side at an insane gallop, sending the battered inmates to the roof, where their heads are banged and beaten; around jutting and dangerous precipices, where one inch too near the edge will pitch the stage, crashing through pines, to destruction. One passenger — an interesting lumberman from Maine, whose fifteen years' exploits in California, as he related them to us, would make a curious and fascinating chapter — remembers when a stage did tip over from reckless driving. Not very long ago. Stage broken all to smash, and a lady killed. This is cheerful. Will it be likely to do so some more? Not impossible. Bang! bang! over rocks and stones. Up we go to the roof, and then down we are crushed on the hard-as-iron seats. The bride from Chicago pays no more attention to her waterfall. Let it flap, let it fly, let it tumble off; she is reckless, poor soul, with suffering. Even yesterday her hysterical laughter as she was flung about the stage broke now and then into a shriek; but today it is the shriek without the laugh. She is in agony. Great black rings show themselves under her eyes, drops of cold sweat break out on her forehead, her hands nervously clutch the window straps; she supplicates with tears to be allowed to get out—to be left upon the road. She is sea-sick as well as sore, and in truth we are all in a pitiable plight, and nobody but ourselves, and other travelled monkeys who have endured this style of tail cutting, to blame for it. And only to think that the worst is yet to come.

But our horses have been watered long before this, and our tortures have again begun. Bang! bang! "Keep your seat Mr. Greeley!" shouts the facetious-minded. And that of all things is just now the most impossible.

Hail, log cabin! Relief has come at last. Here is where we drop the stage, and take the horses. We have dinner here. This is Hodgden's.

The dinner is execrable at Hodgden's. It is composed of salt beef, cold beans, watery potatoes, and boiling tea, as weak as hot. We pay the same price for it, however, as we do for the delicious dinner at the Grand Hotel in "Frisco"; and indeed log-cabin accommodations in the mountains are more expensive (to tourists) than the finest quarters in yon city shut in behind its Golden Gate. And how we all wish we were there!

Dinner over, we mount our steeds—sorry brutes, who look at us with eyes of sullen reproach. I must confess they are badly treated. Not the slightest politeness is shown even the most aged of them.

At first the change from the stage to the horse is pleasant. At least you can now regulate your own miseries, and need no longer be a poor thing beaten and banged by a merciless stage-driver without remorse. This is your theory. It is groundless. Ferguson now takes the place of the stage-driver. He is the guide, a Mexican born in California, and as graceful and as handsome as a picture.

Particularly the bride from Chicago. She moans, she weeps, she bends her poor battered head down upon the horse's neck for relief. Her waterfall is gone—whither we know not. On investigation we find Ferguson has it. It dropped off in the trail, and he thought her head was coming off, but picking it up found she was only painlessly scalped. Without joking, this poor creature's condition is very alarming. We are afraid she will have to be left behind. Her husband is sick. Everybody is sick and sore. Poor idiots, wandering on horseback over these mountain fastnesses, we all get what we deserve for coming!

Ferguson does not want to alarm us, but says if we don't hurry up we won't get to Hamilton's (another H!) at Tamarack Flat to-night. That will be bad, as there is not a single habitation between us and that place. To increase our discomforts, night falls early and a heavy mountain rain sets in. We are drenched and weary—oh, so weary! We let the reins fall over the horse's neck. He follows the trail of his own freewill, and has such an affectionate regard for the blazes, that he scrubs us up against the trees to our infinite discomfort. Another pleasing diversion takes place. Ferguson is driving a pack-mule heavily laden; and with the obstinacy of its race, every ten minutes or so it runs off and has to be followed on the keen gallop by Ferguson, hallooing and shouting, and using the rope about his horse's neck for a whip, driving it back into the path. All our horses being accustomed to drive mules, they all turn out and gallop after the offender, causing their weary riders to perform involuntary circus feats which bring tears to their eyes.

At Tamarack Flat the experienced Hamilton is ready—he is ready every time every saddle train arrives, for he knows the state the arrivers will be in—and he lifts the poor tourist-women off their horses. Our limbs are paralyzed. Some of us are barely alive; the bride from Chicago has swooned. The good wife Hamilton does all she can for us. She offers wine—she rubs us with whiskey; and at last all of us—men, women, and children, married and unmarried, friends and total strangers—lie down in the one only room which composes their cabin, and pass the night in blissful disregard of civilization and modesty at once. *A propos*—lest the reader might forget it, I wish to again remind him here that this is a pleasure trip.

We are up betimes in the morning, and quaff again the delicious mountain air. Time to be off! The rumor is that we shall get to Hutchings's (in the Valley) at noon. Another episode. A rival Ferguson, runner for the other route and the other Valley hotel, makes us more unhappy than we have hitherto been by aspersions on the fair name of Hutchings, the host of the hotel to which we are bound. Hutchings, according to Ferguson No. 2, is a villain who starves his guests, and puts them into beds already habited by another genus. The road over which we are to pass is more dangerous, rockier, more mountainous, more unendurable than any we have seen. These are reassuring tidings to people in our demoralized condition. Ferguson No. 1 denies the aspersions of No. 2, and together they have it hot and heavy. Meantime, to horse! There are only ten miles more of this torture left. At least so we are told by one party; another says there are fifteen. In San Francisco we were told that the whole distance on horseback (of which we have come already considerably more than ten miles) was but eighteen. Doctors and mountaineers disagree.

And now begins the weary trudge again. Oh, positively we shall never live through it. We are obliged to be lifted from our horses every two or three miles, and placed under the shade of trees to rest. The sun creeps higher and higher. It pours its burning rays upon our aching heads, for we are again mounted. The pack-mule runs away; we all run with unpleasant regularity after it, our horses trotting like triphammers, and beating the very breath out of our bodies. And so on and on we go. Eight miles! It is eighty! At length we reach the precipice which is to conduct us into the Valley.

Also here, to represent the dreary period of suffering which elapsed after we began the steep descent of the precipice, and until we reached the goal of our hopes—Hutchings's Hotel.

We do get there at last—all things have an end. But the night has fallen again; we should have reached Hutchings's at noon, but were not able. At any rate, here we are. Our sufferings are at an end now. And to-morrow shall burst upon our enchanted eyes the glorious sight whose beauty is to atone for all. Meantime we are too paralyzed to stir; Hutchings lifts us off our horses—inert masses of what were once tolerably strong-minded and particularly strong-bodied women. Hutchings pours wine down our throats. He tells us we are doing well, as most ladies faint. Mrs. Hutchings rubs us with whiskey; this feels good except in places where the skin is gone; then it makes us moan. We have not strength enough left to squirm.*

---

*It must not be supposed that the women alone suffered. The men were almost as bad. Mr. Greeley visited Yo Semite later, when he was at the zenith of his physical strength; but read in what a condition he was, as told by Hutchings himself in his palavering "Guide": "The mule he rode was considered the hardest trotting brute in America; and Mr. G. (not the mule) being somewhat corpulent, there was but little unabrased cuticle left him. Arriving at the hotel after midnight, *he was lifted from his saddle,* and at his own request put superless to bed. A little after noon the same day, having speaking engagements to fill, he started back without even seeing the lake, or the great sights on the main river."

The dawn breaks in the morning of the next day, and, shining red as fire through the pine knots of the log-cabin where Hutchings dwells, strikes our leaden eyelids and bids us arise. Reluctantly we do so. This is the end of our wanderings. Here is the great prize to obtain a view of which we have come so many weary miles. Now we are to be repaid for all. We make a hurried toilet, and as quickly as our stiffened limbs will permit, we drag out to see the view which "shall awe us, shall make us lose our identity, shall cause us to feel as though we were in the spirit land."*

And what do we see? Tall rocks, a few tall trees, a high and narrow waterfall, a pretty little river! No more. A lovely natural scene, I grant you; but oh! where in this broad and beautiful land of ours are not lovely natural scenes the rule? Words cannot tell the feeling of cold despair which came over me and all our party as we looked about us. Was it for this we had so suffered!

By another day some of us are well enough to mount again and begin our search after Beauty. We find an occasional rattlesnake, unlimited fatigue, and the tombstone of a man who was kicked to death by his horse. The trips are very wearying, the scenery very grand, very beautiful, but we are in no condition to enjoy it.

At the end of three days, homesick, and above all physically sick, we conclude to go home. Hutchings is deeply chagrined at this.

I can truly say that I never in my life saw a more miserable set of people than the poor candle-moth tourists who were gathered this summer in the Yo Semite Valley. The bride from Chicago was stretched in her rough bed alarmingly ill, and no physician nearer than civilization, which seemed so far that we surely must all die before we got back to it. Her husband, who had gone to see Mirror Lake, fell off his horse in a swoon, and lay there for six hours till help came. He was got home with difficulty.

To California women who think nothing of jumping astride an un-broken horse and riding him bareback, the trip to Yo Semite presents few hardships. I refer to women who live in the mountain towns, for California city women are, like most city women, dainty and delicate.

There are numerous other towns with names of mellifluous beauty

---

*These phrases are quoted from divers authorities; any one who has read about the Yo Semite will recognize these old acquaintances.

—Vallejo, San Jose, Oakland, Los Angeles. Go to all these; spend your money freely in California, for they need it, times being hard, and it is better, more fraternal, to give your money to California than to Europe; go to any of the mountain towns where the railroad stops (the railroad, from end to end, is in splendid condition); but *don't* go to the Geysers, *don't* go to Lake Tahoe, *don't* go to Yo Semite—in short, never ride of your own free-will in a California stage.

Notes

CHAPTER 1.

1. Clappe, *California*, I. 27.
2. Colton, *Three Years*, p. 17.
3. Dakin, *Scotch Paisano*, pp. 8-10.
4. McCracken, "When Santa Clara County was Young."
5. Colton, *op. cit.*, p. 93.
6. Vioget's House, pp. 7, 34.

CHAPTER 2.
(Recollections of the Author.)

CHAPTER 3.

1. Andresen, *Historical Landmarks*, p. 31.
2. *Loc. cit.*
3. Powers, *Old Monterey*, p. 231.
4. Bancroft, *California*, III, 378, 672; IV, 743.
5. Monterey county archives. Padron, p. 11.
6. *Ibid.*, Solares, p. 24.
7. San Carlos Church archives. Marriages, p. 67. This entry is almost inelligle, but it is certain that the date as cited is correct.
8. Jochmus, *Monterey*, p. 63; *City of Monterey*, p. 15.
9. Andresen, *op. cit.*, p. 32.
10. Fisher, *The Salinas*, p. 154; Guinn, *Historical*, II, 363. See the last citation for the origin of the name "Julia Liedesdorff."
11. Larkin, Account books, XII, 85, 89; Bancroft, *op. cit.*, IV, 453; V. 751.
12. Elliott & Moore, *Monterey County*, p. 178.
13. Bancroft, *op. cit.*, IV, 566, 711.
14. *Ibid.*, 711.
15. *Ibid.*, V, 575-81; Sandels, *Sojourn*, p. 37; Davis, *Seventy-five years*, p. 180; cf. "Notes and sketches on the bay and river," *Hutchings' Illustrated California Magazine* (July, 1859), p. 4.
16. Bancroft, *op. cit.*, III, 378; IV, 743.
17. Larkin, Documents, I, 1, 31-32.
18. City of Monterey, 1842. This is a sketch that Thomas O. Larkin sent to his cousin, the Rev. William M. Rogers, of Boston, on June 3, 1843. It was published in 1851 as a lithograph, and shows Tresconi's house on the spot that later became the northwest corner of Pearl and Washington streets. Montenegro's house is shown a little to the northward of Tresconi's, and on the line of the latter street. The names of the property owners were added by hand at a later date, and the print was then reproduced. A copy of the original sketch, without the names of the property owners, is the property of Miss Frances M. Molera, of San Francisco, and is on exhibition at the California Historical Society, San Francisco.

19. Englehardt, *San Carlos*, p. 213.
20. Page 8, above.
21. Larkin, Monterey consulate accounts, I. 1-15, *passim*.
22. Colton, *Three Years*, p. 189.
23. Jochmus, *City of Monterey*, p. 19; *Monterey*, p. 42.
24. Monterey county archives. Miscellaneous documents, pp. 57-58.
25. Colton, *op. cit.*, pp. 195-97; *Californian* (Monterey), May 1847.
26. Colton, *loc. cit.*
27. Larkin, *op. cit.*, p. 5.
28. Fisher, *op. cit.*, p. 155.
29. Larkin, *op. cit.*, p. 87.
30. City of Monterey, Note 18, above; Narvaez, Map of Monterey; Toothaker and Westfall, Map of Monterey; Little, Map of Monterey.
31. Ryan, *Personal Adventures*, II, 89, 92-94. Italics are the present writer's.
32. Monterey county archives. Deeds of grants, p. 39.
33. Little, *op. cit.*; Neasham, Map of Monterey; Early photographs of the Washington Hotel and Tresconi's house.
34. Taylor, *Eldorado*, I. 139.
35. *Ibid.*
36. Monterey county archives. Leases, p. 27.
37. *Pacific Sentinel*. June 19, 1858.
38. Julius Tresconi's statements to his sister-in-law, Alice Griffin.
39. Alberto Tresconi's personal papers, *passim*.
40. Jeans, "Architectural remains," p. 26.
41. Andresen, "California's First Hotel."
42. Bancroft, *op. cit.*, IV, 690; V, 529, 741; Colton *op. cit.*, p. 322; Lyman, Chester, Sr., *Around the Horn*, pp. 263, 277.
43. *California Star*, November 14, 1847; Bancroft, *op. cit.*, III, 789.
44. *Californian*, March 9, 1848.
45. Larkin, Official correspondence, II, 74.
46. Colton, *op. cit.*, pp. 247-48; Bourne, "Reminiscences."
47. Hutton, *Glances*, Plates XXX, XL; Colton, *op. cit.*, pp. 195-96.
48. McFarland, *Monterey*, p. 54.
49. Colton, *op. cit.*, p. 196. Italics are the present writer's.
50. Johnson, *Sights*, p. 110.

CHAPTER 4.

1. Bowman, Jean Jacques Vioget, *passim*.
2. Sutter, *Six French Letters*, p. 5.
3. Depending on the author consulted, the *Delmira* was of Peruvian or Ecuadorian registry, and the reader is left to select whichever country he favors. However, the water-color sketch of Yerba Buena that Captain Vioget made in the spring of 1837 shows a brigantine, flying the Swiss flag at her main truck and the Ecuadorian colors at her main-gaff. This ship was unquestionably the *Delmira*, and the question seems thus settled in favor of Ecuador.

4. Vioget, Yerba Buena in the Spring of 1837. The original of this water-color sketch is the property of Mr. Austin Peterson, of Los Angeles, and is on exhibition at the Wells Fargo Bank Museum, San Francisco.

5. Bancroft, Notes on Jean Jacques Vioget. MS. Bancroft Library. *Passim.*

6. Vioget, Autobiography. The alcalde referred to was Francisco Guerrero y Palomares.

7. *Ibid.*

8. Barry and Patten, *Men and Memories,* p. 207.

9. Eldredge, *San Francisco,* II, 511, 732.

10. *Ibid.,* pp. 504-07, *passim.*

11. Dwinelle, *Colonial History,* Addendum, pp. 69, 75.

12. Bancroft, Notes, Vioget, *passim.*

13. Dwinelle, *op. cit.,* pp. 72-73.

14. Davis, *Seventy-five Years,* pp. 92-93.

15. Riesenberg, *Golden Gate,* pp. 53-54.

16. Brown, *Early Days,* pp. 21-22.

17. Barry and Patten, *op. cit.,* p. 211.

18. Davis, *op. cit.,* pp. 258-59.

19. Bancroft, *California,* IV, 179.

20. *Ibid.,* V, 764, *passim.*

21. *Ibid.,* IV, 765; V, 764.

22. Bancroft, Notes, Vioget, *passim;* Finley, *Sonoma County,* p. 87.

23. Davis, *op. cit.,* pp. 257-58; Sandels, *Sojourn,* pp. 37-38.

24. Bancroft, *California,* IV, 673, 674.

25. Finley, *op. cit.,* pp. 83-84, *passim.*

26. Brown, *op. cit.,* p. 24; Bancroft, *op. cit.,* V, 680.

27. Bowman, *op. cit., passim;* cf. Bancroft, *op. cit.,* V, 764.

28. Hendry and Bowman, Adobes, p. 1197.

29. Barry and Patten, *op. cit.,* p. 211.

30. Bowman, The burial place of Jean Jacques Vioget. The late Harry C. Peterson located Captain Vioget's grave about 1900, and photographed it. On November 25, 1942, Dr. Bowman relocated the grave, and identified it as Lot 1, Plot 17, Section 6, in the Oak Hill Cemetery, San Jose, Calif.

31. Brown, *op. cit.,* 1-17, *passim;* Bancroft, *op. cit.,* II, 732-33; Notes, Vioget, *passim.*

32. Brown says that he arrived in Yerba Buena the second time on January 10, 1846 (Brown, *op. cit.,* p. 19), but according to the records of Sutter's Fort he did not leave there until January 14th (Sutter, *New Helvetia Diary,* p. 30). The latter date is reliable, and Brown could not have arrived much before January 20, 1846.

33. Brown, *op. cit.,* p. 13.

34. Bancroft, *op. cit.,* V, 683.

35. Brown, *op. cit.,* p. 24.

36. *Ibid.,* pp. 24-25.

37. Bancroft, *op. cit.,* V, 136; Brown, *op. cit.,* pp. 26-27.

38. Brown, *op. cit.,* p. 30.

39. Bancroft, *op. cit.,* III, 752; IV, 480; Brown, *op. cit.,* p. 31.

40. Sandles, *A Sojourn in California*

41. Brown, *op. cit.,* p. 31.

42. Golden Era (February 27, 1853); *"Saw filings."* cf. Brown, *op. cit.,* p. 32; Bancroft, *op. cit.,* IV, 249; Eldredge, *op. cit.,* II, 540-41.

CHAPTER 5.

1. Brown, *Early Days,* pp. 28-29.

2. Phelps, *Fore and Aft,* pp. 294-95.

3. Brown, *op. cit.,* p. 29.

4. Bancroft, *California,* V, 544, 554; *Times and Seasons,* VI, 1043.

5. Brown, *op. cit., pp.* 37-38.

6. *Ibid.,* p. 39; Phelps, *op. cit.,* pp. 290-91; Eldredge, *San Francisco,* II, 712-13.

7. Swasey, *Early Days,* pp. 63-64.

8. Brown, *op. cit.,* pp. 38-39; *Californian* (Monterey), October 17, 24, 1846.

9. Brown, *loc. cit;* Bancroft, *op. cit.,* II, 721; V, 370, 726.

10. Brown, *op. cit.,* pp. 27-28; Bancroft, *op. cit.,* V, 695.

11. Brown, *op. cit.,* p. 36; Bancroft, *op. cit.,* 773.

12. Brown, *op. cit.,* pp. 39-41.

13. *Ibid.,* pp. 41-42; cf. Alley, Bowen, *Santa Clara,* p. 772.

14. Brown, *op. cit.,* pp. 36-37; Vallejo, Documentos, pt. 3, Doc. 229.

15. Scott, *Brannan,* pp. 98, 105, 124, 143; Bancroft, *op. cit.,* IV, 771.

16. Brown, *op. cit.,* p. 130.

17. John Henry Brown papers, Norris Collection.

18. Brown, *op. cit.,* p. 44.

19. Bancroft, *op. cit.,* V, 645-46 and Note 1; 670-71, Note 3; *Californian* (San Francisco), June 19, 1847.

20. *California Star,* August 3, 1847; Eldredge, *op. cit.,* II, 564; Piper, "Recollections"; Pages 31-32, above.

21. Bancroft, *op. cit.,* V, 646.

22. Contemporary San Francisco newspapers, *passim.*

23. Barry and Patten, *Men and Memories,* pp. 18-19.

CHAPTER 6.

1. Bryant, *What I Saw,* p. 322; Brown, *Early Days,* pp. 20, 131, 134-35; Bancroft, *California,* V, 678; Soulé, *Annals,* illustration, p. 346.

2. Brown, *op. cit.,* p. 31.

3. *Ibid.,* p. 135.

4. *Ibid.,* pp. 44, 61, 75; cf. Bancroft, *op. cit.,* IV, 737.

5. Brown, *op. cit.,* p. 44. Brown says, "...the eldest son of Mrs. Eager...," meaning Mrs. Lucy Eager's son, John. Bancroft, *op. cit.,* II, 787; V, 546; Scott, *Brannan,* pp. 124, 135; *Californian* (Monterey), December 15, 1846; *California Star,* April 24, 1847.

6. Brown, *op. cit.,* pp. 46, 55.

7. *Loc. cit.*; Bancroft, *op. cit.*, V. 379-83.

8. Brown, *op. cit.*, pp. 45-46, 57-59; *Alta California*, September 21, 1851.

9. Brown, *op. cit.*, pp. 62-64; Bancroft, *op. cit.*, II, 783; IV, 723; V, 530-44.

10. Brown, *op. cit.*, pp. 63-64.

11. Swasey, *Early Days*, pp. 83-84.

12. Alley, Bowen, *Santa Clara*, p. 772; Eldredge, *San Francisco*, II, pp. 593, 594

13. Brown, *op, cit.*, pp. 60, 65.

14. *Ibid.*, p. 135. Our description of Brown's, or the City Hotel, does not agree with the conventional second story and *four* dormer windows overlooking Kearny Street, that are so conspicuous in most of the contemporary pictures of San Francisco, but it is nevertheless correct. Soulé, *op. cit.*, illustration, p. 346; Taylor, *Eldorado*, I, 56; cf. Swasey, View of San Francisco, in 1846-1847.

15. Brown, *op. cit.*, p. 64.

16. *Ibid.*, pp. 68-69; Bancroft, *op. cit.*, V, pp. 657, 698.

17. *Californian* (San Francisco), and *California Star*, June 19, 1847; Tuthill, *California*, pp. 222-23; Theodore H. Hittell, *California*, II, 638; cf. Soulé, *op. cit.*, pp. 194-95.

18. Pages 65-66, above.

19. Brown, *op. cit.*, pp. 31, 83; Bancroft, *op. cit.*, V, 645-46, Note 1; Eldredge, *op. cit.*, II, 564; *Californian* (San Francisco), July 10, 1847.

20. Lyman, *Around the Horn*, pp. 205-06. If Lyman referred to San Francisco physician, this was Dr. John Townsend, not Alfred A. Townsend, as Lyman's editor states. Bancroft, *op. cit.*, V, 751.

21. Note 19, above; Lyman, *op. cit.*, p. 209; Bancroft, *op. cit.*, V, 772.

22. Brown, *op. cit.*, pp. 73-74. The man Brown refers to was Thomas Adams, who died in the City Hotel on August 9, 1848. *Californian* (San Francisco), August 14, 1848.

23. Brown, *op. cit.*, pp. 60-61; Bancroft, *loc. cit.*; Eldredge, *loc. cit.*

24. Brown, *op. cit.*, p. 75.

CHAPTER 7.

1. Bancroft, *California*, V, 721; *Pathfinder* (October 31, 1945), p. 16.

2. *California Star*, November 20, 1847; Bancroft, *op. cit.*, V, 646, 781.

3. Bancroft, *op. cit.*, VI, 45; Davis, *Seventy-five Years*, p. 309; Scott, *Brannan*, pp. 1-2.

4. Brown, *Early Days*, pp. 70-72; John S. Hittell, *Mining*, pp. 14-15; William T. Sherman, *Memoirs*, I, 40-41.

5. Brown, *op. cit.*, p. 78. Brown says that he returned to San Francisco in January, 1848, in a Spanish bark owned by a man named Luca. This must have been the Chilian bark *Natalia*, whose owner and supercargo was Juna M. Luco, and that arrived from the Hawaiian Islands on December 26, 1847. *Californian* (San Francisco), December 29, 1847; Bancroft, *op. cit.*, IV, 719; V, 579; cf. Davis, *op. cit.*, p. 408. This bark is not to be confused with the Mexican brig *Natalia*, that was lost at Monterey on December 21, 1834. The latter ship is said to have formerly been Napoleon Bonaparte's *L'Inconstant*, on which the emperor escaped from

Elba in 1815. Bancroft, *op. cit.*, III, 268; Davis, *op. cit.*, p. 404; Rose, *Napoleon* I, II, 441-42.

6. Brown, *op. cit.*, pp. 78-79.

7. It is not known how the expression "seeing the elephant" originated, but it caught the popular fancy and spread all over the country. During the Civil War it was used both by Northern and Southern veterans to impress recruits with what they had to look forward to in their first encounter with the enemy.

8. Brown, *op. cit.*, pp. 79-82.

9. *Ibid.*, pp. 82-83. Brown says that the lease began on January 1, 1848, but this is a slip of the memory. Norris, Brown papers; *California Star,* May 20, June 10, 1848.

10. Sterling, Letter.

11. Brown, *op. cit.*, pp. 108-09. It may well be that one of Brown's hunters was the Marques de Pindray, a French adventurer, who at the time was hunting game for the San Francisco market. Massey, *Frenchman,* p. 15. Later on de Pindrey led a filibustering expedition to the Mexican state of Sonora, where he lost his life. Wyllys, *French in Sonora,* pp. 58-62.

12. *Californian* (San Francisco), September 23, 1848.

13. Brown, *op. cit.*, pp. 72, 84-85, 89.

14. *Ibid,* pp. 85, 89.

15. *Ibid.,* pp. 92-93, 95-96, 97; Taylor, *Eldorado,* I, 61.

16. *California Star,* August 14, 1848; Soulé, *Annals,* p. 205.

17. *Californian* (San Francisco), August 14, 1848.

18. *Ibid.,* September 9, 16, 1848.

19. Brown, *op. cit.*, pp. 84-85, 89.

20. *Ibid.,* pp. 94-95; Bancroft, *op. cit.*, IV, 749.

21. Brown, *op. cit.*, p. 100; Bancroft, *op. cit.*, V, 577; VII, 336 *ff.*

22. Crosby, Statement, p. 12; Taylor, *op. cit.*, I, 205, 305.

23. Crosby, *op. cit.*, pp. 13-14.

24. Swasey, *Early Days,* p. 211; Brown, *op. cit.*, pp. 96-97; cf. Taylor, *op. cit.*, I, 60-61.

25. Taylor, *op. cit.*, I, 56.

26. Shaw, *Golden Dreams,* pp. 37-39; (Letts), *Pictorial,* p. 137.

27. Ryan, *Adventures,* II, 215-16.

28. The suggestion that the City Hotel was either burned or damaged in the fire of December 24, 1849, comes from Brown himself, the statement having been made during his testimony in the case of the United States *vs.* Joel S. Polack, *et al. San Francisco Herald,* March 30, 1857, "Yerba Buena Island." It is probable, however, that Brown was referring to the Parker House rather than to the City Hotel.

29. *Alta California,* September 21, 1851.

30. Scott, *op. cit.*, p. 246.

31. Morgan & Co., *Directory,* 1852, p. 114-A; LeCount & Strong, *Directory,* 1854, pp. 77, 148; Harris, Bogardus & Labatt, *Directory,* 1856.

CHAPTER 8.

1. Brown, *Early Days*, pp. 81-82, 87-88.

2. *Californian* (San Francisco), September 30, 1848; Bancroft, *California*, VI, 188.

3. Brown, *op. cit.*, pp. 88, 105-07; *Californian, loc. cit.*

4. Brown, *op. cit.*, pp. 106, 110; Bancroft, *op. cit.*, IV, 751, 774; V, 721.

5. Brown, *op. cit.*, p. 180; Larkin, Account books, XV, 46, 53.

6. *Californian* (Monterey), March 27, 1847; Ryan, *Adventures*, II, 88-90, 124.

7. Ryan, *op. cit.*, II, 128-29.

8. Brown, *op. cit.*, p. 108.

9. *Ibid.*, pp. 106, 110. Brown's "Libbett" was Francis J. Lippett (Swasey, *Men and Memories*, p. 274; Eldredge, *San Francisco*, II, 554); his "Judge Sutterly" was John Satterlee (Theodore H. Hittell, *California*, IV, 184); his "Dr. Geary" was Dr. S. Russell Gerry (Kimball, *Directory*, 1850, p. 49); and his "Doctor Rogers" was J. H. Rodgers (Kimball, *op. cit.*, p. 94). These are minor examples of the highly original phonetic spelling that John Henry Brown used for proper names throughout his book, that will be referred to later and at greater length. His crowning effort was unquestionably the amazing transformation of Mazatlán, the name of the Mexican Pacific coast seaport, into "Massack Land." This was sheer artistry, and established an all-time record for phonetization.

10. Soulé, *Annals*, pp. 242, 251 (illustrations); Ryan, *op. cit.*, I, 192.

11. Brown, *op. cit.*, pp. 110-11; Soulé, *op. cit.*, p. 254.

12. "Mr. C - -, of Monterey," was James Crane, the enterprising pie merchant of that place, and first manager of the Parker House dining room. He was later collector for the firm of Ward & Smith. Brown, *op. cit.*, pp. 117-18.

13. Ryan, *op. cit.*, II, 203-05.

14. Brown, *op. cit.*, pp. 123-24. "Wright" and "Haight" were Stephen A. Wright and Samuel W. Haight, who with John Thompson owned the Miners' Bank of San Francisco, an institution that loaned money at the rate of ten per cent per month, and sometimes at ten per cent per hour. It is probable that they were the most pressing of Parker's creditors, and the interest they demanded may have been one of the principal reasons for his failure. Brown, *op. cit.*, pp. 102, 123; Bancroft, *op. cit.*, V, 781; Hittell, *op. cit.*, IV, 407. George McDougal appears in the story of Brown's and the City Hotel, and it has been impossible to identify "Hart."

15. Brown, *op. cit.*, p. 125.

16. Bancroft, *op. cit.*, VI, 188; Soulé, *op. cit.*, p. 345; Hittell, *op. cit.*, III, 409; Byington, *San Francisco*, I, 228; Kimball, *op. cit.*, pp. 74, 86, 117; Taylor, *Eldorado*, II, 74.

17. Elliott & Co., *Humboldt County*, p. 101.

18. Brown, *op. cit.*, pp. 123-24; Swasey, *op. cit.*, pp. 210-11; Eldredge, *op. cit.*, II, 582; cf. Bancroft, *op. cit.*, IV, 767; V, 579.

19. Page 40, *above.*

20. Kimball, *op. cit.*, p. 72; Bancroft, *op. cit.*, VI, 174; Brown, John Henry, Biographical Notes; Rowland, letter.

CHAPTER 9.

1. *Calaveras Chronicle*, February 27, 1875.

2. Bancroft, *California*, V, 692.

3. *Ibid.*, VI, 183; V, 723, 725; Brown, *Early Days*, p. 137; *California Star*, December 4, 1847; Pages 58-59, above.

4. *Californian* (San Francisco), April 12, 1848.

5. *Ibid.*, September 9, 16, November 4, 1848; Bancroft, *op. cit.*, V, 685.

6. Brown, *op. cit.*, pp. 91-92; Bancroft, *California Pastoral*, p. 748.

7. Brown, *op. cit.*, p. 137; Bancroft, *California*, II, 790. With his usual quaint phonetic rendering of proper names, Brown spells the last one cited "Aleck." But in this case his version is understandable, as other writers have given it as Alleck, Allig, Ellick and Ellig.

8. Kimball, *Directory*, 1850, p. 38.

9. Ryan, *Adventures*, II, 258.

10. Soulé, *Annals*, p. 556; Eldredge, *San Francisco*, II, 599.

11. Bancroft, *op. cit.*, IV, 768.

12. Ryan, *op. cit.*, II, 242.

13. *Ibid.*, pp. 258-64, *passim*.

14. Bancroft, *op. cit.*, VI, 203.

15. Colville, *Directory*, 1856, p. 198.

16. Bancroft, *op. cit.*, II, 790.

17. Brown, *op. cit.*, pp. 75-76; Bancroft, *op. cit.*, V, 684.

18. *Californian* (San Francisco), November 10, 1847.

19. Bancroft, *op. cit.*, V, 685; Brown, *op. cit.*, p. 135.

20. Brown, *op. cit.*, p. 92.

21. Bancroft, *op. cit.*, II, 716; V, 685.

22. *Ibid.*, II, 779; V, 684.

23. *California Star*, November 20, 1847; Bancroft, *op. cit.*, II, 719.

24. Bancroft, *op. cit.*, V, 586, 663; Alley, Bowen, *Santa Clara*, pp. 339-40; Ryan, *op. cit.*, II, 167.

25. *Californian* (San Francisco), May 17, 1848.

26. Brown, *op. cit.*, pp. 121-22; *Alta California*, September 20, 1849; Bancroft, *op. cit.*, V, 692, 704.

27. Bancroft, *op. cit.*, V, 683, 771; *Californian* (San Francisco), March 15, 1848; *California Star*, April 4, 1848.

28. *Californian* (San Francisco), April 26, 1848; Bancroft, *Pastoral*, p. 745.

29. Ryan, *op. cit.*, II, 190-91; Bancroft, *California*, III, 792.

30. *Californian* (San Francisco), May 6, 1850; Bancroft, *op. cit.*, VI, 202.

31. Johnson, *Gold Region*, pp. 111-12.

32. *Loc. cit.*; Beach, "Reminiscences"; Bancroft, *op. cit.*, IV, 738; V, 685-86; Brown, *op. cit.*, p. 138.

33. Eldredge, *op. cit.*, II, 589.

34. *California Star*, November 27, 1847; Bancroft, *op. cit.*, II, 794.

35. Davis, *Seventy-five Years*, pp. 74-75.

36. *California Star,* January 12, February 12, 1848; *Pony Express Courier,* February, 1937.

37. *Californian* (San Francisco), September 9, 1848.

38. Morgan & Co., *Directory,* 1852, p. 106-A; LeCount & Strong, *Directory,* 1854, p. 147; Langley, *Directory,* 1858, p. 315.

CHAPTER 10.

1. Hall, *San Jose,* p. 50.

2. Alley, Bowen, *Santa Clara,* map facing p. 329; Bryant, *What I Saw,* pp. 315-17.

3. McCracken, "Santa Clara"; page 10, above.

4. Clyman, "Diaries," pp. 134, 135.

5. Bryant, *op. cit.,* p. 315.

6. Sawyer, *Santa Clara,* p. 57; Thompson & West, *Atlas,* p. 10.

7. Wyatt and Arbuckle, *Historic Names,* p. 17; Bancroft, *California,* IV, 695.

8. McCracken, *loc. cit.;* Hall, *op. cit.,* p. 188.

9. Lyman, *Around the Horn,* pp. 245 ff; Wyatt and Arbuckle, *loc. cit.*

10. Alley, Bowen, *op. cit.,* p. 705.

11. *Ibid.*

12. Larkin, *Documents,* Vol. 6, Pt. 1, Doc. 74; Lyman, *op. cit.,* p. 256; Alley, Bowen, *Loc. cit.*

13. Alley, Bowen, *loc. cit.;* William T. Sherman, *Memoirs,* I, 55; *Californian* (San Francisco), July 31, 1847.

14. Lyman, *op. cit.,* pp. 265-67, *passim.*

15. *Ibid.,* p. 268; Alley, Bowen, *loc. cit.;* Bancroft, *op. cit.,* IV, 695.

16. Lyman, *op. cit.,* p. 303.

17. Tinkham, *Stockton,* pp. 55-62, *passim;* Thompson & West, *op. cit.,* p. 10; Sawyer, *loc. cit.*

18. Sutter, Reminiscences, p. 70.

19. Swasey, Statement, p. 4.

20. Hall, *op. cit.,* pp. 147, 150; Bancroft, *op. cit.,* V, 137, 770.

21. Bancroft, *op. cit.,* V, 294.

22. *Californian* (San Francisco), December 1, 1847.

23. Lyman, *op. cit.,* pp. 230, 242.

24. Thompson & West, *Yuba County,* p. 36; *Atlas,* p. 10.

25. Pages 58-59, above.

26. Alley, Bowen, *op. cit.,* pp. 341, 776.

27. Hall, *op. cit.,* pp. 190-91.

28. Lyman, *op. cit.,* p. 269; Alley, Bowen, *op. cit.,* p. 341; Hall, *op. cit.,* p. 192; Tinkham, *op. cit.,* p. 73; Theodore H. Hittell, *California,* II, 693; III, 74, 75.

29. Johnson, *Gold Region,* p. 164; Hall, *op. cit.,* pp. 192-93; Bancroft, *op. cit.,* IV, 749.

30. Tinkham, *op. cit.,* p. 68.

31. Hall, *op. cit.,* p. 135; cf. Bancroft, *op. cit.,* II, 775.

32. Sawyer, *op. cit.,* p. 57.

33. Bancroft, *loc. cit.;* Sawyer, *loc. cit.*
34. Ryan, *Adventures,* I, 264.
35. Bancroft, *op. cit.,* II, 728.
36. Ryan, *op. cit.,* II, 86-87; Hall, *op. cit.,* p. 196.
37. Swan, Gold Mines, pp. 3, 23.

CHAPTER 11.

1. Bryant, *What I Saw,* pp. 309-13; "The Missions of Alta California," *Century,* (January, 1891), p. 400.
2. Forbes, *California Missions,* p. 82.
3. *Californian* (Monterey), October 17, 1846.
4. *Century, loc. cit.*
5. Harlan, *California,* pp. 40, 43.
6. *Ibid.,* pp. 74-75, 80.
7. *Ibid.,* p. 21; Bancroft, *California,* III, 761-62; Slocum & Co., *Contra Costa,* p. 573.
8. Ryan, *Adventures,* II, 83.
9. *Ibid.,* pp. 81-85, *passim.*
10. Citizens' Committee, *Souvenir,* pp. 25-29, *passim;* Bryant, *op. cit.,* p. 317.
11. Bryant, *op. cit.,* p. 318; Wyatt and Arbuckle, *Historic Names,* p. 7; Alley, Bowen, *Santa Clara,* p. 775.
12. Bancroft, *op. cit.,* II, 716; V, 462 ff.
13. *Californian* (San Francisco), February 7, 1848; Alley, Bowen, *op. cit.,* p. 544; Foote, *Pen Pictures,* p. 205.
14. Bancroft, *op. cit.,* II, 715.
15. Knowland, *California,* p. 43.
16. Bancroft, *op. cit.,* III, 353; V, 561; II, 778.
17. Engelhardt, *San Juan Bautista,* pp. 57, 62.
18. California State, "Landmark No. 179," pp. 9-10.
19. Giffin, "Adobes," p. 18.
20. Bancroft, *op. cit.,* II, 751-52.
21. *Ibid.,* 729.
22. *Oakland Tribune,* "Knave," June 18, 1939.
23. Giffin, *loc. cit.*
24. Browne, *Crusoe's Island,* pp. 167, 170-72; Thornton, *Oregon and California,* II, 220; Houghton, *Donner Party,* p. 119. cf. McGlashan, *Donner Party,* pp. 187-88.
25. John and Patrick Breen, Statements.
26. Meyer, *Bound for Sacramento,* pp. x, 69-70.
27. Bancroft, *op. cit.,* II, 729; *Monterey Gazette,* December 31, 1868.
28. Engelhardt, *San Francisco,* pp. 236, 239; Theodore H. Hittell, *California,* II, 204.
29. California state archives, Missions, IV, 445-50.
30. Bancroft, *op. cit.,* V, 659; Engelhardt, *op. cit.,* p. 312.
31. California state archives, *op. cit.,* 723-71.
32. Engelhardt, *op. cit.,* p. 316.

33. Bancroft, *op. cit.*, VI, 187.

34. LeCount and Strong, *Directory*, 1854, p. 149; Langley, *Directory*, 1867, p. 408.

35. Ryan, *op. cit.*, II, 287-88; cf. Gerstacker, *Narrative*, pp. 181-82.

36. *Alta California*, May 27, 1850.

CHAPTER 12.

1. Gates, *Rancho Pastoria*, pp. 14, 23.

2. Lyman, *Around the Horn*, p. 245.

3. Harlan, *California*, p. 116; Alley, Bowen, *Santa Clara*, p. 258; Survey No. 131, Santa Clara county archives, County Engineer's Office, Record of Surveys, Book A, p. 134; Bancroft, *California*, IV, 690; contemporary maps of Santa Clara county.

4. Lyman, *op. cit.*, pp. 245, 248, 252, 253.

5. Harlan, *op. cit.*, pp. 116, 126, 128, 134-35.

6. *Ibid.*, pp. 134-35.

7. *Ibid.*, pp. 137-38.

8. Lyman, *op. cit.*, p. 289.

9. Harlan, *op. cit.*, pp. 141, 146, 148.

10. *Alta California*, September 20, 1849.

11. Ward, "Stage-coach days," pp. 256-57.

12. Alley, Bowen, *loc. cit.*; cf. Bancroft, *op. cit.*, IV, 714; Harlan, *op. cit.*, p. 173.

13. Gates, *op. cit.*, p. 20.

14. Harlan, *op. cit.*, pp. 173-74; Bancroft, *op. cit.*, V, 751; Bidwell, Letter.

15. Gates, *op. cit.*, p. 19; cf. Alley, Bowen, *op. cit.*, p. 784.

16. Gates, *op. cit.*, p. 20.

17. Santa Clara county archives, *loc. cit.*; Hoffman, *Reports*, I, Appendix, 36; Bancroft, *op. cit.*, II, 775.

18. Gates, *op. cit.*, pp. 20, 24.

19. Bancroft, Scrapbooks, XII, 78; Gates, *op. cit.*, p. 20.

20. Bancroft, *California*, VII, 537.

21. Alley, Bowen, *op. cit.*, p. 258; Betty, *Directory*, 1889, p. 58.

CHAPTER 13.

1. As the historical accuracy of this bronze plaque has been challenged, it is only fair to give the full text of its statement, as follows: "Blue Wing Inn. Erected by General Mariano G. Vallejo about 1840 for the accommodation of emigrants and other travelers. Purchased in the Gold Rush days by Cooper and Spriggs, two retired seafaring men and operated as hotel and store. Among the first hostelries in northern California. Notable guests, according to local tradition, included John C. Fremont [sic.], U. S. Grant, Governor Pio Pico, Kit Carson, "Fighting Joe" Hooker, William T. Sherman, Phil Sheridan and members of the Bear Flag party. Classed among the notorious visitors, were bandit Murietta [sic.] and "Three Fingered Jack." Placed by Historical Landmarks Commission Native Sons of the Golden West October 1941." Later on there will be occasion to inquire more

closely into some of the claims made by brazen memorial, and there is no occasion
to say anything more about the matter at this time.

2. Tays, "Mariano Guadalupe Vallejo," pp. 109-14.

3. Charles Brown, Statement, p. 10.

4. Tays, *op. cit.*, pp. 235-44, *passim;* Vallejo, Recuerdos, III, 11; Bancroft, *California*, III, 294; John S. Hittell, *Resources*, p. 426. Lest exception be taken to this
or to any subsequent statements that may seem to suggest that General Vallejo
profited by the secularization of the missions, it must be understood that such
satements are no more than reflections of those made by some of the General's
contemporaries. Eugène Duflot de Morfas, writing in 1842, states categorically
that Vallejo robbed San Solano and San Rafael, and demolished the former mission's church for material to build his house in Sonoma. Duflot, *Exploration*, I,
324-25. General Sutter not only confirms Duflot's accusation, to the effect that
Vallejo appropriated most of the mission property at San Rafael and San Solano,
but refers to alleged acts of a similar nature that occurred at San José, where
Salvador Vallejo, the General's brother, was in charge. Sutter, Personal reminiscences, pp. 121-22. Vicente Perfecto Gómez, who came to California in 1842
with General Micheltorena, as the new governor's secretary, is much more specific in his accusations. According to him Benito Díaz, the collector of customs
at Yerba Buena, openly charged Vallejo with having stolen livestock and other
property from the above missions, including the silver church vessels, ornaments
and utensils of San Solano, to a total value of some $200,000. Díaz's charges were
made in the presence of Micheltorena and Vallejo, and were so serious that the
governor convened a military board of inquiry to hear and take down the evidence. Gómez, who was present throughout the entire affair, states that the testimony, which included letters from the priests of the ex-missions and others,
was so adverse to Vallejo that the governor advised him to be prepared to proceed
to the city of Mexico to appear before a court-martial board, that it seemed the
case called for. Vallejo was so upset by the outcome of a matter that he had
thought to be able to brush off that he became ill, and was confined to his bed.
Influential friends then sought to induce Díaz to withdraw his charges, but he
refused all offers to compromise the matter until Governor Micheltorena called
on him personally. A private conversation followed, and immediately thereafter
Vallejo returned to Sonoma and the case was hushed up. When Micheltorena
returned to Mexico in 1845 he was believed to have taken with him all the records
of the board of inquiry, and these, Gómez says, are supposed to be on file in the
Mexican War Department's archives. Gómez, Lo que sabe, pp. 411-17. When the
History of California was being written by Bancroft's unacknowledged authors
he was fully aware of the foregoing, together with much more evidence of a like
nature, but made no mention of this anywhere in his works. And this despite the
fact that he gives Gómez credit for having dictated voluminous reminiscences of
historic value. Bancroft, *op. cit.*, III, 759. Insofar as is known, the only previous
attempt to throw any light on this and similar passages in General Vallejo's career
was made by Dr. George Tays, when he wrote his "Mariano Guadalupe Vallejo
and Sonoma." This scholarly and profusely documented biography and history

was printed in the *California Historical Society Quarterly*, but all references to the foregoing matters were deleted by the editors before Dr. Tays' manuscript was accepted for publication.

5. Tays, *op. cit.*, pp. 240-41; Bancroft, *op. cit.*, IV, 680-81; Pierce, Journal, *passim.*

6. Hendry and Bowman, Adobes, pp. 215-17.

7. Tays, *op. cit.*, p. 243; Sonoma county archives, Deeds, Book A, No. 2, pp. 4, 5.

8. Tays, *op. cit.*, p. 241; Finley, Sonoma, pp. 233-34. According to José de la Guerra y Noriega, some of the missions were turned into brothels by the government *mayordomos*. Guerra, Documents, VII, 82-83.

9. Tays, *loc. cit.*

10. *Ibid.*, pp. 240, 249; Bancroft, *op. cit.*, II, 721; IV, 750; V, 772, 777, 783.

11. Tays, *op. cit.*, XVII, 152. Vallejo was promoted from the rank of ensign to sub-lieutenant on December 17, 1827, and made a full lieutenant on August 10, 1834. On November 7, 1836, he was appointed *Comandante General* of California, a title that while giving its holder command of all local troops, did not imply that he was of necessity a general officer. To forestall jealousy on the part of higher ranking Mexican officers in California, on November 29th, of the same year, Vallejo was made a colonel of cavalry, his commission being dated December 11, 1836. While he never rose above this rank, he was thereafter known as "General Vallejo." Vallejo, Documentos, I, Doc. 4; Tays, *op. cit.*, XVI, 349, 350.

12. Houghton, *Donner Party*, p. 173; Sandels, *Sojourn*, p. 37.

13. Tays, *op. cit.*, XVI, 351.

14. Bancroft, *op. cit.*, V, 109-10.

15. *Ibid.*, 514.

16. McDonald, Reminiscences, *passim*. The late Miss McDonald was James C. Cooper's granddaughter.

17. *Ibid.*; cf. Murphy, *Sonoma*, p. 132.

18. Murphy, *loc. cit.*; McDonald, *loc. cit.*; Alley, Bowen, *Sonoma*, p. 448.

19. Sonoma county archives, *loc. cit.*

20. Beasley & Cooper, Account book.

21. Larkin, Documents, Vol. 6, Pt. 1, Doc. 4; Bancroft, *op. cit.*, II, 713, 765.

22. Pickett, "A reminiscental"; Murphy, *op. cit.*, p. 132.

23. In 1940 these photographs were in the possession of L. S. Simmons, of Sonoma.

24. Bancroft, *op. cit.*, II, 718; V, 712.

25. Beasley & Cooper, *op. cit.*, *passim.*

26. Houghton, *op. cit.*, p. 192.

27. Beasley & Cooper, *loc. cit.*

28. Houghton, *op. cit.*, p. 203.

29. Hendry and Bowman, *op. cit.*, *passim.*

30. McDonald, *loc. cit.*

31. Black, Statement.

32. Deeds, Sonoma county archives, Recorder's Office, Book D, p. 12.

33. Murphy, *op. cit.*, p. 132.

34. Adler, Statement; McDonald, *loc. cit.*

35. Van Geldern, Description.

36. Houghton, *op. cit.*, p. 203.

37. McDonald, *loc. cit.*

38. cf. Lewis Publishing Co., *Sonoma*, p. 109; Bancroft, *op. cit.*, III, 740.

39. Robert A. Thompson, *Sonoma*, pp. 16, 50; Alley, Bowen, *op. cit.*, p. 450; Houghton, *op. cit.*, p. 195.

40. Overton vs. Atterburg, Sonoma county archives, Superior Court, 3187; Seventh United States Census, Sonoma County, California, October 20, 1850.

41. Helper, *Land of Gold*, pp. 64-67; Morgan & Co., *Directory*, 1852, pp. 35, 107-A.

42. Bancroft, *op. cit.*, VII, 203, Note 13.

43. Murphy, *op. cit.*, pp. 101-03; *San Francisco Call-Bulletin*, August 30, 1941; Knowland, *Landmarks*, p. 162; Hunt, *California*, III, 467-47; cf. Glasscock, *Golden Highway*, p. 201.

44. Thompson, *op. cit.*, pp. 57-58.

45. *Ibid.*; Hoffman, *Reports*, Appendix, p. 76.

46. Thompson, *loc. cit.*; Alley, Bowen, *op. cit.*, p. 447; cf. Bancroft, *op. cit.*, IV, 760.

47. McDonald, *loc. cit.*; Bowers, Map; Thomas A. Thompson & Co., *Atlas*, p. 58; Seventh United States Census, *loc. cit.*

48. McDonald, *loc. cit.*

49. *Ibid.*; *Alta California*, September 12, 1856.

50. McDonald, *loc. cit.*; Sonoma county archives, Deeds, Book B, p. 357.

51. McDonald, *loc. cit.*; *Alta California*, September 8, 13, 1856.

52. McDonald, *loc. cit.*

53. *Ibid.*; Adler, *loc. cit.*; Note 4, above.

54. *Alta California*, *loc. cit.*

55. McDonald, *loc. cit.*; Beasley & Cooper, Account book, note on inside of front cover; Alley, Bowen, *op. cit.*, p. 456; Witsell, *Freemasonry*, III, 1487.

56. McDonald, *loc. cit.*

57. Sonoma county archives, Deeds, Books A and B, *passim.*

CHAPTER 14.

1. Sutter, Reminiscences, p. 72.

2. Moerenhout, *Inside Story*, p. 32.

3. Sutter, *New Helvetia*, October 13, 1845, p. 6.

4. Grimshaw, Narrative, pp. 22-23.

5. Lienhard, *Pioneer*, p. 71.

6. Houghton, *Donner Party*, pp. 132-34, 312.

7. Grimshaw, *loc. cit.*; the following contemporary pictures of Sutter's Fort: Revere, *Tour of Duty*, frontispiece; Colored sketch of Sutter's fort in 1847, original in the Bancroft Library; (Letts), *Pictorial*, p. 62; Edwin A. Sherman, "Sherman was there," p. 352.

8. Sutter, *op. cit.*, August 18, 19, 21, 1847, pp. 70-71; Houghton, *op. cit.*, p. 132.

9. William T. Sherman, *Memoirs,* I, 48.

10. Sutter, *op. cit.,* June 7, 1847, p. 49; Houghton, *loc. cit.*

11. Note 7, above, sketches; Grimshaw, *op. cit.,* p. 30.

12. Houghton, *loc. cit.;* Note 7, above.

13. Sutter, *op. cit.,* June 7, 1847, p. 49.

14. *Ibid.,* June 17 to July 5, 1847, *passim,* pp. 51-56.

15. Sutter, "Diary," *Argonaut,* February 16, 1878.

16. *Ibid.,* February 9, 1878.

17. Sutter, *New Helvetia,* October 12, 1847, p. 84.

18. Bancroft, *California,* II, 728; V, 722; Sutter, Reminiscences, p. 172; Lienhard, *op. cit.,* p. 71; Grimshaw, *op. cit.,* p. 23; Scott, *Brannan,* p. 166.

19. Sutter, *New Helvetia,* January 17, 1848, p. 109.

20. Lienhard, *op. cit.,* p. 74; Jerrett, *California's El Dorado,* pp. 28-30.

21. Sutter, *op. cit.,* January 28, 1848, p. 113.

22. Sutter, Reminiscences, pp. 163-64.

23. Sutter, *New Helvetia,* August 27, 1847, p. 72; March 17, 1848, p. 123; Reminiscences, p. 160.

24. Sutter, *New Helvetia,* February 14, 1848, p. 116.

25. *Ibid.,* April 14, 1848, p. 129.

26. Bancroft, *op. cit.,* VI, 49-50.

27. Morse, *Sacramento,* p. 22.

28. Sutter, *op. cit.,* May 17, 1848, p. 137.

29. *Ibid.,* May 21, 1848, p. 138.

30. Thornton, *Oregon and California,* II, 275.

31. Sutter, Reminiscences, pp. 173-74.

32. William T. Sherman, *op. cit.,* I, 52-53.

33. Journal History, April 5, 1849.

34. William T. Sherman, *loc. cit.*

35. Bailey, *Brannan,* p. 124; Bancroft, *op. cit.,* II, 728.

36. Thompson and West, *Sacramento,* p. 10; Grimshaw, *op. cit.,* pp. 35, 39, 41-42.

37. Sutter, *New Helvetia,* May 22, 1848, p. 138.

38. Note 7, above.

39. *Californian* (San Francisco), July 15, 1848.

40. Bancroft, *op. cit.,* VI, 15, 147.

41. Sutter, "Diary," *Argonaut,* February 16, 1878.

42. Sutter, Reminiscences, pp. 193-96, *passim.*

43. William T. Sherman, *op. cit.,* I, 49.

44. Mason, Letter.

45. Moerenhout, *op. cit.,* pp. 32-33.

46. Gudde, *Sutter's Own Story,* p. 218; Buffum, *Six Months,* p. 63.

47. Grimshaw, *op. cit.,* p. 23.

48. *Ibid.,* pp. 29-30.

49. Thompson and Company, *loc. cit.*

50. Bancroft, *op. cit.,* III, 786.

51. Ryan, *Adventures,* II, 26, 28.

52. Grimshaw, *op. cit.*, pp. 21-22; Buffum, *op. cit.*, p. 31.

53. Grimshaw, *op. cit.*, p. 30.

54. Thompson and Company, *loc. cit.*; Bancroft, *loc. cit.*; *Alta California*, April 13, 1851.

55. Johnson, *Sights*, pp. 131, 141; Grimshaw, *op. cit.*, p. 32; Thompson and Company, *loc. cit.*

56. Moerenhout, *op. cit.*, pp. 65, 66; Sutter, Reminiscences, p. 178; Grimshaw, *op. cit.*, p. 33; Kelly, *Excursion*, II, 25.

57. Pierce, *Forty-Niner*, pp. 33-34.

58. (Luccatt), *Rovings*, II, 353.

59. Thos. H. Thompson & Company, *Atlas*, p. 102.

60. Keefer, Statement.

61. Kelly, *op. cit.*, II, 49-50.

62. Morse, *op. cit.*, pp. 38, 49, 51; Bancroft, *op. cit.*, II, 686; Jones, *Memories*, p. 454.

CHAPTER 15.

1. Richardson, *Beyond the Mississippi*, p. 384; Mrs. Olive Martin, Verbal statement; Browne, *Crusoe's Island*, p. 413.

2. Bancroft, *California*, VI, 467.

3. Browne, *op. cit.*, p. 336.

CHAPTER 16.

1. Day, "Report," p. 80; Galloway, "Comstock," p. 32.

2. Sioli, *El Dorado*, pp. 119-20.

3. Surveyor-general of the state of California, Report, pp. 5, 10.

4. Sioli, *loc. cit.*; Galloway, *op. cit.*, p. 3.

5. *Sacramento Union*, June 15, 1857; cf. Sioli, *op. cit.*, p. 127; Banning, *Six Horses*, p. 175.

6. *San Francisco Bulletin*, April 2, 1861; *Sacramento Union*, July 19, 1861; Sioli, *op. cit.*, pp. 123, 127.

7. Wren, *Nevada*, p. 113.

8. Sioli, *op. cit.*, pp. 128-29; Root and Connelley, *Overland Stage*, p. 138.

9. Sioli, *op. cit.*, p. 130.

10. *Ibid.*, p. 130.

11. *Sacramento Union*, October 26, 1861; Root and Connelley, *op. cit.*, pp. 105-32, *passim*.

12. *Coronet*, December, 1946, p. 72.

13. Bancroft, *Nevada*, p. 86.

14. Hunt, *California*, V, 152; Eldredge, *California*, IV, 231.

15. Bancroft, *op. cit.*, pp. 226-27; Hunt, *loc. cit.*

16. Banning, *op. cit.*, p. 199.

17. Strawberry House register entries; "December 22, 1865. Horis [sic] Greeley Pioneer Stage Driver," "June 1st, 1866, Henry Monk Greeley, Driver, P. S. Co."

18. Clemens, *Roughing It*, p. 156.

19. *Sacramento Union,* August 1, 1859.

20. *San Jose Pioneer,* May 24, 1879.

21. Fitch, *San Francisco Sunday Call,* September 20, 1903.

22. Richardson, *Beyond the Mississippi,* p. 384.

23. California state archives, *Senate Journal,* 1855, pp. 139, 211, 213, 678; *Assembly Journal,* 1855, pp. 426-30.

CHAPTER 17.

1. Authorities for many of our references to and descriptions of the different alignments followed from time to time by the Overland road, and to the many stopping places which lined these routes, are far too numerous for us to attempt to cite them all. We are forced, therefore, to limit ourselves to the most important of these citations, and to assure the reader that on many occasions we have personally explored every part of the routes described, and examined the site of each of the roadhouses mentioned. The field work involved was carried out, first, after the collection and correlation of numberless contemporary manuscripts and printed records, and again after checking and comparing these data with the verbal accounts of all the old-timers who could be contacted, and who possessed personal and first-hand knowledge of the matters under discussion.

2. Borthwick, *Three Years,* pp. 94, 109.

3. *Ibid.,* p. 102. This was doubtless the Crescent City Hotel, that was first succeeded by the Orleans and later by the Union, as Sacramento's staging center.

4. *Ibid.,* pp. 102-11.

5. Herrick & Hooge, *Directory,* 1859.

6. *Sacramento Union,* April 29, 1859.

7. Morse, *Sacramento City,* p. 100; Thompson & West, *Sacramento County,* p. 212; *Sacramento Bee, Guide book,* p. 99.

8. *Sacramento Union,* June 26, 1852; April 30, 1853.

9. *Op. cit.,* April 14, 1860; cf. Root and Cobbelley, *Overland Stage,* p. 110.

10. Morse, *op. cit.,* pp. 63, 99; *Placer Times,* February 23, 1850; *Sacramento Union,* January 10, 1862; Thompson & West, *op. cit.,* p. 211.

11. *Sacramento Union,* January 22; February 8, 1852.

12. *Op. cit.,* January 4, 1873; Thompson & West, *op. cit.,* p. 212.

13. *Sacramento Union,* April 14, 1860; January 4, 1873.

14. *Op. cit.,* January 4, 1873; Thompson & West, *loc. cit.*

15. Gudde, *Place Names,* p. 40.

16. Marryat, *Mountains and Molehills,* p. 206.

17. Sioli, *El Dorado,* p. 252.

18. Marryat, *loc. cit.*

19. *Sacramento Union,* October 13, 1852.

20. Ingalls, *California Letters,* p. 174; Upham, *Voyages to California.*

21. *Sacramento Union,* October 13, 1852; cf. Thompson & West, *op. cit.,* p. 211.

22. Thompson & West, *loc. cit.*

23. Lewis Publishing Company, *Sacramento,* p. 212.

24. *Placer Times,* August 16, 1850; Morse, *Sacramento City,* pp. 83-84; Upham, *op. cit.,* p. 346.

25. This may have been A. H. Crockett, who in the same year was elected inspector at Alder Springs, Mississippi Township, Sacramento County. *Sacramento Union,* August 8, 1851.

26. Marryat, *op. cit.,* pp. 207-08.

27. *Sacramento Union,* September 29, 1852; February 21, 1853.

28. Lewis Publishing Company, *op. cit.,* p. 557.

29. *Ibid.,* p. 470.

30. *Ibid.,* p. 212; Thompson & West, *op. cit.,* 212.

31. Bertschi, Mrs. L. J.

32. *Sacramento Union,* March 1, 1853.

33. Thompson & West, *loc. cit.*

34. *Sacramento Union,* February 27, 1852; Thompson & West, *loc. cit.*

35. Lewis Publishing Company, *op. cit.,* p. 466; California Reports, 79, 347.

36. Lewis Publishing Company, *op. cit.,* p. 436.

37. Johnson, *Gold Region,* p. 195.

38. Thompson & West, *loc. cit.*

39. Bence, Reminiscences.

40. Sacramento Valley Railroad, alignment map, 1854.

41. Bence, *loc. cit.*

42. *Sacramento Union,* October 26, 1861.

43. *Op. cit.,* April 14, 1860.

44. Bancroft, *California,* VII, 152-53; Bence, *loc. cit.*

45. Bancroft, *op. cit.,* p. 696.

46. *Sacramento Union,* July 4, 1855; Bence, *loc. cit.*

47. Deterding, Reminiscences.

48. Lewis Publishing Company, *op. cit.,* p. 422.

49. Deterding, *loc. cit.*

50. Reager, Statement; Deterding, *loc. cit.*

51. Bence, *loc. cit.;* Deterding, *loc. cit.*

52. Bence, *loc. cit.*

53. *Ibid.;* Butler, Reminiscences.

54. *Sacramento Union,* April 13, 1853; Sacramento County Archives, Assessors book, 1863, p. 84. Mr. Ralph H. Cross, Sr.

CHAPTER 18.

1. Bence, Reminiscences; Butler, Reminiscences; Lewis Publishing Company, *Sacramento,* p. 423.

2. Carter Sherman, Letter quoting Vedder family records.

3. *Alta California,* July 24, 1852.

4. Bence, *op. cit.;* Butler, *op. cit.*

5. Goddard, "Report," pp. 128, 133.

6. Thompson & West, *Sacramento,* p. 268; Bence, *loc. cit.;* Butler, *loc. cit.*

7. Bence, *loc. cit.;* Butler, *loc. cit.*

8. *Ibid.;* Euer, Letter; Thompson & West, *op. cit.,* p. 269.
9. Bence, *loc. cit.;* Deterding, Reminiscences.
10. Bence, *loc. cit.;* Euer, *loc. cit.*
11. *Sacramento Union,* November 11, 1854; Bence, *loc. cit.*
12. El Dorado County archives, Road book, p. 233.
13. Ingalls, "California Letters," p. 174.
14. *Sacramento Union,* August 20, 1851.
15. Bence, *loc. cit.,* Atchison, Letter.
16. Deterding, *loc. cit.*
17. Sioli, *El Dorado,* p. 153.
18. *Oakland Tribune,* July 6, 1947, The Knave.
19. Langley, *Pacific Coast Directory,* 1867.
20. *Oakland Tribune, loc. cit.*
21. *Sacramento Union,* July 15, 1854.
22. Gordon, Statements.
23. Sioli, *loc. cit.*
24. *Alta California,* September 23, 1856.
25. Pumpelli, *Reminiscences,* I, 252-53.
26. Atchison, *loc. cit.;* Marks, Reminiscences.
27. Ingalls, *op. cit.,* p. 20.
28. Sioli, *op. cit.,* p. 271; Atchison, *loc. cit.*
29. Atchison, *loc. cit.*
30. Bence, *loc. cit.;* Crawford, Statement.
31. Sioli, *op. cit.,* pp. 200, 201, 245; Rensch and Hoover, *Historic Spots,* p. 90.
32. Raven, *Golden Dreams,* pp. 236-37; Sioli, *op. cit.,* p. 200.
33. Silas Grainger, Statements.
34. Sioli, *op. cit.,* pp. 200, 201.
35. *Sacramento Union,* January 28, 1853; Bence, *loc. cit.;* Atchison, *loc. cit.*
36. E. B. Livingston. Statements.
37. *Mountain Democrat,* May 7, 1864.
38. *Ibid.;* Bence, *loc. cit.*
39. *El Dorado News,* May 21, 1853.
40. Gray. Statement.
41. Sioli, *op. cit.,* p. 230; Bence, *loc. cit.*
42. Bence, *loc. cit.;* Hill, Reminiscences.
43. Sioli, *op. cit.,* p. 203.
44. *Sacramento Union,* October 18, 1851.
45. Sioli, *loc. cit.*
46. Hill, *loc. cit.; Sacramento Union,* July 6, 1855.
47. Hill, *loc. cit.;* Langley, *Directory,* 1867.
48. *Ibid.; Pony Express Courier,* August, 1934.
49. *Sacramento Union,* November 22, 1854.
50. Marks, Reminiscences.
51. Bence, *loc. cit.;* Hill, *loc. cit.*
52. Sioli, *op. cit.,* p. 208; cif. Gudde, *op. cit.,* p. 95.

53. Sioli, *op. cit.,* p. 205; Lewis Publishing Company, *op. cit.,* p. 711.
54. Young, Statement.
55. *Ibid.;* Sioli, *op. cit.,* p. 206.
56. Young, *loc. cit.*
57. Kramp, Reminiscences.
58. Langley, *op. cit.;* Bence, *loc. cit.;* Kramp, *loc. cit.*
59. *El Dorado News,* December 11, 1852.
60. Young, *loc. cit.*
61. Sioli, *loc. cit.*
62. *Ibid.*
63. McKenney & Co., *Directory,* 1884.
64. Young, *loc. cit.*
65. Hill, *loc. cit.*
66. Bence, *loc. cit.;* Hill, *loc. cit.;* Placerville Museum.
67. *Placerville Republican,* June 15, 1925.
68. Young, *loc. cit.*
69. Rensch and Hoover, *op. cit.,* p. 86.
70. Jerrett, *El Dorado,* p. 58.
71. *Sacramento Union,* August 1, 1859.

CHAPTER 19.
1. *Sacramento Union,* August 2, 1859.
2. Alley, Bowen & Co., *Marin,* p. 496.
3. Lewis Publishing Co., *Sacramento,* pp. 212, 213, 450.
4. Bence, Reminiscences.
5. Lewis Publishing Co., *op. cit.,* pp. 423, 486.
6. *Sacramento Union,* May 24, 1851.
7. *Op. cit.,* November 17, 1852.
8. *Op. cit.,* August 2, 1859.
9. Thompson & West, *Sacramento,* p. 222.
10. *Ibid.,* p. 228.
11. Lewis Publishing Co., *op. cit.,* pp. 228, 436.
12. *Loc. cit.*
13. Raven, *Golden Dreams,* p. 91; Mason, (map); Sacramento Valley Railroad, (map).
14. Atchison, Letter.
15. *Ibid.*
16. Bancroft, *California,* VI, 46-51.
17. Kelly, *California,* II, 37-38.
18. *Sacramento Union,* June 21, 1873.
19. *Loc. cit.*
20. Willis, *Sacramento,* p. 340.
21. *Loc. cit.*
22. Thompson & West, *op. cit.,* p. 273.
23. *Ibid.,* p. 231.

24. *Loc. cit.*
25. Smith, Letter.
26. *Sacramento Union*, June 6, 1851.
27. Thompson & West, *op. cit.*, p. 233.
28. Atchison, *loc. cit.;* Wing, map.
29. *Sacramento Evening Star*, June 8, 1864.
30. Atchison, *loc. cit.*
31. Wing, *loc. cit.*
32. Atchison, *loc. cit.;* Wing, *loc. cit.;* Hoxie, Statements.
33. Atchison, *loc. cit.;* Wing, *loc. cit.;* Langley, *Directory*, 1867.
34. Mighels, *Life and Letters*, pp. 40-41.
35. Original photographs; Atchison, *loc. cit.*
36. Wing, map.
37. Atchison, *loc. cit.;* Wing, *loc. cit.*
38. Pelton, Letters.
39. Norton, *Life and Adventures*, pp. 308-12.
40. Atchison, *loc. cit.*
41. Carpenter, Reminiscences; Atchison, *loc. cit.;* Pelton, *loc. cit.*
42. Atchison, *loc. cit.*
43. *Ibid.*
44. *Ibid.*
45. Corle, *Desert Country*, pp. 268-69.
46. Hughes, Statements; Atchison, *loc. cit.*
47. Willis, *Sacramento*, p. 66.
48. Sioli, *El Dorado*, pp. 237-38; Atchison, *loc. cit.*
49. Sioli, *op. cit.*, p. 262; Atchison, *loc. cit.;* Wing, *loc. cit.*
50. Atchison, *loc. cit.;* Wing, *loc. cit.*
51. Sioli, *op. cit.*, p. 241; Wing, *loc. cit.;* Engesser, Statements.
52. Atchison, *loc. cit.;* Wing, *loc. cit.*
53. *Sacramento Union*, May 4, 1852; Sioli, *op. cit.*, p. 252; Wing, *loc. cit.*
54. Gudde, *Place Names*, p. 284.
55. Atchison, *loc. cit.;* Wing, *loc. cit.*
56. Sioli. *op. cit.*, pp. 261, 236, Atchison, *loc. cit.;* Wing, *loc. cit.*
57. Grainger, Statements; Wing, *loc. cit.;* original photographs; Langley, *Directory*, 1867; Sioli, *op. cit.*, pp. 241-45.
58. Wing, *loc. cit.*
59. *Ibid.*

Bibliography

Adler, Adam W. Statements to Ralph H. Cross, Sr., Amplified by Wade H. Wilson, Secretary, Sonoma Chamber of Commerce.

Alley, Bowen & Co. (pubs.). *History of Santa Clara County, California . . .* San Francisco, 1881.

——*History of Marin County, California . . .* San Francisco: Publishers, 1880.

——*History of Sonoma County . . .* San Francisco, 1880.

Alta California (newspaper).

Andresen, Anna Geil. "California's first hotel." *Salinas Daily Journal* (September 4, 1914).

——*Historical Landmarks of Monterey.* Salinas: Salinas Index Press, 1917.

Argonaut (newspaper).

Atchison, Mrs. Elma P. Letters to Ralph H. Cross, Sr.

Bailey, Paul. *Sam Brannan and the California Mormons.* Los Angeles: Westernlore Press, 1943.

Bancroft, Hubert Howe. Brown, John Henry, Biographical Notes. MSS. Bancroft Library, University of California, Berkeley, Calif.

——*California Pastoral.* San Francisco: History Company, 1888.

——*History of California.* San Francisco: A. L. Bancroft & Company and History Company, 1884–1890.

——*History of Nevada, Colorado and Wyoming.* San Francisco: History Company, 1890.

——Scrapbooks. MSS, 1860–64. Bancroft Library.

——Vioget, Jean Jacques, Biographical Notes. MSS. Bancroft Library.

Banning, Captain William, and Banning, George Hugh. *Six horses.* New York: The Century Company, 1930.

Barry, T. A., and Patten, B. A. *Men and Memories of San Francisco in the "Spring of '50."* San Francisco: A. L. Bancroft & Company, 1873.

Beach, George Holton. "My reminiscences." *Society of California Pioneers' Quarterly,* IX, 4, 234.

Beasley & Cooper. Sonoma Store and Saloon Account Book. MS, February 1, 1848, to August 6, 1850. In the possession of J. R. McDonald.

Bence, Robert L. Reminiscences. MS. Ralph H. Cross, Sr.

Bertschi, Mrs. L. J. Letter to Ralph H. Cross, Sr.

Betty, L. L. (comps.). *Santa Clara County Directory; including the City of San Jose; 1889.* San Jose: Compiler, 1889.

Bidwell, John. Letter to Hubert H. Bancroft, May 23, 1884. MS. Bancroft Library.

Black, Eleanor Bosworth. Statement to Donald Page.

Borthwick, J. D. *Three years in California.* Edinburgh: William Blackwood and Sons, 1857.

Bourne, John H. "Reminiscences of Early Days in California." *New York Sun* (January 25, 1898).

Bowers, A. B.   Map of Sonoma County, California, 1867.

Bowman, Jacob N.   The burial place of Jean Jacques Vioget.   MS, December 10, 1942, and photographs.   Bancroft Library.

——Jean Jacques Vioget.   MS, 1938.   Bancroft Library.

Breen, John, and Breen, Patrick.   Statements, January 5, 6, 1889.   Bancroft Scrapbooks, VII, 31.

Brown, Charles.   Statement of recollections of early events in California.   MS. 1878.   Bancroft Library.

Brown, John Henry.   *Early Days of San Francisco; California.*   Oakland: Biobooks, 1949.

Browne, J. Ross.   Crusoe's Island . . . *With Sketches of Adventure in California and Washoe.*   New York: Harper & Brothers, 1872.

Bryant, Edwin.   *What I saw in California . . . in the years 1846, 1847 . . .*   New York: D. Appleton & Company, 1849.

Buffum, E. Gould.   *Six Months in the Gold Mines; from a Journal of Three Years Residence in Upper and Lower California, 1847-8-9.*   Philadelphia: Leo and Blanchard, 1850.

Bunnell, Lafayette Houghton. *Discovery of the Yosemite, and the Indian War of 1851 . . .*   Chicago: Fleming H. Revell, (ca. 1880).

Butler, J. W. S.   Reminiscences.   MS.   Ralph H. Cross, Sr.

Byington, Lewis F.   *The History of San Francisco . . .*   San Francisco: S. J. Clarke Publishing Company, 1931.

Calaveras Chronicle (newspaper).

California Historical Society Quarterly (periodical).

California Reports (see Supreme Court of the state of California).

California state archives.   1856 *Assembly journal.*

——1856 *Senate journal.*

California State Department of Natural Resources, and the State Park Commission, in cooperation with the California State Chamber of Commerce, *Eleventh Report* (March 20, 1935), "Landmark No. 179," pp. 9–10.

California Star (newspaper).

California Star and Alta California (newspaper).

Californian (newspaper).

Carpenter, Mrs. Mary.   Reminiscences.   MS.   Ralph H. Cross, Sr.

Century Illustrated Monthly Magazine (periodical).

Chittenden, Newton H.   *Health and Pleasure Resorts of the Pacific Coast.*   (2nd edit.).   San Francisco: A. A. Murdock & Co., 1884.

Citizens' Committee of Santa Clara, *Souvenir; Golden Jubilee of Santa Clara College; 1851–1901.*   Santa Clara: Chas. A. Nace, 1901.

Clappe, Mrs. Louise Amelia Knapp Smith.   *California in 1851; the Letters of Dame Shirley.*   San Francisco: Grabhorn Press, 1933.

Clemens, Samuel L. (Mark Twain, pseud.).   *Roughing it.*   Hartford: American Publishing Company, 1872.

Clyman, James.   "James Clyman; his Diaries and Reminiscences."   *California*

Historical Society Quarterly, IV, 105-41, 272-83, 307-60; V, 44-84, 109-38, 255-82, 378-401; VI, 58-68.

Colton, U.S.N., Rev. Walter. *Three Years in California.* New York: S. A. Rollo & Co., 1859.

Colville, Samuel (comp.). *Colville's San Francisco Directory*, Vol. 1. *For the Year Commencing October, 1856.* San Francisco: S. Colville, 1856.

Corle, Edwin. *Desert country.* New York: Duell, Sloan & Pearce, (c1941).

Coronet (peridical).

Cossley-Batt, Jill L. *The Last of the California Rangers.* New York: Funk & Wagnalls Company, 1928.

Crawford, R. T. Statement to Ralph H. Cross, Sr.

Crosby, Elisha O. Statement of events in California. MS, 1878. Bancroft Library.

Dakin, Susanna Bryant. *A Scotch Paisano; Hugo Reid's Life in California. 1832– 1852 . . .* Berkeley: University of California Press, 1939.

Davis, William Heath. *Seventy-five Years in California . . .* San Francisco: John Howell, 1929.

Day, Sherman. "Report on the immigrant wagon road explorations." *Annual Report of the Surveyor-general of the state of California.* 1856. Assembly Document No. 5.

Deterding, Charles W. Reminiscences. MS. Ralph H. Cross, Sr.

Directories:

City and county, 1884. McKenney & Co.
Pacific coast business directory, 1867. Langley.
San Francisco, 1850. Kimball.
San Francisco, 1852. Morgan & Co.
San Francisco, 1853. Parker.
San Francisco, 1854. LeCount & Strong.
San Francisco, 1856. Colville.
San Francisco, 1856. Harris, Bogardus & Labatt.
San Francisco, 1858. Langley.
San Francisco, 1859. Herrick & Hooge.
San Francisco, 1860. Langley.
San Francisco, 1861. Langley.
Sna Francisco, 1865. Langley.
San Francisco, 1867. Langley.
San Francisco, 1871. Langley.
San Jose, city of, 1889. Beatty.
Santa Clara county, 1889. Beatty.

Duflot de Mofras, Eugène. *Exploration du Territoire de l'Orégon, des Californies et de la Mer Vermeille, executée pendant les années 1840, 1841 et 1842.* Paris: A. Bertrand, 1844.

Dwinnelle, John W. *The Colonial History of San Francisco . . .* San Francisco: Towne & Bacon, 1863.

El Dorado County archives. Road book. MS. Recorder's office, Placerville.

El Dorado News (newspaper).

Eldredge, Zoeth Skinner. *The Beginnings of San Francisco* ... San Francisco: Author, 1912.

Elliott & Co., Wallace W. (pubs.). *History of Humboldt County, California* ... San Francisco: Publishers, 1882.

Elliott & Moore (pubs.). *History of Monterey County, California* ... San Francisco: Publishers, 1881.

Engelhardt, Fr. Zephyrin. *Mission San Carlos Borromeo (Carmelo)* ... Santa Barbara: Mission Santa Barbara, 1934.

——*Mission San Juan Bautista* ... Santa Barbara: Mission Santa Barbara, 1931.

——*San Francisco Mission Dolores*. Chicago: Franciscan Herald Press, 1924.

Engesser, Albert. Statements to Ralph H. Cross, Sr.

Euer, Robert S. Letter to Ralph H. Cross, Sr.

Finley, Ernest L. (ed.). *History of Sonoma County, California* ... Santa Rosa: Press Democrat Publishing Co., 1937.

Fisher, Anne B. *The Salinas; Upside-down River*. New York: Farrar & Rinehart, Inc., 1945.

Fitch, Thomas. *San Francisco Sunday Call*, September 20, 1903.

Fitzhamon, E. G. "The Streets of San Francisco," *San Francisco Chronicle*, (ca. 1928–29). Pioneer Scrapbook, California Society of Pioneers, San Francisco.

Folsom Telegraph (newspaper).

Foote, Horace S. (ed.). *Pen Pictures from the Garden of the World, or Santa Clara County, California* ... Chicago: Lewis Publishing Co., 1888.

Forbes, Mrs. Armitage S. C. *California Missions and Landmarks* ... Los Angeles: Author, 1903.

Galloway, John Debo. "Early engineering works contributary to the Comstock." *University of Nevada Bulletin*, Geological and mining series No. 45, June, 1947.

Gates, Mary J. *Rancho Pastoria de las Borregas, Mountain View, California*. San Jose: Cottle & Murgotter, 1895.

Gerstacker, Friedrich W. C. *Narrative of a Journey around the World* ... London: Hurst and Blackett, 1853.

Giffin, Helen S. "Some two-story adobe houses of old California." *Historical Society of Southern California Quarterly* (March, 1938), p. 18.

Glasscock, G. B. *A Golden Highway* ... Indianapolis: The Bobbs-Merrill Company, (ca. 1934).

Goddard, George H. "Report of a survey of a portion of the eastern boundary of California, and of a reconnaissance of the old Carson and Johnson immigrant roads over the Sierra Nevada." *Annual report of the Surveyor-general of the state of California*. 1856 Assembly Document No. 5.

Golden Era (newspaper).

Gómez, Vicente Perfecto. Lo que sabe sobre cosas de California ... MS, 1878. Bancroft Library.

Gordon, Mrs. Emma Hare. Statements to Ralph H. Cross, Sr.

Grainger, Silas. *Ibid.*

Gray, Euell. *Ibid.*

Grimshaw, William Robinson. His narrative of life and events in California during 'flush times,' particularly the years 1848–50. MS, 1872. Bancroft Library.

Gudde, Erwin G. *Sutter's Own Story* ... New York: G. P. Putnam's Sons, 1936.

——*California place names.* Berkeley: University of California Press, 1949.

Guerra & Noriega, José de la. Documentos para la historia de California. MS, 1878. Bancroft Library.

Guinn, James M. *Historical and Biographical Record of Monterey and San Benito Counties* ... Los Angeles: Historical Record Co., 1910.

Hall, Frederic. *The History of San Jose and Surroundings* ... San Francisco: A. L. Bancroft and Company, 1871.

Harlan, Jacob Wright. *California; '46 to '88.* San Francisco: Bancroft Company, 1888.

Harlow, Neal (comp. ed.). *The Maps of San Francisco Bay from the Spanish Discovery in 1769 to the American Occupation.* San Francisco: The Book Club of California, 1950.

Harris, Bogardus and Labatt (comps.). *San Francisco City Directory for the Year Commencing October, 1856.* San Francisco: Whitton, Towne & Co., 1856.

Helper, Hinton R. *The Land of Gold. Reality versus Fiction.* Baltimore: Author, 1855.

Hendry, George W., and Bowman, Jacob N. The spanish and Mexican adobe and other buildings in the nine San Francisco bay counties, 1776 to about 1850. MS, 1940. Bancroft Library.

Herrick, W. F., and Hooge, Octavian (comps.). *San Francisco almanac for the year 1859.* San Francisco: Compilers, 1859.

Hill, Seymour. Reminiscences. MS. Ralph H. Cross, Sr.

Hittell, John S. *A History of the City of San Francisco* ... San Francisco: A. L. Bancroft & Co., 1878.

Hittell, Theodore H. *History of California.* San Francisco: Occidental Publishing Co., 1885.

Hoffman, Ogden. *Report of the land cases determined in the United States District Court for the Northern District of California. June term, 1853, to June term, 1858, inclusive.* San Francisco: Numa Hubert, 1862.

Houghton, Eliza P. Donner. *The Expedition of the Donner Party and its Tragic Fate.* Chicago: A. C. McClurg & Co., 1911.

Hoxie, Mrs. Addie C. Statements to Ralph H. Cross, Sr.

Huges, John. *Ibid.*

Hunt, Rockwell D. (ed.). *California and Californians.* Chicago: Lewis Publishing Company, 1926.

Hutchings' Illustrated California Magazine (periodical).

Hutton, William Rich. *Glances at California; 1847–1853* . . . San Marino: Huntington Library, 1942.

Ingalls, John. "California letters of the gold rush period; the correspondence of John Ingalls; 1849–1851." *Proceedings of the American Antiquarian Society*, New series, vol. 47, part 1.

Jeans, Raymond William. Architectural remains of old Monterey. M.A. thesis, 1917, Universiay of California.

Jerrett, Herman Daniel. *California's El Dorado; Yesterday and Today*. Sacramento: J. Anderson, 1915.

Jochmus, Augustus C. *The City of Monterey* . . . Pacific Grove, Calif., (ca. 1925).

——*Monterey; All of its Between two Covers; 1542–1930*. Pacific Grove, (ca. 1934).

Johnson, Theodore T. *Sights in the Gold Region* . . . New York: Baker and Scribner, 1849.

Jones, M.D., J. Roy. *Memories, Men and Medicine* . . . (Sacramento): Sacramento Society for Medical Improvement, 1950.

Journal History of the Latter Day Saints' Church. Church Historian's Office, Salt Lake City, Utah.

Keefer, Alice F. Verbal statements to Ralph H. Cross, Sr.

Kelly, William. *An Excursion to California . . . With a stroll through the Diggings and Ranches of that Country*. London: Chapman and Hall, 1851.

Kimball, Charles (comp.). *The San Francisco City Directory . . . September 1, 1850*. San Francisco: Journal of Commerce Press, 1850.

Knowland, Joseph R. *California, a Landmark History* . . . (Oakland): Tribune Press, ca. 1941.

Kramp, Mrs. Ettie Barlos. Reminiscences. MS. Ralph H. Cross, Sr.

Langley, Henry G. (comp.). *The San Francisco Directory for the Year 1858* . . . San Francisco: S. D. Valentine & Son, 1858.

——*Ibid., commencing July, 1860* . . . San Francisco: S. F. Valentine & Co., 1860.

——*Ibid., September, 1861* . . . San Francisco: S. F. Valentine & Co., 1861.

——*Ibid., December, 1865* . . . San Francisco: Henry G. Langley, 1865.

——*Ibid., September, 1867* . . . San Francisco: Henry G. Langley, 1867.

——*Ibid., April, 1871* . . . San Francisco: Henry G. Langley, 1871.

——*The Pacific coast business directory for 1867* . . . San Francisco: Compiler, 1867.

Larkin, Thomas Oliver. Account books. MSS. Bancroft Library.

——City of Monterey, 1842. Black and white sketch. Property of Miss Frances Moler, San Francisco. California Historical Society.

——Documents for the history of California. *Ibid.*

——Monterey consulate accounts. *Ibid.*

——Official correspondence. *Ibid.*

LeCount, Josiah J., and Strong, E. Y. (comps.). *LeCount and Strong's San Francisco City Directory for the Year 1854*. San Francisco: San Francisco Herald, 1854.

Letts, John M. *California Illustrated* ... New York: W. Holdredge, 1853.

Lewis Publishing Company (pubs.). *An Illustrated history of Sacramento County, California* ... Chicago: Publishers, 1890.

——*An Illustrated history of Sonoma County, California* ... Chicago: Publishers, 1889.

Lienhard, Heinrich. *A Pioneer at Sutter's Fort, 1846–1850* ... Los Angeles: Calafía Society, 1941.

Little, W. C. Map of Monterey, 1901.

Livingston, E. B. Statements to Ralph H. Cross, Sr.

(Luccatt, Edward). *Rovings in the Pacific, from 1837 to 1849. with a glance at California* ... London: Longman, Brown, Green, and Longmans, 1851.

Lyman, Chester S. *Around the Horn to the Sandwich Islands and California; 1845–1850* ... New Haven: Yale University Press, 1924.

Lyman, George H. *The saga of the Comstock lode* ... New York: Charles Scribner's Sons, 1934.

MacFarland, Grace. *Monterey: Cradle of California's Romance* ... Monterey: Weybret-Lee Co., 1914.

Macracken, Elizabeth. "When Santa Clara County was Young." *San José Evening News* (January 12, 1942), 2nd News Section.

Maps:
    Monterey, 1849. Narvaez.
    Monterey, 1885. Toothaker and Westfall.
    Monterey, 1901. Little.
    Monterey, 1938. Neasham.
    Overland road, Folsom to Coloma (n.d.). Wing.
    Sacramento County and Delta region (n.d.). Thomas Bros.
    Sacramento to Folsom, 1854. Sacramento Valley Railroad.
    Sonoma county, 1867. Bowers.
    Upper and lower gold mines, 1848. Mason.

Marks, Henry. Reminiscences. MS. Ralph H. Cross, Sr.

Marryat, Frank. *Mountains and molehills* ... New York: Harper & Brothers, 1855.

Martin, Mrs. Olive. Statement to Donald Page.

Mason, U.S.A., Colonel Richard B. Letter to Brigadier General R. Jones, Adjutant General, U.S.A., Washington, D. C., Dated Headquarters Tenth Military Department, Monterey, September 10, 1848. Quoted in Revere, *A Tour of Duty* ..., p. 129.

——Position of the upper and lower gold mines on the South Fork of the American River, California. July 20, 1848. (map). United States, House Executive Document No. 1, 30th Congress, Second Session, Washington, D. C., 1848. (Accompanying Colonel Mason's report, published with President Polk's message to Congress, December 5, 1848. Copy in the Bancroft Library.

Massey, Ernest de. "A Frenchman in the Gold Rush." *California Historical Society Quarterly*, V, 3-43, 139-77, 219-54, 342-77.

McDonald, Ruth B.   Reminiscences.   MSS, 1938–50.   Ralph H. Cross, Sr.

McGlashen, C. F.   *History of the Donner Party* ...   (11th edition).   San Francisco: A. Carlisle & Co., 1918.

McKenney & Company, L. M. (comps.).   *City and county directory including Sacramento city and county, Amador, El Dorado and Placer counties.*   San Francisco: Compilers, 1884.

Meyer, Carl.   *Bound for Sacramento* ...   Claremont, Calif.: Saunders Studio Press, 1938.

Mighels, Ella Sterling (Aurora Esmeralda, pseud.).   *Life and letters of a Forty-niner's daughter.*   San Francisco: Harr Wagner Publishing Company, (c1929).

Moerenhout, Jacques Antoine.   *The Inside Story of the Gold Rush.*   California Historical Society Special Publication No. 8.   San Francisco, 1935.

Monterey County archives.   Padron general de Monterey, April 14, 1836.   MS.   Bancroft Library.

——Solares de Monterey, 1835–1850.   Grants, Book A.   MS.   Recorder's office, San Jose.

——Miscellaneous documents, VIII.   MS.   *Ibid.*

——Deeds of grants, Vol. C.   MS.   *Ibid.*

——Leases, Book A.   MS.   *Ibid.*

Monterey Gazette (newspaper).

Morgan & Co., A. W. (comps.).   *A. W. Morgan & Co's. San Francisco City Directory; September, 1852.*   San Francisco: F. A. Bonnard, 1852.

Morse, John Frederick.   *The First History of Sacramento City* ...   Sacramento: Sacramento Book Collectors Club, 1945.

Mountain Democrat (newspaper).

Murphy, Celeste G.   *The People of the Pueblo* ...   Sonoma: W. L. and C. G. Murphy, 1935.

Narvaez, Pedro.   Map of Monterey, 1849.

Neasham, Audrey.   Map of Monterey (ca. 1938).

Newspapers:

Alta California, San Francisco.
Argonaut, San Francisco.
Calaveras Chronicle, Mokelumne Hill.
California Star, San Francisco.
California Star and Alta California, San Francisco.
Californian, Monterey and San Francisco.
El Dorado News, Placerville.
Folsom Telegraph, Folsom.
Golden Era, San Francisco.
Monterey Gazette, Monterey.
Mountain Democrat, Placerville.
New York Sun, New York.
Oakland Tribune, Oakland.
Pacific Sentinel, Santa Cruz.

Placer Times, Placerville.

Placerville Republican, Placerville.

Pony Express Courier, Placerville.

Sacramento Bee, Sacramento.

Sacramento Evening Star, Sacramento.

San Francisco Bulletin, San Francisco

San Francisco Call-Bulletin, San Francisco.

San Francisco Chronicle, San Francisco.

San Francisco Herald, San Francisco.

San Francisco Sunday Call, San Francisco.

San José Evening News, San Jose.

San José Pioneer, San Jose.

Times and Seasons, Nauvoo, Ill.

Norris, Thomas W., Monterey, California. Collection of John Henry Brown papers.

Norton, Col. L. A. *Life and adventures of* . . . Oakland: Pacific Press Publishing House, 1887.

Pathfinder (periodical).

Parker, James M. (comp.). *The San Francisco Directory for the Years 1852–53* . . . San Francisco: Compiler, 1852.

Peirce, Henry A. Journal. MS, April 21, 1839, to March 31, 1842. Bancroft Library.

Pelton, Aylmer E. Letters to Ralph H. Cross, Sr.

Periodicals:

    California Historical Society Quarterly, San Francisco.

    Century Illustrated Monthly Magazine, New York.

    Coronet, Boulder, Colorado.

    Historical Society of Southern California Quarterly, Los Angeles.

    Hutchings' Illustrated California Magazine, San Francisco.

    Pathfinder, Washington, D. C.

    Society of California Pioneers' Quarterly, San Francisco.

Phelps, William D. (Webfoot, pseud.). *Fore and Aft* . . . Boston: Nichols & Hall, 1871.

Pickett, Charles Edward. "A pioneer reminiscental." Undated clipping, *San Francisco Bulletin* (ca. 1882). In John C. Maynard's Scrapbook, I, 205, California Historical Society.

Pierce, Hiram Dwight. *A Forty-Niner Speaks* . . . Oakland: Keystone-Inglect Printing Co., 1930.

Piper, Asabel D. "Recollections of San Francisco twenty years ago." *Alta California* (February 17, 1867). Supplement.

Powers, Laura B. *Old Monterey, California's Adobe Capital*. San Francisco: San Carlos Press, 1934.

Pumpelli, Raphael. *My reminiscences*. New York: Henry Holt & Co., 1918.

Raven R. (George Payson, pseud.). *Golden dreams and leaden realities*. New York: G. P. Putnam & Co., 1853.

Reager, Lewis Martin. Statements to Ralph H. Cross, Sr.

Rensch, H. E. and E. G., and Hoover, Mildred Brooke. *Historic spots in California; valley and sierra counties.* Stanford: Stanford University Press, (c1933).

Revere, Joseph Warren. *A Tour of Duty in California* . . . New York: C. S. Francis & Co., 1849.

Richardson, Albert D. *Beyond the Mississippi* . . . *1857–1867.* Hartford: American Publishing Company, 1867.

Riesenberg, Jr., Felix. *Golden Gate; the story of San Francisco Harbor.* New York: A. A. Knopf, 1940.

Robinson, Fayette. *California and its Gold Regions* . . . New York: Stringer & Townsend, 1849.

Root, Frank A., and Connelley, William Elsey. *The overland stage to California* . . . Topeka: Authors, 1901.

Rose, John Holland. *The life of Napoleon I* . . . London: G. Bell and Sons, Ltd., 1924.

Rowland, Leon. Letter, May 29, 1951, to Ralph H. Cross, Sr.

Ryan, William Redmond. *Personal Adventures in Upper and Lower California, in 1849-50* . . . London: William Shoberl, 1850.

Sacramento Bee (newspaper, pubs.). *Guide book.* Sacramento: Publishers, 1939.

Sacramento County archives. Assessor's book, 1863. MS. Ralph H. Cross, Sr.

Sacramento Valley Railroad. Alignment map, Sacramento to Folsom, 1854. Copy in Bancroft Library.

Salinas Daily Journal (newspaper).

San Carlos church archives, First book of marriages. MS. San Carlos church, Monterey.

Sandels, G. M. Waseurtz af (The King's Orphan, pseud.). *A Sojourn in California* . . . San Francisco: Book Club of California, 1945.

Sawyer, Eugene T. *History of Santa Clara County, California* . . . Los Angeles: Historic Records Company, 1922.

Scott, Reva. *Samuel Brannan and the Golden Fleece* . . . New York: Macmillan Company, 1944.

Shaw, William. *Golden Dreams and Waking Realities* . . . London: Smith, Elder and Co., 1851.

Sherman, Edwin A. "Sherman was there; recollections of Major Edwin A. Sherman . . ." *California Historical Society Quarterly,* XXIII, 259-81, 349-77.

Sherman, Mrs. Emilinn Carter. Letter to Ralph H. Cross, Sr.

Sherman, William Tecumseh. *Memoirs of General William T. Sherman* . . . New York: D. Appleton and Company, 1875.

Simmons, L. S. Early photographs of Sonoma.

Sioli, Paolo (pub.). *Historical souvenir of El Dorado County, California* . . . Oakland: Publisher, 1883.

Slocum & Co., W. A. (pubs.). *History of Contra Costa County, California* . . . San Francisco: Publishers, 1882.

Smith, Mrs. Louis. Letter to Ralph H. Cross, Sr.

Society of California Pioneers' Quarterly (periodical).

Sonoma County archives. Deeds, Book A, No. 2. MS. Recorder's Office, Santa Rosa.

——Deeds, Book B. *Ibid.*

Soulé, Frank (and others). *The Annals of San Francisco* . . . New York: D. Appleton & Company, 1855.

Sterling, Charles B. Letter to Thomas O. Larkin, dated San Francisco, July 14, 1848. Larkin Documents, Vol. VI, Pt. 2, P. 292, Doc. 144.

Strawberry House register. MS. Bancroft Library.

Supreme Court of the state of California. *Reports of cases determined by the Supreme Court of the State of California.* San Francisco: Bancroft-Whitney Company.

Surveyor-general of the state of California. "Annual report." 1856 *Assembly Journal*, Document No. 5.

Sutter, John Augustus. "General Sutter's Diary." *Argonaut* (January 26; February 2, 9, 16, 1878).

——*New Helvetia Diary; a Record of Events kept by John A. Sutter and his Clerks at New Helvetia, California, from September 9, 1845, to May 25, 1848.* San Francisco: Grabhorn Press, 1939.

——Personal reminiscences. MS. Bancroft Library.

——*Six French Letters; Captain John Augustus Sutter to Jean Jacques Vioget; 1842-1843* . . . (Sacramento): Nugget Club, C. K. McClatchy High School, (ca. 1942).

Swan, John A. Trip to the gold mines in 1848. MS, 1872. Bancroft Library.

Swasey, William F. *The Early Days and Men of California.* Oakland: Pacific Press Publishing Company, 1891.

——Statement. MS, 1878. Bancroft Library.

——View of San Francisco, formerly Yerba Buena, in 1846-7 before the discovery of gold . . . San Francisco as it really appeared in March 1847. Colored lithograph. Bancroft Library.

Taylor, Bayard. *Eldorado, or Adventures in the Path of Empire* . . . New York: George P. Putnam, 1850.

Tays, George. "Mariano Guadalupe Vallejo and Sonoma . . ." *California Historical Society Quarterly*, XVI, 99-121, 216-55, 348-72; XVII, 50-72, 141-67, 219-42.

Thomas Bros. (pubs.). Map of Sacramento County and the Delta region. Oakland: Publishers, (n.d.).

Thompson and Company (pubs.). *Historical and Descriptive Review of the Industries of Sacramento, 1886* . . . Sacramento: Publishers, 1886.

Thompson & Co., Thos. H. (pubs.). *Historical Atlas Map of Sonoma County, California* . . . Oakland: Publishers, 1877.

Thompson, Robert A. *Historical and Descriptive Sketch of Sonoma County, California.* Philadelphia: L. H. Everts & Co., 1877.

Thompson & West (pubs.). *Historical Atlas Map of Santa Clara County, California* ... San Francisco: Publishers, 1876.

——*History of Sacramento County, California* ... Oakland: Publishers, 1880.

——*History of Yuba County,* California ... Oakland: Publishers, 1879.

Thornton, J. Quinn. *Oregon and California in 1848* ... New York: Harper & Brothers, 1849.

Times and Seasons (newspaper).

Tinkham, George A. *A History of Stockton* ... *including a sketch of San Joaquin County* ... San Francisco: W. M. Hinton & Co., 1880.

Tothaker, L. S., and Westfall, A. Map of Monterey, 1885.

Tresconi, Alberto. Personal papers in the possession of Alice Griffin, Monterey.

Tresconi, Julius. Verbal statements.

Tuthill, Franklin. *The History of California.* San Francisco: H. H. Bancroft & Company, 1866.

Upham, Samuel C. *Notes of a voyage to California* ... *1849–1850.* Philadelphia: Author, 1878.

Vallejo, Mariano Guadalupe. Documentos para la historia de California. MSS, 1769–1850. Bancroft Library.

——Recuerdos historicos y personales tocante á la Alta California. MS, 1875. Bancroft Library.

Van Geldern, Dr. Charles. Description of Sonoma as it was in October, 1849. Alley, Bowen & Co., *Sonoma County,* p. 447 ff.

Van Nostrand, Jeanne, and Coulter, Edith M. (comp. eds.). *California Pictorial; a History in Contemporary Pictures, 1786 to 1859* ... Berkeley: University of California Press, 1948.

Vioget, Jean Jocques. Autobiography. MS fragment, one folio page. Sutter's Fort Museum, Sacramento.

——Yerba Buena, in the spring of 1837. Water color sketch. Property of Austin Peterson, Los Angeles. Wells Fargo Bank Museum, San Francisco.

Ward, Henry C. "Stage-coach days in California . . ." *California Historical Society Quarterly,* XIII, 255.

Whitsell, Leon O. *One Hundred Years of Freemasonry in California.* San Francisco: Grand Lodge, Free and Accepted Masons of California, (ca. 1950).

Willis, William L. *History of Sacramento County, California* ... Los Angeles: History Record Company, 1913.

Wilson, Wade H. See Adler, Adam W.

Wing, Mrs. Pearle. Sketch map of the Overland road, Folsom to Coloma, (n.d.).

Wood, Alley & Co. (pubs.). *History of Solano County* ... San Francisco: Publishers, 1879.

Wren, Thomas. *A history of the state of Nevada* ... New York: Lewis Publishing Company, 1904.

Wyatt, Roscoe D., and Arbuckle, Clyde. *Historic Names, Persons and Places in Santa Clara County*. San Jose: California Pioneers of Santa Clara County, 1948.

Wyllys, Rufus Kay. *The French in Sonora (1850–1854)* ... Berkeley: University of California Press, 1932.

Young, Garrard. Statement to Ralph H. Cross, Sr.

Index

500 COPIES

Designed and printed by Lawton Kennedy